The Future of Finance

The Future of Finance

THE LSE REPORT

Adair Turner
Andrew Haldane
Paul Woolley
Sushil Wadhwani
Charles Goodhart
Andrew Smithers
Andrew Large
John Kay
Martin Wolf
Peter Boone
Simon Johnson
Richard Layard

THE LONDON SCHOOL OF ECONOMICS AND POLITICAL SCIENCE

Published by The London School of Economics and Political Science

Published in association with the London Publishing Partnership
www.londonpublishingpartnership.co.uk

ISBN 978-0-85328-458-1 (pbk.)

A catalogue record for this book is available from the British Library

This book has been composed in Lucida using TeX
Typeset by T&T Productions Ltd, London

Cover design: LSE Design Unit

Contents

Preface

The financial crisis of 2007–8 has been the most damaging economic event since the Great Depression—affecting the lives of hundreds of millions of people. The most immediate problem now is how best to prevent a repeat performance.

Much has been written about reforming the world financial system. But it is rarely based on a searching in-depth analysis of the underlying weaknesses within the system. Nor does it usually tackle the key question of what a financial system is for.

To correct this omission, we invited eighteen leading British thinkers on these issues to form a Future of Finance Group.[1] They included journalists, academics, financiers and officials from the Financial Services Authority, the Bank of England and the Treasury. We have met twelve times, for what many of those present described as the best and most searching discussions they had ever participated in. The result is this book.

The issues at stake are extraordinarily difficult and profound. The central question is what the financial system is for. Standard texts list five main functions—channelling savings into real investment, transferring risk, maturity transformation (including smoothing of life-cycle consumption), effecting payments and making markets. But if we study how financial companies make their money, it is extraordinarily difficult to see how closely this corresponds to the stated functions, and it is often difficult to explain why the rewards are often so high. Any explanation must also explain why the system is so prone to boom and bust.

Chapters 1, 2 and 3 of the book deal with these fundamental issues: the ideal functions of the system; the way the system has actually operated; and the sources of boom and bust. To answer these questions, much of the abstract theory of finance has to be abandoned in favour of a more

---

[1] Other regular members of the group (apart from the authors) were Alastair Clark, Arnab Das, Howard Davies, Will Hutton, Martin Jacomb, Jonathan Taylor, Dimitri Vayanos and David Webb.

realistic model of how the different agents actually behave. Central to this is opacity and asymmetric information, combined with short-term performance-related pay. For example, the asset price momentum which accompanies booms occurs because the owners of giant funds expect fund managers to shift into the fastest rising stocks. (They would do better to invest on a longer-term basis.)

The opacity of the system has increased enormously with the growth of derivatives. Did this contribute to high long-term growth? The issue remains open. On one side, people point to the high real growth in 1950–73 (an era of financial repression) and the real cost of the present downturn. On the other side, many studies, discussed in chapter 4, point to real benefits from financial deepening. But apart from this chapter, all others in the book propose the need for a radically simplified and slimmer financial system.

There are four aims of such a reform. The first is to prevent the financial system destabilizing the real economy, as it has in the recent past. The second (closely related) is to protect taxpayers against the possible cost of bailouts. The third is to reduce the share of real national income which accrues as income to the financial sector and its employees for reasons not related to the benefits it confers—thus absorbing into the sector talent that could be more usefully used elsewhere. And all of this has to be done in a way that works.

There are two main lines of approach. The first is *regulation*: higher capitalization of all financial institutions, and levels of required capital that rise in a boom and fall in a slump. These are discussed in chapters 5, 6 and 7. Chapter 5 points to some of the difficulties involved in any such regulation; chapter 6 shows that asset price booms can be identified, at least sometimes; and chapter 7 discusses how such information could be used if there were an independent committee specifically charged with 'macroprudential regulation'. (Chapter 4 argues by contrast that financial booms should be mainly controlled via interest rates.)

The second main approach to a more stable system is *institutional reform*. Chapter 8 argues strongly for the introduction of narrow banking. In such a system, only deposit-taking institutions could expect to be insured through the state, and they would not be allowed to build up a balance sheet of risky assets. This is a version of the so-called Volcker rule.

Faced with these two possible lines of approach, chapter 9 comes down in favour of strong regulation, linked perhaps to some institutional reform, aimed especially at greater competition. It argues that the state would in fact bail out any major financial institution threatened with bankruptcy, whether deposit-taking or not; it must therefore regulate all institutions.

Moreover, managers must face totally different incentives and pay. In particular, chapter 9 suggests that managers should be liable to repay a substantial proportion of their pay if their institution requires state assistance or goes bankrupt within ten years of their getting that pay.

All these proposals would directly reduce the profitability of banks and the pay of bankers. Do they have a chance? Chapter 10 documents the huge influence that banks exert in the political sphere worldwide. And it argues strongly that only a worldwide system of regulation embodied in a worldwide treaty organization, like the WTO, could have a chance. In this context it is encouraging that the working party of the G20 Financial Stability Board which will deliver proposals to the G20 Summit this November is chaired by our first author, Adair Turner.

It has been an extraordinary privilege to chair the discussion of these chapters. The book was presented at a major conference at Savoy Place, London, on 14 July 2010. Both the conference and the work of the group have been funded by The Paul Woolley Centre for Capital Market Dysfunctionality at the LSE. We are extremely grateful to Paul Woolley for his financial support and for his foresight in establishing his Centre well before the crash.

The Group and the Conference have been jointly planned by Paul Woolley in his Centre and by myself in the Centre for Economic Performance. The Group has been superbly organized by Harriet Ogborn, and the Conference likewise by Jo Cantlay.

Richard Layard

Contributors

Adair Turner
Chairman, Financial Services Authority

Andy Haldane
Executive Director of Financial Stability, Bank of England

Paul Woolley
Senior Fellow, The Paul Woolley Centre for the Study of Capital Market Dysfunctionality, London School of Economics

Sushil Wadhwani
CEO, Wadhwani Asset Management; Visiting Professor, London School of Economics and Cass Business School

Charles Goodhart
Emeritus Professor of Banking and Finance, London School of Economics

Andrew Smithers
Founder, Smithers & Co

Andrew Large
Former Deputy Director, Bank of England

John Kay
Visiting Professor, London School of Economics

Martin Wolf
Financial Times

Peter Boone
Executive Chair, Effective Intervention

Simon Johnson
Ronald A. Kurtz Professor of Entrepreneurship, MIT Sloan School of Management; Senior Fellow, Peterson Institute for International Economics

Richard Layard
Emeritus Professor of Economics, London School of Economics

The Future of Finance

———————————————————————————————

PART 1
DIAGNOSIS

What Do Banks Do? Why Do Credit Booms and Busts Occur? What Can Public Policy Do About It?

By Adair Turner

Over the last thirty to forty years the role of finance within developed economies has grown dramatically: debt to GDP ratios have increased, trading volumes exploded, and financial products have become more complex. Until the recent crisis this growing scale and complexity were believed to enhance both efficiency and stability. That assumption was wrong. To understand why, we need to recognize specific features of financial markets, credit contracts and fractional reserve banks. The recent crisis was particularly severe because of the interaction between the specific characteristics of maturity transforming banks and securitized credit markets. The regulatory response needs to distinguish the different economic functions of different categories of credit: only a fraction of credit extension relates to capital formation processes. The response should combine much higher bank capital requirements than pre-crisis, liquidity policies which reduce aggregate maturity transformation, and countercyclical macroprudential tools possibly deployed on a sectorally specific basis.

INTRODUCTION AND SUMMARY

In 2007–8 the world faced a huge financial crisis, which has resulted in major losses in wealth and employment and which has imposed great burdens on the public finances of developed countries. The latest stage of the crisis—its mutation into sovereign debt concerns—is still ongoing. We still need to manage our way out of the crisis; and we need to learn the lessons of what went wrong so that we can reduce the probability and severity of future crises. To do that effectively, we need to ask fundamental questions about the optimal size and functions of the financial system and about its value added within the economy, and about whether and under what conditions the financial system tends to generate economic stability or instability. We need to debate what the 'future of finance' should be. That is the purpose of the essays combined in this book.

The recent past of finance, the last twenty to thirty years, has been striking, with three important developments:

(i) a very major growth in the scale of financial activities relative to the real economy;

(ii) an explosion of the complexity of financial products and services, in particular linked to the development of securitized credit and of credit and other derivatives; and

(iii) a rise in intellectual confidence that this growth in scale and complexity was adding economic value, making the global economy both more efficient and less risky.

It is now clear that the third assumption was quite wrong: we need to understand why.

Many aspects of what went wrong are obvious and have been set out in numerous official and academic reports. Risk management practices were often poor, relying on over-simplistic mathematical models; governance arrangements—the role of boards, risk committees and risk managers—were often inadequate, as sometimes was supervision by regulatory authorities. Rating agencies were beset by conflicts of interest. Complex structured products were sometimes sold to investors who failed to understand the embedded options; and in derivatives markets, huge counterparty exposures appeared, creating severe risks of interconnected failure. The policy response now being designed at European and global level needs to address, and is addressing, these clear deficiencies.

But even if these deficiencies are addressed, the future financial system could remain dangerously unstable. Regulatory reform needs to address more fundamental issues. To do that effectively it must recognize that financial markets and systems have highly specific characteristics which distinguish them from other markets within a capitalist economy. In particular,

(i) financial markets are different because they are inherently susceptible to destabilizing divergences from equilibrium values;

(ii) credit contracts create highly specific risks which increase economic volatility, and different categories of credit perform different functions and create different risks;[1] and

(iii) banks are highly specific institutions which introduced their own specific risks into the economy.

---

[1] Three features of credit contracts carry important implications for cyclical tendencies within a market economy: specificity of tenor; specificity of nominal value; and the rigidity and irreversibility of default and bankruptcy. See Turner (2010) for a discussion of these features.

Understanding these distinctive characteristics is central to understanding the potential dynamics of modern market economies; too much of modern economics has ignored them almost completely, treating the financial system as neutral in its macroeconomic effect.

This chapter considers their implications. Its key conclusions are as follows.

(i) There is no clear evidence that the growth in the scale and complexity of the financial system in the rich developed world over the last twenty to thirty years has driven increased growth or stability, and it is possible for financial activity to extract rents from the real economy rather than to deliver economic value. Financial innovation and deepening may in some ways and under some circumstances foster economic value creation, but that needs to be illustrated at the level of specific effects: it cannot be asserted *a priori* or on the basis of top-level analysis.

(ii) The most fundamental development in several developed economies in the last forty to fifty years has been the growth in private-sector debt to GDP, and it is essential to understand the role which debt/credit plays within our economy. In many current discussions about the potential impact of higher capital requirements on growth, the focus is almost exclusively on credit extension as a means of intermediating household savings into corporate investment, with a direct potential link between credit extension and GDP growth. But in many developed economies the majority of credit extension plays no such role and instead either (i) supports consumption smoothing across the life-cycle, in particular through residential mortgages, or (ii) supports leveraged 'asset play' investments in already existing assets, in particular in commercial real estate. Lending against property—residential or commercial—dominates credit extension and is inherently susceptible to self-reinforcing cycles of credit supply and asset price.

(iii) Fractional reserve banks facilitate all categories of credit extension through maturity transformation, which in turn creates significant risks. There is a reasonable case that financial deepening via bank credit extension plays a growth-enhancing role in the early and mid stages of economic development, but it does not follow that further financial deepening (i.e. a growing level of private-sector credit and bank money relative to GDP) is limitlessly value creative. Less maturity transformation in aggregate and a reduced role for bank credit in the economy, compared with that which emerged pre-crisis in several developed economies, may be optimal in the long run.

5

(iv) While volatile credit supply in part derives specifically from the existence of banks, which introduce both leverage and maturity transformation into the financial system, the development of securitized credit and mark-to-market accounting has also contributed to that volatility, increasing the extent to which credit pricing and the quantity of credit supplied are driven by self-referential assessments of credit risk derived from the market price of credit.

(v) The essential reason why the 2007–8 crisis was so extreme was the interaction of the specific features of bank credit and the specific features of securitized credit.

(vi) Looking beyond banking and credit supply to the more general development of trading activity in non-credit derivatives, foreign exchange and equities, a pragmatic approach to the economic value of liquid traded markets should replace the axiomatic belief in the value of increased liquidity which characterized the pre-crisis years. Market liquidity delivers economic value up to a point, but not limitlessly. Liquid foreign exchange markets play a role in lubricating trade and capital flows, but can overshoot equilibrium values. Equity markets may be reasonably efficient at setting relative prices, but are susceptible to huge aggregate overshoots. Volatility in equity markets, however, is less harmful than volatility in debt markets. Market-making can be an economically useful function, but some proprietary trading (e.g. many foreign exchange carry trades) perform no useful economic purpose and can generate instability. The ability of regulators to distinguish useful market-making from destabilizing proprietary trading is, however, limited. Conversely, however, it is not nil.

If the essential causes of the crisis lay in the interaction between the specific risky characteristics of banks and of securitized credit markets, the regulatory response must address these fundamental issues.

The implications for policy are as follows.

(i) No 'silver bullet' structural reform can be an adequate response.

- Addressing the 'too big to fail' issue is a necessary but not sufficient response. Destabilizing volatility of credit supply could arise in a system of multiple small banks.
- The objective behind the Volcker rule is highly desirable, but a system of completely separate commercial and investment banks could still generate destabilizing credit and asset price swings.

- Narrow banking proposals to separate insured deposit-taking from lending activities will fail to address the fundamental drivers of credit and asset price instability.
- Proposals for replacing banks with 100% equity-financed loan funds, while useful in stimulating thinking about radical increases in bank capital requirements, might exacerbate price and valuation driven instability.

(ii) The most important elements of the regulatory reform instead need to be as follows.

- Much higher capital requirements across the whole of the banking system, and liquidity requirements which significantly reduce aggregate cross-system maturity transformation in both banks and shadow banks.
- The development of countercyclical macroprudential tools which can lean against the wind of credit and asset price cycles, and which may need to do so on a sector-specific basis.

(iii) Other elements of reform are appropriate but less fundamental.

- Improvements in and regulation of remuneration, risk governance and rating agencies practices have a role to play.
- More effective and intense supervision of individual firms is important.
- Fiscal policies—levies and taxes—can legitimately raise revenue and can be designed to complement capital and liquidity regulation.
- A pragmatic attitude towards the value of liquid traded markets implies that constraints on specific products or practices, such as short-selling, may be useful elements in the regulatory tool kit and should not be rejected as axiomatically harmful.

But none of these other policies is as important as higher capital and liquidity standards and the development of a macroprudential approach; it is vital that focus on other aspects of the reform does not divert attention from these priorities.

To make these points, this chapter is structured in six sections.

Section 1.1 addresses what a financial system does and, in particular, what banks do: their theoretical value added within the economy.

Section 1.2 looks at trends in the banking and financial system over the last fifty years, illustrating a dramatic increase in the overall scale of the financial sector, and important changes in the mix of activities performed.

7

Section 1.3 focuses on the provision of credit to the real economy, and the relationship between credit, economic growth and human welfare, and an argument in favour of new macroprudential policy tools, focused directly on the dynamics of credit extension, is given.

Section 1.4 looks at the complex securitization which developed over the last fifteen years. Was it truly valuable? Will it return and do we want it to return? What policy measures are required to make sure that it plays its appropriate function in the real economy?

Section 1.5 focuses on the provision of market liquidity and on the trading and position-taking activities which support it. How valuable is it? And what policy implications follow if we do not accept that more trading activity is always beneficial in all markets?

Section 1.6 gives implications for the regulatory reform agenda.

1.1 THE FINANCIAL SYSTEM'S VALUE ADDED TO THE ECONOMY

What does the financial system do, and how does it deliver economic value added or welfare benefits? There are many different ways of categorizing financial system activities. For the purposes of this chapter, I will start with a fourfold distinction between

(1) the provision of payment services, both retail and wholesale,

(2) the provision of pure insurance services, life or general, wholesale and retail, which enable people or businesses to lay off exposure to risks by pooling their exposure with others,

(3) the creation of markets in spot or short-term futures instruments in, for instance, foreign exchange and commodities, and finally

(4) financial intermediation between providers of funds and users of funds, savers and borrowers, investors and businesses, an intermediation which plays a crucial role in capital allocation within the economy.

Of course, specific products and activities span these four categories. A bank current account is a bundled mix of (1) and (4). Most life insurance products bundle elements of (2) and (4). And commodities trading via the futures market can be a form of investment, competing with other categories of investment to which savers might wish to devote their funds. But the conceptual distinctions nevertheless remain valuable.

My focus in this chapter will be almost entirely on category (4), with some comments in the final section on category (3). It is in these category (4) activities that the problems arose in the latest crisis: nothing went

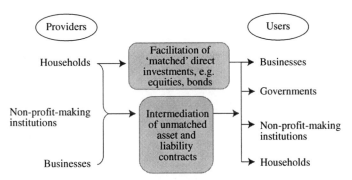

Figure 1.1. Linking fund providers with fund users.

wrong with the payment system, or with insurance pooling services, or with spot foreign exchange markets. Indeed, it is within this category (4) set of activities that problems have arisen in most past financial crises and where they are most likely to lie in future.

The function we are focusing on here (figure 1.1) is that of linking providers of funds (which can be either households or businesses or other corporate bodies) with users of funds, which again can be either households, businesses or other corporate bodies, or indeed the government. And the claims which exist between the providers and the issuers can take debt or equity (or intermediate) form, and can be a variety of different maturities.

One function that parts of the financial system perform is simply to help make a match between specific providers of funds and specific users, so that a direct investment can be made. Equity research and underwriting and distribution, for instance, can result in an individual household or corporate body owning a share of a specific company—similarly for bond research underwriting and distribution. But this match-making function is actually only a small part of what the financial system does. Indeed, the core of what the financial system does is to intermediate *non-matching* providers and users of funds, enabling the pattern of providers' assets to differ from the pattern of users' liabilities.

This intermediation of non-matching assets and liabilities entails four functions.

(i) First, a pooling of risks, with each depositor of a bank having an indirect claim on all the mortgages, business loans, or credit card receivables owed to the bank rather than a claim on one specific mortgage or loan.

(ii) Second, maturity transformation via balance-sheet intermediation, with banks lending at longer average maturities than they borrow. The

9

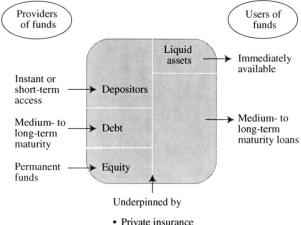

Figure 1.2. Maturity transformation via bank intermediation.

clear risks inherent in this transformation are offset by the equity cushion, but also by the holding of a fractional reserve of highly liquid assets, by liquidity insurance achieved through lines available from other banks and by the central bank lender-of-last-resort function (figure 1.2). This maturity transformation function enables, for instance, savers within the household sector to hold short-term deposits, while borrowers within the household sector can borrow on long-term mortgages.

(iii) Third, maturity transformation via the provision of market liquidity, which gives the holder of a contractually long-term asset the option of selling it immediately in a liquid market. The matching process I referred to earlier can result in a company issuing perpetual equity which is bought by a specific investor who intends to hold the equity in perpetuity, taking the dividend stream. But if there is a liquid market in equities, that investor does not have to hold the equity perpetually but has the option of selling the equity.[2]

(iv) Fourth, and finally, risk–return transformation: the creation of a different mix of debt and equity investment options for savers than arises naturally from the liabilities of the borrowers. Thus, what a bank balance

---

[2]Of course, this form of liquidity provision comes with uncertainty with regard to capital value, while maturity transformation on balance sheet enables the depositor to enjoy both liquidity and (almost, it is hoped) capital certainty. But it is still a form of maturity transformation, giving the fund provider a different set of asset options than is inherent in the maturity of the liabilities faced by fund users.

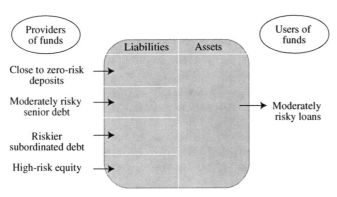

Figure 1.3. Risk–return transformation via bank intermediation: 'tranching'.

sheet essentially does is take a set of debt liabilities from final users and, in the language of securitization, to 'tranche' them, with some investors buying bank equity, some buying bank subordinated debt, some senior debt, and some making deposits (figure 1.3). As a result, depositors and senior debt holders hold a debt claim of much lower risk than the average pooled quality of the asset side of the banks' balance sheet, but also lower return, while equity holders have a higher-risk and higher return investment.

These four transformation functions can deliver value added to the economy in three different ways.

(i) The first function, pooling, entails the intermediary allocating capital to end projects. The financial system plays an indirect role in the capital allocation process even when it facilitates and informs direct matched investments—via, for instance, equity research and distribution. But it plays an even more active role in capital allocation when it performs pooling functions, either via asset management or via the pooling of bank debt claims. And it is important that it is done well, since a more efficient allocation of capital will tend to produce a higher level of income for any given level of investment.[3]

(ii) Second, and within the household sector, functions two and three enable individuals to hold the maturity mix of assets and liabilities which they want with, for instance, savers able to have short-term deposits,

---

[3]This financial intermediary function does not perform the whole of the capital allocation process. A significant amount of capital allocation occurs de facto within large firms, which make decisions about the use of retained earnings. But while it does not perform the whole of the capital allocation process, the financial system does play an important role.

while borrowers can have long-term maturity mortgages. This provides assurance of access to liquid assets in the face of either fluctuating consumption or unanticipated income shocks. It enables more extensive smoothing of consumption across the life cycle. And as a result it can deliver direct consumer welfare benefits independent of any impact on aggregate savings rates, investment levels, the efficiency of capital allocation or economic growth.

(iii) Third, all four functions together enable individual household sector savers to hold a mix of assets (as defined by risk, return and liquidity) which is different from the mix of liabilities owed by business users of funds. This transformation may under some circumstances produce a higher rate of savings, more productive investment and, for a period of time, higher growth.[4] Thus, for instance, maturity transformation makes possible a term structure of interest rates more favourable to long-term investment than would otherwise pertain, making long-term loans available on better terms. But in general, the impact of transformation of risk–return and/or liquidity possibilities will be to produce a level of savings which is *optimal* even if not necessarily higher, i.e. a level of savings which best reflects individual preferences and which thus maximizes welfare. Under some circumstances this welfare-maximizing savings rate might be lower than would pertain in a less developed financial system: underdeveloped financial systems, by constraining financial investment options and life-cycle consumption smoothing choices, can sometimes constrain individuals to choose savings rates higher than they would have chosen if a wider set of investment and borrowing options was available.

The first of these benefits, capital allocation, derives from the pooling function. The second and third derive from the risk–return transformation and the maturity transformation processes. Essentially, what these do is increase the range of options for investment in different combinations of risk–return/maturity beyond that which would exist if investors had to invest directly in the individual untransformed liabilities of business or households, or in pools of these untransformed liabilities.

Finally in this description of the theory, it is useful to note that the wave of complex credit securitization which occurred over the last fifteen to twenty years was not entirely new in its economic function, but rather it was an intensification of the four financial system transformations

---

[4]A higher rate of investment will produce a period of higher growth and a higher level of income at any one time than would otherwise pertain, but not a permanently higher growth rate.

described above and an application of those transformation functions to more assets and at a finer level of differentiation. This intensification entails four developments.

- Complex securitization pooled previously un-pooled assets such as mortgages.
- It transformed the risk–return characteristics of assets by tranching, taking, for instance, a set of mortgages with an average untransformed credit rating of A and manufacturing some AAA securities, some AA, some BBB and some equity.
- It introduced new forms of contractual balance-sheet maturity transformation, via structured investment vehicles (SIVs), conduits and mutual funds, which enabled short-term providers of funds to fund longer term credit extensions.[5]
- And it was underpinned by extensive trading in credit securities, providing market liquidity so that the holder of a contractually long credit security could sell it immediately if they wanted.

By doing all this, complex securitization increased the extent to which assets offered to investors could be tailored to their specific preferences for specific combinations of risk–return and liquidity. As a result, its proponents asserted before the crisis that it must have increased economic efficiency and economic welfare. Whether that argument was valid is considered in section 1.4.

1.2 Trends in Banking, Securitization and Trading

Section 1.1 has considered the functions which a banking and financial system can in principle perform. A striking fact about the last thirty to forty years of economic history is that the scale on which it performs those functions, the overall size of the financial system relative to the real economy, has dramatically increased. There are several different dimensions to this increase (figure 1.4)

Leverage, measured by debt to GDP, has increased significantly in many countries including the US shown in figure 1.4(a), with households in particular becoming more indebted, and with a particularly striking

---

[5]Indeed, it also applied the technologies of rotating 'master trusts' to achieve maturity transformation in the other direction, creating longer term credit securities out of mortgages whose average expected repayment maturity might (but might not) be relatively short term.

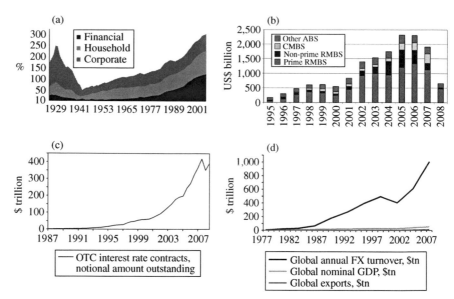

Figure 1.4. Measures of increasing financial intensity. (a) US debt as a percentage of GDP by borrower type. (b) Global issuance of asset-backed securities. (c) Growth of interest rate derivatives values, 1987–2009. (d) Foreign exchange trading values and world GDP 1977–2007.

Notes (for part (b)): public issuance only. Full-year issuance, except for 2008 which is up to and including September. 'Other ABS' includes auto, credit card and student loan ABS. *Source*: Bank of England.

increase in *intra*-financial system leverage, i.e. claims by one financial firm upon another.

Innovation has driven complexity, with a massive development over the last twenty years of complex securitization and derivatives products.

Trading volumes have increased hugely, relative to underlying real economic variables, with foreign exchange trading, for instance, increasing from eleven times global trade and long-term investment flows in the 1970s to over seventy times today and with similarly dramatic increases in oil and derivatives trading.

There has thus been an increasing 'financialization' of the economy: that is, an increasing role for the financial sector. Financial firms as a result have accounted for an increased share of GDP, of corporate profits and of stock market capitalization. And there has been a sharp rise in income differential between many employees in the financial sector and average incomes across the whole of the economy.

This increasing financial intensity reflected in part the globalization of world trade and capital flows, and the floating exchange rate regimes which followed the breakdown of the Bretton Woods system in the 1970s, but also deliberate policies of domestic financial liberalization.

A crucial issue is therefore whether this increased financial intensity has delivered value added for the real economy—whether it has improved capital allocation, increased growth, or increased human welfare and choice in ways which do not show up in growth rates. And whether it has made the economy more or less volatile and vulnerable to shocks.

Three observations are striking when we pose that question.

(i) First is the relatively little attention to that question paid by mainstream economics, with many theories of growth and development, and many models of the economy used by policymakers in finance ministries and central banks, treating the financial system as a neutral pass through. As Alan Taylor and Moritz Schularick (2009) note in a recent paper which considers the same issues I will address in this chapter,

> In the monetarist view of Friedman and Schwartz (1963) and also in the recently dominant neokeynesian synthesis, macroeconomic outcomes are largely independent of the performance of the financial system.

(ii) Second, however, is that while the recently dominant neoclassical school of economics has often been uninterested in the detailed transmission mechanisms which link actual financial institutions to real economic variables, it has provided strong support for the belief that increased financial activity—financial deepening, innovation, active trading and increased liquidity—must be a broadly positive development. This is because more financial activity helps complete markets. The first fundamental theorem of welfare economics, demonstrated mathematically by Kenneth Arrow and Gerard Debreu (1954), illustrates that a competitive equilibrium is efficient, but only if markets are complete, i.e. if there are markets in which to strike all possible desired contracts, including insurance contracts and investment contracts linking the present and the future, as well as markets for current goods, services and labour. Therefore, the more that the financial sector provides the transformation functions described in section 1.1, the more that innovation allows investors to choose precise combinations of risk, return and liquidity, and the more that trading activity generates market liquidity, the more efficient and welfare-maximizing the economy must be.

These theoretical propositions have, moreover, had a major influence on policymakers. Keynes famously suggested that 'practical men, who

15

believe themselves quite exempt from any intellectual influences, are usually the slaves of some defunct economist'. But the bigger danger may be that reasonably intellectual men and women who play key policymaking roles can be over-influenced by the predominant conventional wisdom of the current generation of academic economists. Certainly in the UK Financial Services Authority, the idea that greater market liquidity is in almost all cases beneficial, that financial innovation was to be encouraged because it expanded investor and issuer choice, and that regulatory interventions can only be justified if specific market imperfections can be identified, formed key elements in our institutional DNA in the years preceding the crisis. And the predominant tendency of the International Monetary Fund in the years before the crisis was to stress the advantages of free capital flows, financial deepening and financial innovation, making reference to theories of market completion and allocative efficiency.

(iii) The third observation, however, is that at the most general level there is no clear and always present correlation between the financial intensity of an economy and, say, the overall rate of economic growth. Carmen Reinhart and Ken Rogoff (2009) in their recent survey of eight centuries of financial folly, crashes and debt defaults (*This Time It's Different*) identify the period between 1945 and the early 1970s as one of 'financial repression' in which the role of the financial system was subdued in many countries. And in some developing countries that 'financial repression' probably was one among a package of market restrictive policies which hampered economic growth. But equally there were countries which in that period achieved historically rapid growth with fairly depressed financial systems (for instance Korea) and in the more developed economies—the US, Europe and Japan—this period of financial repression was one of significant and relatively stable growth, comparing well with the subsequent thirty years of increased financial activity and financial liberalization.

To assess the question properly, however, we need to consider specific financial activities and the economic functions they perform. This section therefore sets out a detailed description of what has changed, under four headings.

(i) The growth and changing mix of credit intermediation through UK bank balance sheets over the last fifty years.

(ii) The growth of complex securitization as a new form of credit intermediation over the last ten to twenty years.

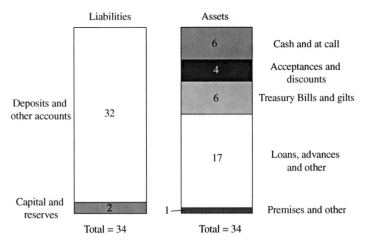

Figure 1.5. What the UK banking system did: 1964. UK banks' aggregate balance sheet as percentage of GDP.
Source: Sheppard (1971).

(iii) The difficulty in quantifying the vitally important change in aggregate maturity transformation, which the first two sets of changes have almost certainly produced.

(iv) And finally, the growth of financial trading activity over the last thirty years, linked in part to complex credit securitization, but also visible in a far wider range of markets than credit securities alone.

1.2.1 Growth and Changing Mix of Bank Intermediation

First, then, trends in bank intermediation. What did UK banks do fifty years ago and what do they do today: what has changed? Well, for data availability reasons my figures actually start forty-six years ago in 1964. Figure 1.5 shows the balance sheet of the UK banking system in that year, with the quantities expressed as percents of GDP, the aggregate balance sheet of all UK banks then just 35% of GDP. And one of the things banks then did was to use deposits from the household sector to fund government debt, with banks holding large holdings of government debt as part of their liquidity policies, and with the UK government's debt level, at 93.2% of GDP, still reflecting the aftermath of high debts incurred during the war. But the other thing the banking and building society sections together did (figure 1.6) was take net funds from the household sector, which deposited 40% of GDP but borrowed only 14%, and lend it to the private, non-financial and corporate sector, which deposited 8% of GDP

17

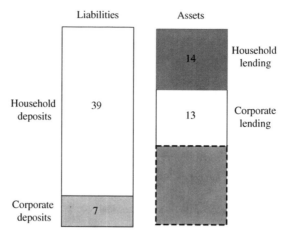

Figure 1.6. What the UK banking system did: 1964 (continued). Banks and building societies' lending/deposits (£bn). Private non-financial sector as percentage of GDP.
Source: Bank of England (2009).

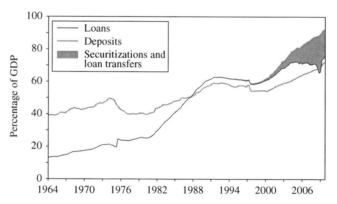

Figure 1.7. Household deposits and loans: 1964–2009.
Source: Bank of England (2009, tables A4.3, A4.1).

but borrowed 13%. In other words, it intermediated net household savings into business investment.

Over the subsequent forty-five years, however, the pattern changed significantly (figure 1.7). Household and unincorporated business borrowing from the banking and building society sectors grew from about 14% of GDP to 76% of GDP, while deposits also grew, but less dramatically from 39% to 72%. In addition, however, from the late 1990s, securitization made possible loans to the household sector that were not, or not

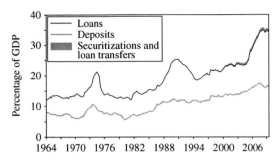

Figure 1.8. Private non-financial corporate deposits and loans: 1964–2009.
Source: Bank of England (2009, tables A4.3, A4.1).

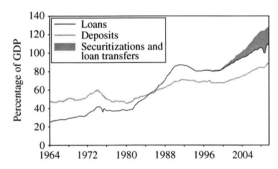

Figure 1.9. Household and private non-financial corporate deposits and loans: 1964–2009.
Source: Bank of England (2009, tables A4.3, A4.1).

necessarily, held on bank balance sheets, these reaching 17% of GDP by 2007 (the grey shaded area in figure 1.7).

Meanwhile (figure 1.8), a somewhat similar, but more volatile, pattern was observed for the corporate sector, with lending growing from 13% of GDP to 35% (but with sudden surges and setbacks on the path) and with deposits growing from 8% to 17%.

So, putting the two sectors together (figure 1.9) we get a far more dynamic growth in total lending than we do in deposits and the emergence on bank and building society balance sheets (figure 1.10) of what is labelled 'a customer funding gap': a deficiency of customer deposits (household or corporate) versus loans to those sectors. This funding gap was bridged by increased wholesale funding, including wholesale funding from abroad, made easier by the fact that by 2007, unlike in 1964, the UK banking system's relationship with the UK real economy (captured in figure 1.10) was within the context of London's role as a very large wholesale financial entrepot. Thus the total balance sheet of the UK banking

19

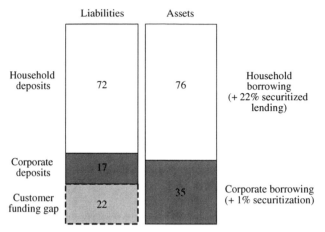

Figure 1.10. UK banks and building societies lending/deposits (£bn) to/from private non-financial sector: 2007 as percentage of GDP.

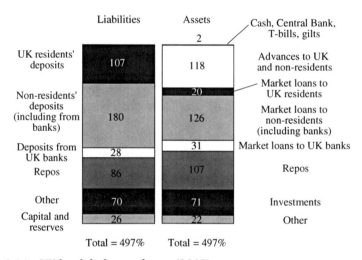

Figure 1.11. UK bank balance sheets (2007).

system, defined to include all legal banking entities operating in London, had by 2007 reached around 500% of GDP, compared with 34% in 1964, and was dominated not by the banks' relationship with UK households and companies, but by a complex mesh of intra-financial system claims and obligations (figure 1.11).

This funding gap and reliance on wholesale funding created significant vulnerabilities for the UK banking system which crystallized in 2007 and 2008 and new liquidity policies are being introduced to reduce such

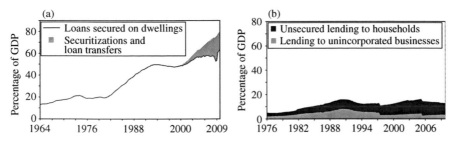

Figure 1.12. Household and 'non-profit institutions serving households' lending: 1964–2009. (a) Residential mortgage lending. (b) Other lending to household and non-profit institutions serving households.

Source: Bank of England (2009, tables A4.3, A4.1).

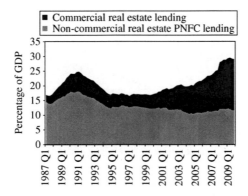

Figure 1.13. Corporate loans by broad sector: 1987–2008.

Source: ONS, Finstats. *Note*: part of the increase in real estate lending may be due to recategorization of corporate lending following sale and lease-back of properties and public finance initiative lending, but we do not think these elements are large enough to change the overall picture. Break in series from 2008 Q1 due to inclusion of building society data. Sterling borrowing only.

vulnerabilities in future. But it is not on the important risks and policies related to this funding gap that I wish to comment here, but on the increase in leverage in both the household and corporate sectors.

In both sectors, debt to GDP has increased significantly and the leverage has been focused on the financing of real estate assets.

In the household and unincorporated business sector (figure 1.12) the increase has been dominated by mortgage lending, up from 14% to 79% of GDP. Unsecured personal sector lending has increased from 3% at end 1975 to 9% but is still far less important than mortgage lending. Lending to unincorporated businesses meanwhile remains trivial in the big picture.

21

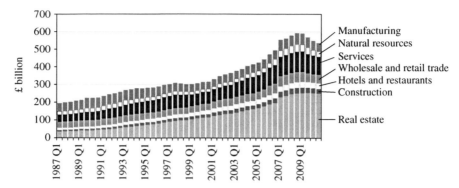

Figure 1.14. Corporate loans by sector: 1998-2008.
Source: Bank of England (2009).

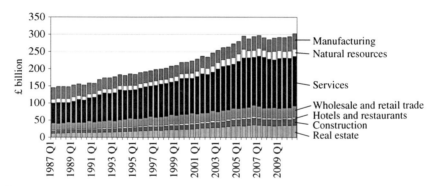

Figure 1.15. Corporate deposits by sector: 1998-2009.
Source: Bank of England (2009).

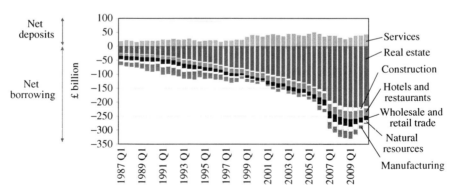

Figure 1.16. Corporate sector net deposits/borrowing: 1998-2009.
Source: Bank of England (2009).

In the corporate sector, meanwhile, the dramatic increase in the debt to GDP ratio in the last two decades has been dominated by the commercial real estate sector (figure 1.13), with very little increase in the leverage of non-commercial real estate related businesses; a dominance which looks even greater if we look at net lending. Thus, if, for the last ten years, we look at gross lending to different corporate sectors (figure 1.14) and gross deposits by different sectors into the banking system (figure 1.15), then we can calculate each sector's *net* deposits to or net lending from the banking sector (figure 1.16). What this illustrates is that the vast majority of net lending to the corporate sector is explained by lending to commercial real estate with, for instance, manufacturing only a marginal net borrower from the banking system, and indeed borrowing less in nominal terms than in 1998. The service sector excluding wholesale and retail, hotels and restaurants, by contrast, is a net depositor, for understandable reasons given its inherent characteristics.

Summing up, therefore, the striking features of UK banking sector trends over the last forty-five years are as follows.

- First, a very significant financial deepening, i.e. an increase in both loans and deposits as a percentage of GDP.
- Second, significant increases in the income leverage of both the household and corporate sectors, i.e. of indebtedness relative to GDP, and thus to income measures such as household income, corporate profit or property rentals.[6]
- Third, the fact that leverage growth has been dominated by increasing debt levels secured against assets, and predominantly against residential houses and commercial real estate.

1.2.2 *The Growth of Complex Securitization*

These changes in the scale and mix of banking intermediation have occurred gradually since the 1960s, with a strong acceleration after the financial liberalization of the 1970s.[7] The second overall trend I will highlight—the growth of the complex securitization—accrued primarily over the last two decades, though with important initial developments in the 1970s and 1980s.

---

[6]Details of the several different ways of measuring leverage (relative to income or assets) are set out in FSA (2010).

[7]In the UK, key policy measures were the liberalization of the domestic banking system via 'Competition and credit control' (1971) and the abolition of exchange controls in 1979.

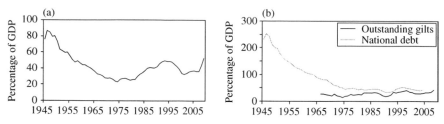

Figure 1.17. Government bonds outstanding as percentage of GDP. (a) US government bonds outstanding (source: Federal Reserve Flow of Funds Accounts; Datastream). (b) UK government bonds outstanding.

Notes: total gilts outstanding at 2009 Q4 was £796.3 billion. *Source*: 'national debt' from HM Treasury Public Finances Databank; 'outstanding gilts' from ONS Financial Statistics Consistent; Datastream.

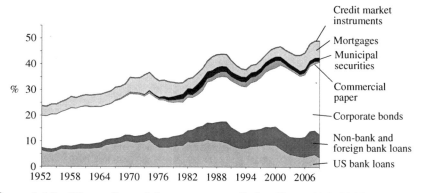

Figure 1.18. US non-financial corporate credit funding: 1952–2009 as percentage of GDP.

Notes: in 2009 the outstanding value of credit market instruments was $7.2 trillion and the outstanding value of corporate bonds was $4.1 trillion. *Source*: US Flow of Funds. *Note*: municipal securities refers to bonds issued to fund public–private partnerships and are not traditional local government issued securities. Mortgages can be defined as commercial property lending.

I use the term 'complex securitization' to stress the fact that marketable credit securities had been around for a long time before the securitization wave of the last twenty to thirty years. These straightforward credit securities, government bonds and corporate bonds were non-pooled and non-tranched: each security was the liability of a single government or corporate; and there was no process for creating multiple credit quality tiers out of the liabilities of one issuer. But they were credit securities which connected providers of funds to users of funds in a debt contract form, without the intermediation of a bank balance sheet. And

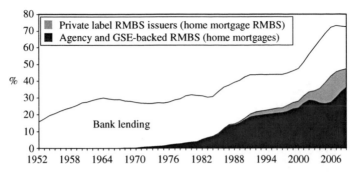

Figure 1.19. Securitization of US residential mortgages: 1960–2009.
Source: US Flow of Funds.

the markets for these instruments were and are very big, illustrating the large potential investor base for medium and long-term debt contracts (figure 1.17). US government debt to GDP reached 76% in 1945 and is 53% today with $7.5 trillion of T-bonds outstanding. US single-name corporate bonds (figure 1.18) accounted for 50% of all corporate credit financing even back in the 1950s, and there are now $4.1 trillion of these straight-forward single-name corporate bonds outstanding.

So securitized credit—i.e. credit extension through purchase of marketable credit securities rather than through loans on bank balance sheet—is not new. But what 'complex securitization' did was to extend the potential role of marketable credit securities to a wider range of final borrowers.

The initial, and still most important, application of this new technology was in residential mortgages, with two phases of development.

- First (figure 1.19), the growth of US agency and government-sponsored enterprise (GSE) mortgage-backed securities from 1971 onwards, initially in a simple pass-through, non-tranched form, but with tranching introduced with the creation of collateralized mortgage obligations (CMOs) from 1983 onwards.

- Second, the growth of private label (i.e. non-GSE) mortgage-backed securities from the mid 1980s onwards, with these usually using the new technique of tranching.

This growth of mortgage securitization was then followed, from the late 1980s onwards, by the extension of securitization to other asset categories (figure 1.20), in particular consumer credit and commercial mortgages.

25

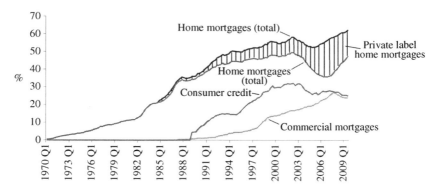

Figure 1.20. Securitized credit as percentage of total category: 1970–2009.
Source: US Flow of Funds.

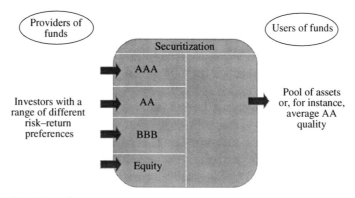

Figure 1.21. Tranching via securitization.

In essence, what this complex securitization did was to achieve, outside a bank balance sheet, two of the functions which, as we saw earlier, a bank balance sheet can deliver (figure 1.21): pooling of multiple small credit risks and tranching so that different providers of funds can hold a variety of different combinations of risk and return. As a result, complex securitization made it possible to extend the role of credit securities beyond the sphere of governments and single named corporates. In addition, its advocates asserted that it delivered efficiency and welfare benefits arising from the fact that investors could select precisely that combination of risk and return which met their preferences. They could then continually and smoothly adjust this combination over time, not only by buying or selling the underlying credit instruments but also through use of the credit derivatives markets (figure 1.22) that developed alongside complex securitization.

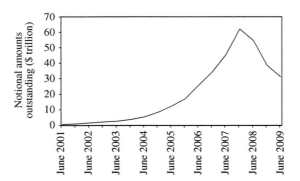

Figure 1.22. Global credit derivatives outstanding.
Source: ISDA Market Survey.

1.2.3 *Increasing Aggregate Maturity Transformation*

In addition to choosing their precise desired combination of risk and return, moreover, it appeared that securitization enabled investors to enjoy precisely the liquidity that they desired, given the marketable nature of credit securities. The long-term buy and hold investor could hold a credit security for its long-term contractual maturity, but the short-term investor could sell at any time.

Securitization, therefore, by increasing the range of credits which could be securitized, played a role in what is almost certainly another key feature of the financial system of the last several decades—an increasing aggregate maturity transformation. Aggregate maturity transformation is the extent to which the financial sector in total (eliminating all *intra*-financial system claims) holds assets which are longer term than liabilities, and thus is the extent to which the non-financial sector is enabled to hold assets which are shorter term than its liabilities. And it is frustratingly difficult to measure with any precision the level and trend of aggregate maturity transformation given the complexity introduced by the large scale of intra-financial system claims.

But the figures for household deposits and lending in the UK (figure 1.23) clearly suggest that a significant increase in aggregate maturity transformation must have occurred. Loans to the UK household sector have increased dramatically as a percentage of GDP, and these loans are primarily mortgages, with long-term contractual terms of twenty or thirty years or more. Deposits have also increased but these deposits are predominantly short term; indeed, many are instant access. And buffers of highly liquid assets held by banks have significantly reduced. It therefore must be the case that the UK banking system, and banking systems in

27

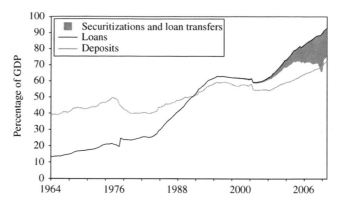

Figure 1.23. Household deposits and loans: 1964–2009.
Source: Bank of England (2009).

other countries, are performing more aggregate maturity transformation than in the past and, as a result, are running greater liquidity risks.

In addition, however, to increased maturity transformation on bank balance sheets, securitization, combined with other financial innovations, resulted in an increasing level of maturity transformation *off* bank balance sheets. SIVs and conduits were major buyers of contractually long-term credit securities, but were funded by short-term commercial paper. Mutual funds had liabilities to investors who believed they enjoyed both immediate access to funds and deposit-like security of capital value. But these funds were investing in long-term credit securities, or in the commercial paper of SIVs and conduits, which in turn bought long-term securities. They were thus involved in either one-step or two-step maturity transformation processes. And the trading books of commercial investment banks included large portfolios of contractually long credit securities, funded short term by repo financing arrangements.

All these new forms of maturity transformation rely crucially on the idea that 'market liquidity' would be available whenever needed—all helping to give investors more choice in respect to the liquidity of their investments but all creating new financial stability risks.

1.2.4 *Increasing Trading Activity Across Multiple Markets*

Fourth, and finally in this review of key financial trends, the last thirty years have seen a quite remarkable explosion in the scale of financial trading activities relative to real economic variables.

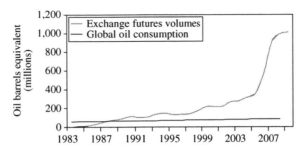

Figure 1.24. Increased trading activity relative to real economy: oil.
Notes: global oil consumption versus traded oil futures 1983–2009. *Source*: NYMEX.

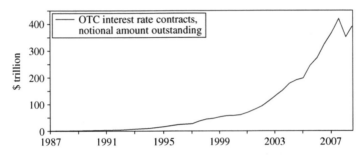

Figure 1.25. Interest rate derivatives trading: 1980–2009.
Source: ISDA Market Survey (1987–97); BIS Quarterly Review (1998–2009). Includes interest rate swaps and interest rate options.

- The value of foreign exchange trading has exploded relative to the value of global GDP or global trade (figure 1.4(d)): from eleven times global trade value in 1980 to seventy-three times today.
- The value of oil futures traded has increased from 20% of global physical production and consumption in 1980 to ten times today (figure 1.24).
- Interest rate derivatives trading has grown from nil in 1980 to $390 trillion in mid 2009 (figure 1.25).

Summing up, therefore, increasing financial intensity in the UK, US and other advanced economies over the last forty to fifty years, and in particular the last thirty, has been driven by the following factors.

- Increased leverage of non-financial sectors, in particular driven by increased lending against real estate assets, both residential and commercial.
- The growth of complex securitization, which has in particular supported more residential mortgage lending.

29

- An increased level of aggregate maturity transformation.
- Increased trading activity and market liquidity.
- As a result of these other trends, an increase in the scale and complexity of *intra*-financial system claims, claims between financial institutions rather than between them and the real economy.

The crucial question is whether this increase in financial activity has delivered human welfare benefits and, if so, how.

- Via the direct welfare benefits of more effective consumption smoothing?
- Or via improved allocation of capital?
- Or via increased savings rates and growth rates?
- Or via optimal savings rates and growth rates, even if not necessarily increased rates?

1.3 BANK CREDIT EXTENSION: OPTIMAL ROLE AND MIX

The development of the modern market economy over the last 200 years has been accompanied by a pervasive development of banking systems, performing the first three functions outlined in section 1.1: pooling of risks, maturity transformation and risk–return transformation via the introduction of an intermediating equity slice. As a result, depositors enjoy high certainty of capital value combined with short contractual maturity: equity fund providers take much greater risk, but with that risk still bounded by limited liability.

So fundamental and pervasive are these features of banking systems within market economies that there is a tendency to think that they are inherent and inevitable. In fact, however, there have always been economists concerned that these features create market instability: Irving Fisher and Milton Friedman warned against the dangers of a classic fractional reserve banking model, and in the last year Professor John Kay (2009) in Britain and Professor Laurence Kotlikoff (2010) in the US have produced 'narrow bank' or 'limited-purpose bank' proposals that would completely reject the model in which short-term deposits of certain value can, via transformation, fund risky household and commercial loans.

I am not going to argue in this chapter for either of those radical change models. Indeed, I believe that the proposals of Professors Kay and Koltikoff would not effectively address the fundamental problem we face—which is volatility in the supply of credit to the real economy, and biases in the sectoral mix of that credit. A volatility and bias which, as I shall describe in section 1.4, can occur as much in a non-bank securitized form of credit extension as when credit is extended on balance sheet. But the fact that there are respected economists arguing that the entire structure of banking is inappropriate does mean that we need to go back to the basics of whether and why and under what circumstances banks as we currently know them add value to the real economy.

A classic statement of how fractional reserve banking adds value was set out in Walter Bagehot's *Lombard Street*. He argued that banking enabled the mobilization of savings, that, for instance, Britain enjoyed an economic advantage over France because the UK's more advanced banking system fostered the productive investment of savings rather than leaving them 'dormant':

> Much more cash exists out of banks in France and Germany and in the non-banking countries than can be found in England or Scotland, where banking is developed. But this money is not ... attainable... The English money is 'borrowable money'. Our people are bolder in dealing with their money than any continental nation ... and the mere fact that their money is deposited in a bank makes it attainable. A place like Lombard Street where in all but the rarest times money can be obtained on good security or upon decent proposals of probable gain is a luxury which no other country has ever enjoyed before.

Bagehot's argument rests essentially on the positive benefits of the transformation functions considered in section 1.1, with the pooling, maturity and risk–return transformation functions of Britain's banking system enabling individuals with secure liquid deposits to finance trade and investment through loans to borrowers with whom they had no direct contact, and whose liabilities were of longer term; while in France, with a less developed banking system, the capital formation process depended to a greater extent on the creation of precise matches—people with money who happened also to have entrepreneurial and management capability, or who could make direct contracts with specific businesses.

Bagehot's initial insight is reflected in the predominant belief that 'financial deepening' is good for an economy: that more financial intermediation, measured by credit as a percentage of GDP, will mean higher investment and thus higher GDP. And a number of studies have indeed illustrated either cross-sectoral or time serves correlations between the development of basic banking and financial systems and economic growth (see, for example, King and Levine 1993; Rousseau and Sylla 1999). And from the current position of a developing nation like, say, India, the positive benefits of some financial deepening do seem clear. But the paper by Moritz Schularick and Alan Taylor that I quoted earlier questions whether this positive relationship pertains as economies move beyond the level of financial maturity reached in the advanced countries thirty to forty years ago. It documents the growth of leverage and credit extension which liberalization and innovation have facilitated, but finds little support for the preposition that this liberalization and innovation has led to a corresponding increase in real growth rates for the countries in their sample.

It is on this question of financial deepening beyond the level reached in the advanced countries thirty to forty years ago that I will focus here. And in doing so I will focus solely on what one might label the long-term comparative statics issue, not the issue of transitional dynamics.

- By long-term comparative statics I mean the question of whether the UK, for instance, would be better or worse off if in, say, 2025 if we had a debt to GDP ratio of 120%, or 100% or 80%. Or indeed would we be better or worse off if today we had 80% debt, with debt never having grown to today's level of 125%? To answer that question we need to consider the impact of credit on the long-term savings rate and the efficiency of capital allocation, and thus on the long-term productive potential of the economy. We also need to consider the direct welfare benefits that credit can deliver through life-cycle consumption smoothing.

- The transitional dynamics question, by contrast, is quite different. It accepts as a necessary given that we start with private debt to GDP of 125% and asks what the optimal evolution of this level over the medium term, say the next five years, is. To answer that question we need to consider the implications of changes in credit supply for aggregate nominal demand, and thus for the path of actual GDP (and employment) relative to productive potential.

We need to know the answers to both questions, and the answers might well pose a policy timing dilemma, with deleveraging being beneficial over the long term but harmful over the short. And both questions are highly relevant to the design of the new capital and liquidity regulatory regime on which the global institutions—the Financial Stability Board and the Basel Committee—are engaged this year. Higher capital and liquidity requirements together will probably mean less plentiful credit supply. The newly established Macroeconomic Assessment Group jointly established by the Bank for International Settlements (BIS) and the Financial Stability Board (FSB) will therefore need to consider both the long term

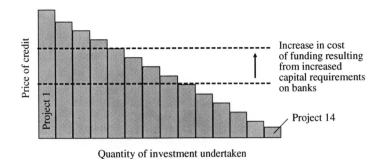

Figure 1.26. Credit prices and productive investment: the commonly assumed model.

and the transitional implementations of such restriction. For now, however, I will focus solely on the long-term question.

And I will begin by assuming that higher capital and liquidity requirements will increase the cost of credit intermediation and thus increase the price and/or decrease the quantitative supply of credit. I say 'assume' because, at least in respect to higher capital requirements, there is a theoretical debate. If, for instance, the propositions of Modigliani and Miller hold, higher equity capital requirements ought to produce a lower cost of bank equity and a lower cost of bank debt (since the riskiness of both would reduce), and in a taxless world those effects would fully offset the higher proportionate role for relatively more expensive equity (Miller and Modigliani 1958, 1963). In the real world of tax biases in favour of debt, however, there is clearly a private cost penalty to higher equity requirements, and the case that tighter liquidity requirements increase the cost of long-term credit provision appears fairly clear.

So assuming that higher capital and liquidity requirements do mean more expensive and less plentiful credit supply, what economic consequences follow?

A common and apparently obvious answer assumes that a higher cost of credit and more restricted supply of credit will mean that capital investment will be reduced as productive investments go unfinanced. The assumed model here is that of a marginal efficiency of capital schedule (figure 1.26) with possible investment projects ranked by order of return, and with the level of investment in the economy, i.e. the number of projects that get financed, determined by how many deliver a return higher than the cost of capital. Increase the cost of credit intermediation and fewer projects will be financed.

Under this model it can still be socially optimal to raise capital requirements since the impact of increased credit intermediation costs in good

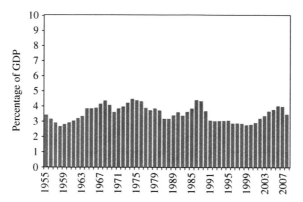

Figure 1.27. Residential dwellings investment as percentage of GDP.

years can be offset by a decreased risk of financial crises. Models which assume that this is the balance to be struck, such as the NIESR model which the Financial Services Authority (FSA) has been using to consider the tradeoffs involved in the setting of new capital liquidity requirements, can still suggest that significant increases in capital and liquidity requirements are socially optimal.[8] But such models still assume that increased bank capital means decreased investment and thus reduced growth in good times. And this is the quite explicit assumption behind much private-sector input to the regulatory debate.

What I would like to question, however, is whether this model of the impact of credit supply constraint is actually relevant to all, or indeed more than a small proportion of, the total credit supply described in my earlier charts. Consider for instance, the growth of UK mortgage credit, which has gone over the last forty-five years from 14% to 79% of GDP. To some extent, mortgage credit obviously indirectly helps finance new investment in housing. But over the last fifty years capital investment in UK housing as a percentage of GDP (figure 1.27) has oscillated but with no particular trend. And the net capital stock of investment in residential housing measured as accumulated past investment minus depreciation has as a result not risen as a percentage of GDP (figure 1.28). Instead, what we have is a phenomenon in which mortgage debt as a percentage

---

[8]See FSA (2009b) for a description of the modelling approach using the NIESR model. Note that the NIESR model does distinguish the impact of credit restrictions on the corporate versus household sector, but does not distinguish within the corporate sector between different categories of credit (e.g. commercial real estate versus all others) in the way considered later in this section.

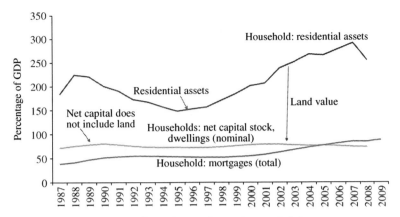

Figure 1.28. Housing capital stock, market value and debt.

of GDP and the market value of housing have risen in a fashion largely detached from the processes of capital investment.[9]

Which does not, I must immediately stress, mean that mortgage finance has no economic or social value but rather that in countries with relatively stable populations and with large housing stocks inherited from the past, the economic function of mortgage finance is only to a very limited extent related to the financing of new investment, and to a very large extent supporting the ability of individuals to smooth consumption over the life cycle, with younger generations buying houses off the older generation who already own them.[10] The extent to which this is the case varies with national characteristics such as the density of population and the growth rate of the population (or of household numbers) but it is at least possible to imagine an economy which was making no new net investment in housing but which had a high and rising level of mortgage debt to GDP.

An assumed model in which an increased cost of credit intermediation would curtail investment, and thus growth, is therefore largely irrelevant to residential mortgage debt in the UK, and therefore for 63% of all bank lending. Instead, when we think about the value added of different levels of mortgage debt, the trade-off is as follows.

---

[9]The difference between the market value of housing and the net capital stock illustrated in figure 1.28 is to a significant extent explained by land values. Mortgage credit in a rich, densely populated but stable population country is therefore to a very significant extent financing the purchase of a fixed supply of land by one generation from another.

[10]The key element of consumption that is smoothed is the flow of housing services that ownership of a house delivers.

- A plentiful supply of residential mortgage debt will increase human welfare by enabling individuals to smooth the consumption of housing services through their life cycle. It enables the individual without inherited resources to use future income prospects to purchase houses today. And it lubricates a process by which one generation first accumulates housing assets and then sells them to the next generation, achieving an inter-generational resource transfer equivalent to a pension system. A more restricted supply of mortgage finance makes access to home ownership more dependent on the vagaries of inheritance, and tends to produce an inefficient use of housing resources, with older people facing few incentives to trade down from large houses and to release housing resources for use by the younger generation.

- Conversely, however, the easy availability of mortgage credit can generate a credit/asset price cycle, and can encourage households on average to select levels of income leverage which, while sustainable in good and steady economic times, increase vulnerability to employment or income shocks. It can therefore create macro-economic volatility. And it can tempt some individuals, in pursuit of prospective capital gain, into debt contracts which harm their individual welfare rather than maximize it.

There are therefore very important advantages and risks created by extensive mortgage credit supply, which need to be taken into account in decisions about bank capital and liquidity (or any other policy levers which might impact on credit supply). But the optimal resolution of this balance has no necessary implications either way for the overall level of investment and growth in the economy, on which discussions of the impact of capital adequacy regimes frequently focus.

Similar considerations may apply when thinking about some subsets of corporate lending, and in particular lending to the corporate real estate sector, which has grown so dramatically in the last twenty years as a percentage of GDP and as a share of total corporate lending.

And here again I definitely do not suggest that all lending to commercial real estate is somehow socially useless and that, as it were, 'real bankers only lend money to manufacturing companies'. Indeed, in a mature economy high-quality investment in commercial real estate—high-quality hotels, office space and retail parks—and the related investment in the public urban environment is definitely part of the wealth-creation process. Fixed capital formation in buildings and structures at around 6% of GDP is now slightly higher than total investment in all plant,

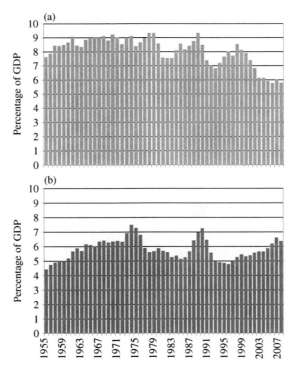

Figure 1.29. Gross capital investment in buildings and machinery structures: 1955–2007. (a) Plant, machinery, vehicles, ships and aircraft. (b) Other new buildings and structures (commercial real estate).

machinery, vehicles, ships and aircraft, and that may well be what we should expect in a mature rich economy (figure 1.29).

But note that it was just as high as a percentage of GDP in 1964, when total lending to real estate developers was much lower.

Which suggests that alongside the role which lending to commercial real estate plays in financing new productive real estate investment, what much commercial real estate lending does is to enable investors to leverage their purchase of already existing assets, enjoying as a result the tax benefit of interest deductibility, often in the expectation of medium-term capital gain, and in some cases exploiting the put option of limited liability.

Thus, in both residential and commercial real estate lending, the model in which we assume that more expensive credit would restrict productive investment is only partially applicable. In both, moreover, we need also to recognize the role that credit can play in driving asset price cycles which in turn drive credit supply in a self-reinforcing and potentially

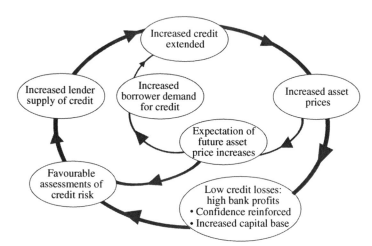

Figure 1.30. Credit and asset price cycles.

destabilizing process. Thus (figure 1.30), increased credit extended to commercial real estate developers can drive up the price of buildings whose supply is inelastic, or of land whose supply is wholly fixed. Increased asset prices in turn drive expectations of further price increases which drive demand for credit, but they also improve bank profits, bank capital bases and lending officer confidence, generating favourable assessments of credit risk and an increased supply of credit to meet the extra demand.

Overall, as we look at the drivers and economic functions of credit we must, I believe, distinguish between different categories (figure 1.31), which have different economic functions and whose dynamics are driven by different factors. Household credit, 74% of the total, is essentially about life-cycle consumption smoothing and inter-generational resource transfer not productive investment. Real estate lending, which, combining household and commercial real estate, amounts to over 75% of all lending in the UK, is at times strongly driven by expectations of asset appreciation. Commercial real estate and indeed leveraged buyout borrowing has quite a lot to do with exploiting the tax shield of debt and the put option of limited liability. Only lending to non-real estate companies therefore appears to accord fully with the commonly assumed model in which credit finances investment and trade and is serviced out of capital flows, and in which a higher cost of credit will curtail productive investment. But in the UK at least, such lending accounts for a relatively small proportion of the total (figure 1.32).

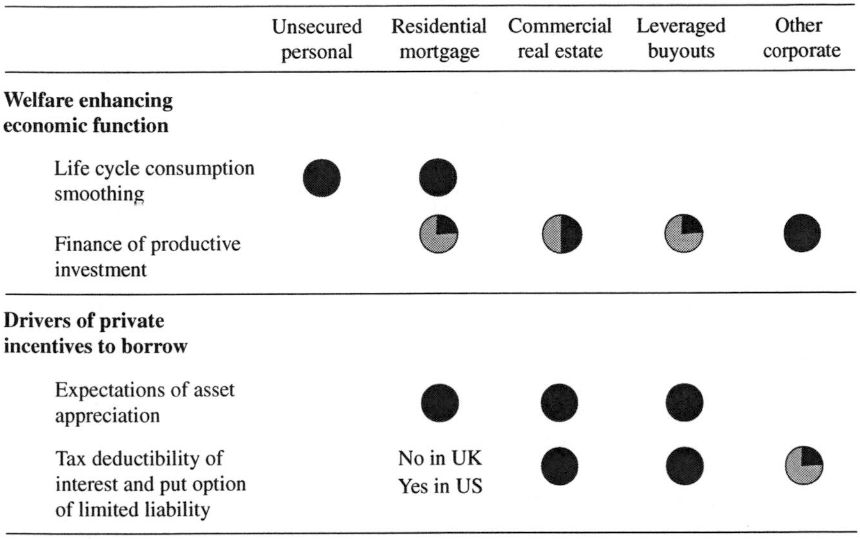

	Unsecured personal	Residential mortgage	Commercial real estate	Leveraged buyouts	Other corporate
Welfare enhancing economic function					
Life cycle consumption smoothing	●	●			
Finance of productive investment		◔	◑	◕	●
Drivers of private incentives to borrow					
Expectations of asset appreciation		●	●	●	
Tax deductibility of interest and put option of limited liability	No in UK Yes in US	●	●		◕

Figure 1.31. Drivers and economic function of different categories of debt.

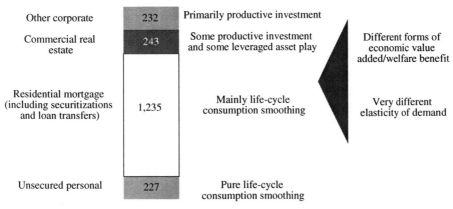

Figure 1.32. Bank and building society lending (£bn) to UK economy by function: 2009.

In deciding optimal levels of capital and liquidity for the banking system we therefore need to consider the possible impact on different categories of lending whose economic value or direct welfare benefit is quite different. We also need to recognize, however, that the elasticity of response of different categories of credit to interest rate changes is likely to be hugely varied and to vary over time in the light of changing expectations of future asset prices.

39

- The company which is thinking of investing in a new project—be it a new manufacturing product development, a new energy investment, or a new retailing concept—and intending to repay the loan out of project cash flows may be very sensitive to minor variations in expected interest rates. So, to a lesser but still significant extent, might be the individual using unsecured credit to smooth short-term cash flows.

- But when expectations of property (or other asset) price inflation have become strongly embedded, even quite large increases in interest rate may have little short-term impact—to the homeowner or commercial real estate investor who expects medium-term capital appreciation of say 15% per annum, small increases in lending rates may make little difference to their propensity to borrow.

There is therefore a danger that at some points in the credit/asset cycle appropriate actions to offset the economic and financial stability dangers of exuberant lending will tend to crowd out that element of lending which is indeed related to the funding of marginal productive investments.

This in turn carries implications for optimal policy. The analysis presented in this section suggests three conclusions.

(i) First, that we cannot base our assessment of optimal capital and liquidity levels solely on the 'marginal productive investment' model, but that we do need to understand what impact higher capital requirements would have on fixed capital investment.

(ii) Second, that optimal policy almost certainly needs to distinguish between different categories of credit, which perform different economic functions and whose interest rate elasticity of demand is likely, at least at some points in the cycle, to vary hugely.

(iii) And third, that optimal policy needs to be able to lean against credit and asset price cycles.

These conclusions together suggest the need for macroprudential through-the-cycle tools, and perhaps for those tools to be differentiated in their sectoral application.[11] We need new tools to take away the punch bowl before the party gets out of hand. Four approaches could be considered.

---

[11] The case for such tools and the complexities involved in their application are discussed in Bank of England (2009).

(i) The first is for interest rate policy to take account of credit/asset price cycles as well as consumer price inflation. But that option has three disadvantages: that the interest elasticity of response is likely to be widely different by sector—small and medium-sized non-commercial real estate enterprises start hurting long before a real estate boom is slowed down; that higher interest rates can drive exchange rate appreciation; and that any divergence from current monetary policy objectives would dilute the clarity of the commitment to price stability.

(ii) The second would be across the board countercyclical capital adequacy requirements, increasing capital requirements in the boom years, on either a hardwired or discretionary basis. But that too suffers from the challenge of variable elasticity effects, given that capital levers also work via their impact on the price of credit.

(iii) The third would be countercyclical capital requirements varied by sector, increased against commercial real estate lending, say, but not against other categories. That certainly has attractions, but might be somewhat undermined by international competition, particularly within a European single market. If, for instance, Ireland had increased capital requirements for commercial real estate lending countercyclically in the years before 2008, the constraint on its own banks would have been partially offset by increased lending from British or other foreign competitors.

(iv) The fourth would entail direct borrower-focused policies, such as maximum limits on loan-to-value ratios, for instance, either applied continuously or varied through the cycle.[12] There are no easy answers here, but some combination of new macroprudential tools is likely to be required. And a crucial starting point in designing them is to recognize that different categories of credit perform different economic functions and that the impact of credit restrictions on economic value added and social welfare will vary according to which category of credit is restricted.

---

[12]Note that while national borrower-focused limits are also susceptible to cross-border leakage problems (e.g. it is possible for a company operating in the UK to borrow money through a legal entity in another country), these leakage problems are least in respect to lending secured against real estate. This is because, given the immovable nature of property, it is possible to design restrictions on the level of debt which can be secured against specific properties.

1.4 Complex Securitized Credit: Reducing or Increasing Risk?

The growth of complex securitized credit was discussed in section 1.2.2 and its role in driving increased maturity transformation was discussed in section 1.2.3. It played a major role in the 2008 crisis. It was not the sole driver of that crisis: the rapid expansion of poor quality on-balance-sheet lending, financed by wholesale funding, was also important. And securitization and related trading played no significant role in some of the biggest individual bank failures; it was, for instance, irrelevant to HBOS's over expansion into commercial real estate. Clearly, though, securitization was an important part of the story: complex securitization supported an explosion of low-quality mortgage credit origination in the US and new forms of off-bank-balance-sheet maturity transformation created major new risks. And excessive complexity created problems of intransparency, imperfectly understood risks, and confidence and contagion effects driven by uncertainties over the value of 'toxic assets'.

Before the crisis, however, securitization and the associated growth of credit and other derivatives were widely lauded as favourable developments, improving investor and borrower choice, economic efficiency and risk management. In the wake of the crisis we should therefore ask the following questions.

- Were the positive benefits attributed to securitization and credit derivatives significant, or could they have been?
- Are the risks that complex securitization helped generate inherent to the provision of credit in a securitized form, or did they arise simply because of bad features of the pre-crisis securitization—features we can fix via better regulation or market practice?

Four related arguments were advanced in favour of credit securitization.

(i) First, that it enabled banks to better manage their balance-sheet risks (see, for example, Bryan 1988). Rather than, say, a regional bank in the US holding an undiversified portfolio of credit exposures in its region, it could instead originate loans and distribute them, and it could hedge credit exposure via credit derivatives and interest rate exposure via interest rate derivatives. In some past banking crisis—such as the US banking system collapse of the early 1930s or the savings and loans crisis of the 1980s—the problems were in part the undiversified nature of specific bank exposures, or the lack of instruments to separate credit risk exposure from interest rate mismatch. Securitization appeared to fix these problems.

(ii) Second, it was argued that complex securitization achieved market completion, with pooling, tranching and marketability enabling each investor to hold precisely that combination of risk–return/liquidity which best met their preferences. It was assumed by axiom that this must in some way be good—either, presumably, in a direct welfare sense, or because it enabled the attainment of a higher, or at least an optimal, savings rate.

(iii) Third, and as a result, it was asserted that securitization not only made individual banks less risky, but the whole system more stable, because risk was dispersed into the hands of precisely those investors best suited to manage different combinations of risk.

(iv) Fourth, it was argued that securitization supported increased credit supply. Complex securitization of subprime mortgage credit in the US was valuable because it enabled new classes of borrower to enjoy the benefits of life-cycle consumption smoothing, and the use of credit default swaps (CDSs) was beneficial because it enabled banks to better manage credit risk, economizing on the use of bank capital and enabling them to extend more credit off any given capital base.[13]

Obviously something went badly wrong with this rosy vision, and in particular with the proposition that complex securitization would reduce individual bank and system-wide risks. And the easy thing, with the benefit of hindsight, is to list the specific features of pre-crisis securitization which created major risk.

- Inadequacies in credit ratings, as rating agencies with conflicts of interest were tempted into putting ratings on securities for which no sound rating methodology existed.
- Poor incentives for good underwriting: originators and traders who cared little whether the credit was good as long as they could sell it before any problems arose.
- Overcomplexity—particularly in the final decade before the crisis, with a proliferation of the alphabet soup of ever more exotic resecuritizations, such as constant proportion debt obligations (CPDOs)

---

[13]In the pre-crisis years, 'using bank capital more efficiently' (i.e. being able to support more lending on any given level of bank capital) was perceived as not only a rational private objective for individual banks, but as a valuable social objective. Thus, the Basel II capital adequacy regime was designed around the overt principle that if banks could develop more sophisticated risk management systems, they should be allowed to operate with higher leverage.

and CDO squareds, combined with a general lack of transparency about underlying credit quality.

- Poorly understood embedded options—again, particularly a problem in the most complex products which emerged in the final decade.
- Far too low capital requirements against the holding of credit securities in trading books, creating massive capital arbitrage opportunities, and resulting in a model of securitized credit which was called 'originate and distribute', but which was actually 'originate, distribute, and then acquire somebody else's credit securities', so that when the music stopped the biggest losses actually arose on the balance sheets of banks and investment banks.[14]

In response to this list of now obvious problems, an extensive regulatory reform programme is in hand, involving the following.

- Regulation of credit rating agencies to guard against conflicts of interest.
- Various forms of risk retention requirements to ensure that credit originators have 'skin-in-the-game'.
- Requirements for better disclosure of underlying risk.
- A radical reform of trading-book capital. The Basel Committee has already announced specific changes, for implementation by 2011, which will increase capital requirements against specific trading activities several times, and a fundamental review of all trading-book capital requirements will be completed over the next twelve months.

Alongside these regulatory responses, meanwhile, a market reaction ('once bitten, twice shy', as it were) is likely in itself to mean that when securitized credit returns it will do so without some of the past excesses. The marketplace is likely to demand simple and transparent structures and, even if regulators allowed it, to have no appetite for the hypercomplex instruments of the final stage of pre-crisis exuberance.

So the regulators and the market together have a clear view of past problems, and I think we will fix them. But what we do not know is whether fixing these problems means that complex securitization bounces back in a new, less risky form or whether it never returns, or at least not on anything like the same scale. Because what is not clear is

---

[14] See, for example, the estimates of the incidence of losses set out in IMF (2008).

how far previous market volumes were only possible because of intrinsically risky practices.

So, beyond the immediate agenda of obvious things we should do and are doing, two questions remain.

- Did complex securitization deliver economic value?
- Were the risks it generated fixable or inherent?

1.4.1 Securitization and Related Derivatives: What Economic Value Added?

Let's consider the 'economic value added' case for securitization under three headings.

The first is market completion, the idea that complex securitization and derivatives must have delivered value added because they completed markets, making possible particular contracts that were not previously available, and thus allowing investors to pick precisely that combination of risk, return and liquidity which best met their preferences. In theory these benefits of 'market completion' follow axiomatically from the Arrow–Debreu theorem, and in the pre-crisis years many regulators, and certainly the FSA, were highly susceptible to this argument by axiom. We were philosophically inclined to accept that if innovation created new markets and products, that must be beneficial, while if regulation stymied innovation, that must be bad. We are now more aware of the instability risks which might offset the benefits of such innovation. But we also need to question how big the benefits could possibly have been, even if securitization had not brought with it risks of instability. And here two perspectives are important.

- The first is that to the extent that complex structuring was driven by either tax or capital arbitrage, reducing tax payments or reducing capital requirements without reducing inherent risk, then it clearly falls in the category of the 'socially useless' (i.e. delivering no economic value at the collective social level), even if it generated private return. And a non-trivial proportion of complex securitization was indeed driven by tax and capital arbitrage.
- Second, that while there clearly is an economic value in market completion, it must be subject to diminishing marginal return. That beyond some point, the additional welfare benefit of providing ever more tailored combinations of risk, return and liquidity must become minimal.

45

Together these two perspectives argue for a far greater scepticism about market completion arguments in future than was common pre-crisis.

As for the second argument—that complex securitization made possible increased credit extension—that is undoubtedly true. In the US, the UK and several other markets, securitization of residential mortgages made possible the extension of mortgage credit to segments of the population previously excluded from credit access. But deciding whether or not that was truly beneficial takes us back to precisely the considerations about the economic function and value of credit that I discussed in section 1.3, and to the different functions that different categories of credit perform. And just as with mortgage credit extended on balance sheet, so with securitized mortgage credit, the key issues are whether increased life-cycle consumption smoothing was socially beneficial, and whether increased supply of credit drove asset prices in a volatile cycle, rather than the extent to which more credit enabled marginal productive investment. Even from a direct consumer welfare point of view, let alone from a macro volatility point of view, it is clear that much of the extension of credit to new categories of borrowers which was made possible by mortgage securitization in the US, and to a degree in the UK, was harmful rather than beneficial to the individuals concerned.[15,16]

The third, and final, argument relates to better risk management, both at the individual firm level and at the system level. Given how spectacularly the system blew up, it might seem obvious that this is the least convincing of the arguments for complex securitization. But in principle, and providing securitization was done well and distribution truly achieved, this might be the most convincing of the three arguments put forward. In principle it would be better if small and medium-sized banks did not hold undiversified credit exposure to particular sectors or regions and the use of credit default swaps to enable banks to adjust and diversify their

---

[15]FSA (2009a), for instance, describes how securitized lending in the UK, extended credit to new categories of previously excluded borrower, but also the extent to which arrears and repossessions are concentrated in these sectors.

[16]The high credit losses incurred on US subprime and Alt-A lending ultimately derive from the fact that the individuals concerned did not have the income levels to sustain the debt they took on, which could only have been made affordable via further house price appreciation. This illustrates that while the extension of credit to previously excluded sectors can enhance welfare by making possible consumption smoothing, it cannot in a sustainable and non-risky way increase the lifetime earnings/consumption which are being smoothed. If customers are excluded from credit access because their lifetimes earnings prospects are low, the extension of credit cannot overcome and could make worse problems which can only be addressed through income enhancement or redistribution.

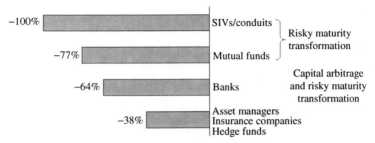

Figure 1.33. Investors in US and European prime RMBSs: change in number of investors between 2006–7 and 2009.

credit risks can have an economic value. As a result, securitized credit and credit derivatives probably will and should play a significant role in the financial system of the future. But recognizing that fact should not lead us to fall into the trap of believing that ever more complex innovation is beneficial because it completes more markets, or that an increased aggregate supply of credit is a valid argument in favour of innovation and light regulation.

1.4.2 Risks in the Securitized Credit Model: Fixable or Inherent?

As discussed above, pre-crisis complex securitization was made risky by a number of apparently fixable problems. But risks were also created by two more fundamental factors, which together imply that securitization is unlikely to return on the scale which existed pre-crisis, and that new tools for macroprudential management of the credit cycle—discussed in section 1.3—are as relevant to securitized credit as to on-balance-sheet credit.

Maturity transformation. The first of these fundamental factors is maturity transformation. As discussed in section 1.2.3, investor demand for securitized credit was supported before the crisis by new forms of maturity transformation, contributing to the increase in aggregate maturity transformation which made the financial system more vulnerable to shocks. SIVs and conduits bought contractually long securities funded with short-term commercial paper; mutual funds with very short-term liabilities bought either long-term securities or the commercial paper of SIVs and conduits; and banks and investment banks financed large trading-book securities portfolios with repo finance. The proportion of the securitized credit investor base which was only present because of these unsafe forms of maturity transformation is difficult to quantify, but it may have constituted more than half of the total, and it is these sources of demand which collapsed most precipitously during the crisis (figure 1.33). While the origination and distribution of pooled and tranched securities are likely to play a significant role in the future system, it will likely be a much smaller role than that which existed pre-crisis.[17]

Securitized credit, self-referential pricing and instability. The second fundamental issue is whether a financial system in which securitized credit plays a greater proportionate role is likely to be one in which the volatility of the credit and asset price cycle described in section 1.3 is still more severe. Securitization is certainly not the only cause of credit cycles: purely bank-based credit systems can and have generated self-reinforcing credit and asset price upswings of the sort described on figure 1.30, followed by credit crunches when the cycles swing into reverse. There have been many past banking crises in systems where securitized credit played an insignificant role.[18]

But a pervasive role for securitized credit can further increase the potential for volatility by increasing the extent to which credit risk assessment and credit pricing becomes self-referential, with credit security investors and bank loan officers deriving their assessment of an appropriate price for credit not from independent analysis of credit risks but from the observable market price. Thus, for instance, the International Monetary Fund (IMF) *Global Financial Stability Report* of April 2006 noted that credit derivatives 'enhance the transparency of the market's collective view of credit risks … [and thus] provide valuable information about broad credit conditions and increasingly set the marginal price of credit'. But a marginal price of credit set by a liquid market in credit derivatives is only economically valuable if we believe, as per the efficient market hypotheses, that 'the market's collective view of credit risks' is by definition a correct one. If instead we note the movement in the CDS spreads for major banks shown on figure 1.34, with spreads falling relentlessly to reach a historic low in early summer 2007, and providing no

---

[17]Note that this fact is highly pertinent to the 'transitional dynamics' issue which this chapter does not consider but which is extremely important. In a long-term comparative static sense, the disappearance of securitized credit extension based on unsafe maturity transformation may be strongly positive but, over the medium term, the likelihood that securitized credit markets will not return to their pre-crisis scale makes still more acute the issues of transition management in implementing new capital and liquidity requirements which will restrict on-balance credit extension.

[18]For instance, the US savings and loan crisis of the 1980s, and the Japanese and Swedish banking crises of the 1990s.

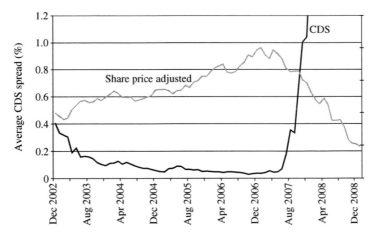

Figure 1.34. Financial firms' CDS and share prices.

Sources: Moody's KMV; FSA calculations. *Note*: firms included Ambac, Aviva, Banco Santander, Barclays, Berkshire Hathaway, Bradford & Bingley, Citigroup, Deutsche Bank, Fortis, HBOS, Lehman Brothers, Merrill Lynch, Morgan Stanley, National Australia Bank, Royal Bank of Scotland and UBS. The CDS series peaks at 6.54% in September 2008.

forewarning at all of impending financial disaster, we should be worried that an increased reliance on market price information to set the marginal price of credit could itself be a source of credit and asset price volatility, particularly when combined with mark-to-market accounting.

A credit system which combines both maturity transforming banks *and* a significant role for traded credit securities could therefore be even more susceptible to self-reinforcing exuberant upswings and subsequent downswings than a pure bank system (figure 1.35).

- With mark-to-market profits reinforcing management's, investors' and traders' confidence and animal spirits, and swelling bank capital bases and thus supporting more trading or more lending.

- And with the link from high asset prices to favourable credit assessments now hardwired into the system, as high asset prices drive higher credit securities prices and lower spreads, which are then used to set the marginal price of credit.

- A set of self-reinforcing cycles clearly evident in the years running up to the crisis, reversing into the self-reinforcing downward spiral of confidence and credit extension which has caused such economic harm.

The reasons why the latest financial crisis was so severe may therefore have been rooted in the interaction between the specific character-

49

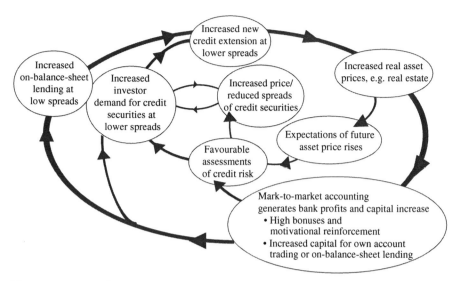

Figure 1.35. Credit and asset prices with securitized credit and mark-to-market accounting.

istics of maturity transforming banks and those of a securitized credit system.

Two implications follow. First, that the emergence of a global credit supply system which combines bank balance sheet and securitized elements has increased the importance of macroprudential tools. Second, that in considering the design of new macroprudential tools to address the volatility of the credit cycle, we need to consider the potential volatility of securitized credit extension as well as on-balance-sheet credit. Tools which solely address on-balance-sheet credit, such as variations in capital requirements against particular categories of credit, might be undermined if overexuberant credit supply simply migrates to an off-balance-sheet form. This might, along with the cross-border competition factors already noted, imply the need to consider borrower-focused restraints (e.g. maximum loan-to-value ratios) rather than concentrating solely on lender focus credit supply.

Let us sum up, therefore, on complex securitization and related credit derivatives markets.

- It seems highly likely that securitization will continue to play a significant role in the credit intermediation process, and with appropriate regulation and market discipline, could perform a socially useful function of enabling improved risk management.

- But the pre-crisis ideology that 'market completion' arguments justified ever more complex innovation, which regulators should never impede, ignored the fact that returns from market completion must be subject to diminishing marginal returns, ignored the extent to which much innovation was based on tax and capital arbitrage, and ignored the risks which complexity created.

- The fact that a considerable proportion of investor demand relied crucially on risky maturity transformation means that securitization's role in future is likely to be more limited than in the past.

- Finally and crucially, a system of securitized credit *interacting with* a system of maturity transforming banks can further increase the risks of self-reinforcing credit and asset priced cycles and therefore further increase the case for new macroprudential tools.

1.5 Market Making and Position Taking: Valuable up to a Point?

One of the functions which banks and investment banks perform in the market for credit securities and credit derivatives is to trade and thus provide liquidity, enabling end investors and other market users to buy and sell at reasonably low bid–offer spreads. That activity is one among many trading activities in which banks have been increasingly involved, with, as shown in section 1.2.4, an explosion over the last thirty years in the volume of trading activity relative to real economic variables.

What value did this explosion of trading actually deliver: how valuable is the liquidity which position-taking, or, as some would label it, speculation, makes possible?

The question is a politically sensitive one, because market-making and proprietary trading to support it are at times highly profitable for firms and for individuals. Lending officers guilty of lending badly to commercial real estate firms in an irrationally exuberant upswing may have been overpaid relative to the economic value added of their activity for society, but it is not in that area of financial services but within the trading rooms of banks, investment banks and hedge funds that remuneration sometimes reaches levels which to the ordinary citizen are simply bewildering. There is therefore strong popular support for measures to curtail either trading volume or the profits derived from it, whether by direct regulation of trading room bonuses, 'Volcker rule limits on commercial banks' involvement in proprietary trading, or financial transaction taxes such as that proposed by James Tobin.

The high profitability of market-making and proprietary trading—to the firms and to individuals—reflects two facts: first, that end customers appear to place great value on market liquidity; second, that market-makers with large market share and high levels of skill are able to use their knowledge of underlying order flow and of interconnections between different traded markets to make position-taking and complex arbitrage profits.[19]

And the fact that end customers greatly value liquidity is in turn taken by the proponents of ever more active trading as proof that more trading and more liquidity must be socially valuable as well as privately profitable. The dominant ideology of financial liberalization and innovation has therefore argued that increased liquidity is wholly beneficial in all markets for five reasons.

- Increased liquidity enables end customers to trade at low bid–offer spreads and in large amounts: for any given scale of activity this decreases their costs.

- If faced with this lower cost per transaction, customers transact more and therefore provide more net revenues to the market-makers and professional position takers, which must be because they derive value from it.

- Liquidity is indeed directly valuable because, in the classic argument of market completion, it provides investors with a wider set of options: in this case the option to sell whenever they want.

- Liquidity creates value by ensuring efficient 'price discovery', with a wider set of market participants able to contribute to the collective judgement of the rational market and with correct prices driving allocative efficiency.

- Finally, these benefits of liquidity are likely to be accompanied by reduced volatility, since liquidity is in part created by professional position takers who spot divergences of prices from rational levels and by their speculation correct these divergences.

---

[19]The proponents of separating 'casino' banking from commercial banking often argue in support that proprietary trading activity and market-making is only profitable because risk-taking is cross-subsidized by 'too big to fail' status and a significant taxpayer guarantee. It is notable however that some of the most profitable market-making activities, either at all times (e.g. spot and foreign exchange) or at particular times (government bonds during 2009) are actually relatively low risk, and have very rarely resulted in losses which have harmed individual bank solvency or total system stability. Several market-making functions appear to deliver super normal returns even when fully risk adjusted.

These arguments reflect the dominant conventional wisdom of the last several decades based on the assumptions of rational expectations and of efficient and self-equilibrating markets. They have been frequently and effectively deployed to argue against regulations which might limit trading activity. And some of these arguments are compelling, up to a point: reduced bid–offer spreads on forward foreign exchange must, for instance, have delivered value to exporters and importers.

But Keynes believed that

> of the maxims of orthodox finance, none surely, is more anti-social than the fetish of liquidity and the doctrine that it is a positive value on the part of institutional investors to concentrate their resources on the holding of 'liquid' securities.

And scepticism about the limitless benefits of market liquidity supported by speculative trading is justified on at least three grounds.

(i) First, the fact that the benefits of market liquidity must be, like the benefits of any market completion, of declining marginal utility as more market liquidity is attained. The additional benefits deliverable, for instance, by the extra liquidity which derives from flash or algorithmic training, exploiting price divergences present for a fraction of a second, must be of minimal value compared with the benefits of having an equity market that is reasonably liquid on a day-to-day basis.

(ii) Second, the fact that greater market liquidity and the position-taking and speculation required to deliver it can, in some markets, produce destabilizing and harmful momentum effects—cycles of overvaluation and then undervaluation. Such swings can be explained by the insights of behavioural economics—human tendencies, rooted in our evolutionary history, which condition us to be swept along with herd psychology,[20] or they can be explained in terms of relationships between different market participants, operating under conditions of inherent irreducible uncertainty, imperfect information and complex principal–agent relationships, which make it rational for individual participants to act in ways which produce collectively unstable results, with continual oscillations around rational equilibrium levels (see Vayanos and Woolley 2008; Soros 2008).

(iii) And third, an emerging body of analysis which suggests that the multiple and complex principal–agent relationships which exist

---

[20]See Kahneman *et al.* (1982) for a discussion of how economic agents made decisions on the bases of rough heuristics, i.e. rules of thumb. The widespread application of these rules by multiple agents can then generate self-reinforcing herd effects.

throughout the financial system mean that active trading, which both requires and creates liquid markets, can be used not to deliver additional value to end investors or users of markets, but to extract economic rent. Additional trading, for instance, can create volatility against which customers then seek to protect themselves by placing value on the provision of market liquidity. The fact that customers place great value on market liquidity, and thus support large market-marking profits, therefore in no way proves that the increased trading activity is value added at the social level.

So faced with these two schools of thought, what should we conclude? Has all the increased trading activity of the last thirty years delivered economic value via lower transaction costs and more efficient and liquid markets, or has it generated harmful volatility and enabled market traders to extract economic rent? My answer is that I don't know the precise balance of these possible positives and negatives, because there are many issues of complex theory and empirical analysis not yet resolved and very difficult to resolve. But we certainly need to have the debate rather than accepting as given the dominant argument of the last thirty years which has asserted that increased liquidity, supported by increased position-taking, is axiomatically beneficial. And a reasonable judgement on the economic value added of increased liquidity may be that increased liquidity does deliver benefits but that those benefits are subject to diminishing marginal utility, and that the increased financial speculation required to deliver increased liquidity creates an increasing danger of destabilizing herd and momentum effects the larger pure financial activity becomes relative to underlying real economic activity (figure 1.36).

There is an optimal level of liquidity, with increased liquidity and speculation valuable up to a point but not beyond that point. The complication for policymakers is, however, that the point of optimal benefit is impossible to define with any precision, that it varies by market, and that we have highly imperfect instruments through which to gain the benefits without the disadvantages. There is, for instance, no economic value that I can discern from the operation of speculators in currency 'carry trades', which are among purest examples of what Professor John Kay labels 'tailgating strategies'—riding an unsustainable trend in the hope that you will be clever enough to get out just ahead of the crash (see Kay 2010). But there may be no instruments that can eliminate carry trade activities without undermining useful foreign exchange market liquidity of value to non-financial corporations.

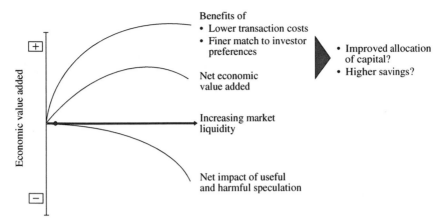

Figure 1.36. How valuable is increased market liquidity? A possible conceptual framework.

But the fact that we do not have perfect discriminatory instruments does not mean that a more nuanced assessment of the benefits of market liquidity will have no implications for public policy. Instead three implications follow.

(i) The first is that in setting trading-book capital requirements for commercial and investment banks, we should shift from a bias in favour of liquidity to a bias to conservatism. If regulators believe that the level of capital required for prudential purposes needs to increase, and the industry argues that this will restrict liquidity in some specific markets, we should be more willing to question whether the liquidity serves a useful economic purpose and more willing in some cases to wave it goodbye.

(ii) The second is that policymakers need to be concerned with the potential danger of destabilizing speculative activity, even if it is performed by non-banks. Speculative trading activity can cause harm, even when it poses no threat to commercial bank solvency. If necessary, highly leveraged hedge fund speculation should be constrained by leverage limits.

(iii) And third, we should certainly not exclude the potential role for financial transaction taxes which might, in James Tobin's words, 'throw some sand in the wheels' of speculative activity. It may well be the case that a generalized and internationally agreed financial transactions tax, whether on foreign exchange flows or on a wider set of financial transactions, is not achievable. One of the interesting features of the transaction tax debate is that it is littered with articles by academics who have been convinced of the theoretical case in favour of a financial transaction tax, but who have subsequently failed to promote the idea. In 1989, Larry Summers coauthored an article entitled 'When financial markets work too well: a cautious case for a securities transaction tax' (Summers and Summers 1989), but in office subsequently he did not pursue it. Rudi Dornbusch argued in 1990 that 'it's time for a financial transactions tax', but was subsequently sceptical about the feasibility of comprehensive capital controls.[21] But at the very least we should take financial transaction taxes out of the 'index of forbidden thoughts'.

1.6 Reforming Global Finance: Radicalism, Structural Solutions and Inherent Instability

Let me sum up then and draw some overall conclusions about the need for radical reform, and what we should mean by radical. I started by describing the quite startling increases in the scale of the financial system which have occurred over the last thirty to fifty years, and I have then considered the value added of this increased financial activity under three headings.

(i) First, the huge growth in bank balance sheets relative to GDP, and in the level of leverage in the real economy. Here I concluded that whether this increase was value added depends crucially on the economic and social functions that credit performs, and that these functions vary by category of credit. Whereas some credit extension enables more productive investment, in fact much credit (for instance most mortgage credit) plays the economic functions of enabling life-cycle consumption smoothing and inter-generational resource transfer, and is valuable to the extent that such smoothing delivers welfare benefits but should not be expected to spur investment or long-term economic growth. I also argued that credit extension to finance real assets, such as property, can be subject to self-reinforcing and potentially unstable cycles, particularly given the corporate tax deductibility of interest payments and the existence of limited liability. I therefore argued that we need to recognize the credit/asset price cycle as a crucial economic variable, and that we need new macro-prudential policy tools to manage that cycle—tools that may need to be differentiated by category of credit, given the hugely different elasticity

---

[21]See Dornbusch (1990). Note that while Dani Rodrik has argued that Dornbusch's subsequent scepticism about capital controls ('Capital controls: an idea whose time is past', 1997) is inconsistent with Dornbusch's earlier position, in fact it is quite possible to be opposed to legislated prohibition of capital flows but in favour of taxing them.

response of different categories and their different economic and social value.

(ii) Second, I looked at the growth of complex securitization, the growing role of tranched and pooled credit securities within total credit supply, and again concluded that the economic and social value of these innovations depended crucially on the value of the credit extension which it enabled. I also stressed the danger that a securitized system of credit extension can make credit assessments and pricing decisions increasingly self-referential, and that mark-to-market accounting of credit securities can reinforce procyclical tendencies in credit extension, both in its securitized and its on-balance-sheet form. What made the latest financial crisis so severe was therefore the interaction between the specific features of maturity transforming banks and of traded credit securities markets. Banks are special because they can create both money and credit in a self-reinforcing fashion; credit securities markets can be subject to cycles in which credit assessment and pricing become self-referential. Either can introduce volatility into the financial system, but it is their interaction which maximizes that volatility. This interaction, I argued, increases the importance of effective macroprudential tools.

(iii) Finally, I considered the huge growth of trading activity, across multiple markets and relative to underlying real economic variables, and argued that we must reject the efficient market hypothesis that more trading and more market liquidity is axiomatically beneficial, working instead on the assumption that position-taking which supports liquidity is valuable up to a point but not beyond that point. I therefore argued for a bias to conservatism in the setting of capital requirements against trading activities, a greater willingness to accept that in some circumstances there can be a case for restricting specific categories of trading activities, and for the removal of the idea of financial transaction taxes from the 'index of forbidden thoughts'.

Overall, therefore, I am arguing for a radical reassessment of the too simplistic case in favour of financial liberalization and financial deepening which strongly influenced official policy in the decades ahead of the crises, and which reflected the dominant conventional wisdoms of neoclassical economics.

We need to challenge radically some of the assumptions of the last thirty years and we need to be willing to consider radical policy responses. Those radical responses, however, are not necessarily those, or not only those, often defined as radical in current debates.

In those debates many commentators have tended to define radicalism along three specific dimensions.

- How far we go in addressing the 'too big to fail' problem, by making large banks resolvable or if necessary smaller.
- Whether we are willing to separate 'casino banking', i.e. proprietary trading, from utility or commercial banking.
- And whether we embrace major structural reforms to create narrow banks or limited-purpose banks of the sort proposed by Professors John Kay and Laurence Kotlikoff.

But the implication of this chapter is that none of these structural solutions will be sufficient to address the potential for instability inherent in the specific characteristics of financial markets, credit contracts, and maturity transforming banks.

Addressing 'too big to fail'.   The 'too big to fail' agenda is undoubtedly important and a key focus for the Financial Stability Board's Standing Committee on supervisory and regulatory cooperation which I chair. It is not acceptable that taxpayers have to bail out large failing banks, and the *ex ante* expectation that they will undermines market discipline. In the latest crisis as in previous ones, however, direct taxpayer costs of bank rescue are likely to account for only a very small proportion of the total economic costs. IMF estimates suggest that they are unlikely to exceed 2–3% of GDP in the developed economies most affected by the crisis, and they may turn out significantly less once bank equity stakes are sold.[22] But public debt burdens in the developed economies are likely, as a result of this crisis, to increase by something like 50% of GDP. These much larger costs derive essentially from volatility in credit supply, first extended too liberally and at too low prices—especially to real estate and construction sectors—and then restricted. This has two implications. The first is that when we say that in future all banks, however big, must be allowed to 'fail', the objective should not be to put them into insolvency and wind-up, since that will produce a sudden contraction of lending, but instead to ensure that we can impose losses on subordinated debt holders and senior creditors sufficient to ensure that the bank can maintain operations, under new management, without taxpayer support. The second is that the multiple failure of small banks could be as harmful to the real economy as the failure of one large bank, even if all such banks failed

---

[22]IMF (2010) estimates that 'Net of amounts recovered so far, the fiscal cost of direct support has averaged 2.7% of GDP for advanced G20 countries'.

at no taxpayer cost, and even if the market knew *ex ante* that no tax-payer support would be forthcoming.[23] The American banking crisis of 1930–33 was primarily a crisis of multiple relatively small banks.

Separating commercial from investment banking. Limiting the in-volvement of commercial lending banks in risky proprietary trading is undoubtedly also desirable. Losses incurred in trading activities can gen-erate confidence collapses, which constrain credit supply and *in extremis* necessitate public rescue. The interaction between trading activity and classic investment banking played a crucial role in the origins of the lat-est crisis: indeed, the thesis of this chapter is that it was precisely the interaction of maturity transforming banks and of self-referential credit securities markets that drove the peculiar severity of this latest crisis. But for three reasons legislated separation of commercial and investment banking will not prove a straightforward or sufficient solution.

(i) First, because a precise legislated distinction is extremely difficult, as the terms of the 'Volcker rule' now introduced in US legislation illus-trate. That legislation defines proprietary trading as the purchase, sale or underwriting for profit of any tradable security or contract, but it then exempts from the definition any such position-taking for the purposes of market-making, customer facilitation or hedging, leaving it to regulators to enforce the distinction and to devise tools to prohibit position-taking unrelated to value added activities. Underpinning the authority of regula-tors with the principle of a legislated Volcker rule may well be desirable; but the implementation of the rule is likely to depend crucially on appro-priate design of trading-book capital rules.

(ii) Second, because while large integrated commercial and investment banks (such as Citi, RBS and UBS) played a major role in the crisis, so too did large or medium-sized commercial banks (such as HBOS, Northern Rock and IndyMac) which were not extensively involved in the proprietary trading activities which a Volcker rule would constrain.

(iii) Third, that even if proprietary trading of credit securities was largely conducted by institutions separate from commercial banks, im-portant and potentially destabilizing interactions could still exist be-tween maturity transforming banks and credit securities trading. A credit supply and real estate price boom could be driven by the combination of

---

[23] See BIS (2010, p. 16): 'A financial landscape dotted with a large number of small but identical institutions will be just as prone to collapse as a system with a small number of financial behemoths'.

commercial banks originating and distributing credit and non-banks buying and trading it, with the two together generating a self-referential cycle of optimistic credit assessment and loan pricing, even if the functions were performed by separate institutions.

Volcker rules are in principle desirable, but they are not a sufficient response.

Separating deposit-taking from commercial banking. Professor John Kay's proposed structural solution is quite different from Paul Volcker's. Rather than splitting commercial from investment banking, it would separate insured deposit-taking from lending. All insured retail deposits would be backed 100% by government gilts, while lending banks would be funded by uninsured retail or commercial deposits or by wholesale funds, and would compete in a free, unregulated and unsupervised market. The underlying assumption is that the existing system is unstable only because explicit deposit insurance and implicit promises of future rescue undermine the market discipline which would otherwise produce efficient and stable results. If instead we believe that financial markets, maturity transforming banks, and credit extension against assets which can increase in value, are inherently susceptible to instabilities which cannot be overcome by identifying and removing some specific market imperfection, then Professor Kay's proposal fails to address the fundamental issues. It would create safe retail deposit banks which would never need to be rescued, but it would leave credit supply and pricing as volatile, procyclical and self-referential as it was pre-crisis.

Abolishing banks: 100% equity support for loans. Professor Kotlikoff's proposal, in contrast, suggests a truly radical reform of the institutional structure for credit extension. Lending banks would become mutual loan funds, with investors sharing month by month (or even day by day) in the economic performance of the underlying loans. This is equivalent to making banks 100% equity funded, performing a pooling but not a tranching function. And it would clearly exclude the possibility of publicly funded rescue: if the price of loan fund assets fell, the investors would immediately suffer the loss. But it is not clear that such a model would generate a more stable credit supply. As section 1.4 argued, a system of securitized credit combined with mark-to-market accounting can generate self-referential cycles of overconfidence and underconfidence. And while Kotlikoff's loan funds might seem to abolish the maturity transforming bank, with investors enjoying short-term access but not capital certainty, investors would be likely in the upswing to consider their investments as safe as bank deposits. Investments in loan funds would therefore be likely to grow in a procyclical fashion when valuations were on an upswing and then to 'run' when valuations and confidence fell, creating credit booms and busts potentially as severe as in past bank-based crises. The essential challenge indeed is that the tranching and maturity transformation functions which banks perform do deliver economic benefit, and that if they are not delivered by banks, customer demand for these functions will seek fulfilment in other forms. We need to find safer ways of meeting these demands, and to constrain the satisfaction of this demand to safe levels, but we cannot abolish these demands entirely.

There is therefore a danger that if radicalism is defined exclusively in structural terms—small banks, narrow banks or the replacement of banks with mutual loan funds—that we will fail to be truly radical in our analysis of the financial system and to understand how deep-rooted are the drivers of financial instability. An exclusive focus on structural change options, indeed, reflects a confidence that if only we can identify and remove the specific market imperfections which prevent market disciplines from being effective, then at last we will obtain the Arrow–Debreu nirvana of complete and self-equilibrating markets. If, instead, we believe that liquid financial markets are subject for inherent reasons to herd and momentum effects, that credit and asset price cycles are centrally important phenomena, that maturity transforming banks perform economically valuable but inherently risky functions, and that the widespread trading of credit securities can increase the procyclicality of credit risk assessment and pricing, then we have challenges which cannot be overcome by any one structural solution.

Instead two elements should form the core of the regulatory response to the crisis: much higher bank capital and liquidity requirements and the development of new macroprudential through-the-cycle tools. Together these can help address the fundamental issues of volatile credit extension and asset price cycles.

(i) Higher capital and liquidity requirements will create a more resilient banking system—one that is less likely to suffer crisis and bank failure. But they will also, by constraining but not eliminating the extent to which the banking system can perform its tranching and maturity transformation functions, constrain total leverage in the real economy and thereby reduce the vulnerability which derives from the rigidities of credit contracts. And by reducing the likelihood of bank failure, they will reduce the danger that confidence collapse leads to sudden constraints on credit supply. Even if not varied through the cycle, higher bank capital and liquidity requirements will therefore tend to reduce the procyclicality inherent in banking systems and credit markets. In the long run, moreover, there is no reason to believe that a more restricted credit supply and lower financial system and real economy leverage will result in lower steady-state growth, given in particular that much credit supply and demand in rich developed countries is unrelated to productive investment, instead performing a different (but still valuable) consumption smoothing effect. While the transition to higher capital and liquidity standards needs to be managed with care, there is therefore a strong argument for long-term capital standards which are *much* higher than pre-crisis, and for liquidity policies which seek deliberately to constrain aggregate maturity transformation well below pre-crisis levels.

(ii) Higher continuous capital and liquidity requirements will still, however, leave the economy vulnerable to destabilizing upswings in credit supply and asset prices, deriving from the interaction between maturity transforming banks, credit securities markets and self-reinforcing credit and asset price cycles. In addition, therefore, the regulatory response needs to involve the deployment of countercyclical macroprudential tools which directly address aggregate credit supply. These could include automatic or discretionary variation of capital or liquidity requirements across the cycle, or constraints, such as loan-to-value limits, which directly address borrowers rather than lenders. Such policy levers may, moreover, need to be varied by broad category of credit (e.g. distinguishing between commercial real estate and other corporate lending) given the very different elasticity of response of different categories of credit to both interest rate and regulatory levers.

References

Arrow, K., and G. Debreu. 1954. Existence of an equilibrium for a competitive economy. *Econometrica* **22**(3), 265–90.

Bank of England. 2009. The role of macroprudential policy. Discussion Paper, November.

BIS. 2010. *80th Annual Report* (June).

Bryan, L. 1988. *Breaking Up the Bank: Rethinking an Industry Under Seige.* Irwin Professional.

Dornbusch, R. 1990. It's time for a financial transactions tax. *International Economy* **20**, 95–96.

FSA. 2009a. *Mortgage Market Review* (October).

FSA. 2009b. *The Turner Review.* Conference Discussion Paper (October).

FSA. 2010. *Financial Risk Outlook.*

IMF. 2008. *Global Financial Stability Report* (October).

IMF. 2010. A fair and substantial contribution by the financial sector. Interim Report prepared for the G20 (April).

Kay, J. 2009. *Narrow Banking: The Reform of Banking Regulation.* London: CSFI.

Kay, J. 2010. Tailgating blights markets and motorways. *Financial Times* (19 January).

King, I. R. G., and R. Levine. 1993. Finance and growth: Schumpeter might be right. *Quarterly Journal of Economics* **108**(3), 717–37.

Kotlikoff, L. 2010. *Jimmy Stewart Is Dead: Ending the World's Ongoing Financial Plague with Limited Purpose Banking.* John Wiley & Sons.

Kahneman, D., P. Slovic and A. Tversky (eds). 1982. *Judgement Under Uncertainty Heuristics and Biases.* Cambridge University Press.

Modigliani, F., and M. Miller. 1958. The cost of capital, corporation finance and the theory of investment. *American Economic Review* **48**(3), 261–97.

Modigliani, F., and M. Miller. 1963. Corporate income taxes and the cost of capital: a correction. *American Economic Review* **53**(3), 433–43.

Reinhart, C. M., and K. Rogoff. 2009. *This Time It's Different: Eight Centuries of Financial Folly.* Princeton University Press.

Rousseau, P., and R. Sylla. 1999. Emerging financial markets and early US growth. NBER Working Paper 7448.

Schularick, M., and A. M. Taylor. 2009. Credit booms gone bust: monetary policy, leveraged cycles and financial crises 1870 to 2008. NBER Working Paper 15512 (November).

Soros, G. 2008. *The New Paradigm for Financial Markets.* New York: PublicAffairs Books.

Summers, L. H., and V. P. Summers. 1989. When financial markets work too well: a cautious case for a securities transaction tax. *Journal of Financial Service Research* **3**, 261–86.

Turner, A. 2010. Something old and something new: novel and familiar drivers of the latest crisis. Lecture to the European Association of Banking and Financial History (May).

Vayanos, D., and P. Woolley. 2008. An institutional theory of momentum and reversal. LSE Working Paper (November).

What Is the Contribution of the Financial Sector: Miracle or Mirage?

By Andrew Haldane, Simon Brennan and Vasileios Madouros

This chapter considers the contribution made by the financial sector to the wider economy. The measured GDP contribution of the financial sector suggests it underwent a 'productivity miracle' from the 1980s onwards, as finance rose as a share of national output despite a declining labour and capital share. But a detailed decomposition of returns to banking suggests an alternative interpretation: much of the growth reflected the effects of higher risk-taking. Leverage, higher trading profits and investments in deep-out-of-the-money options were the risk-taking strategies generating excess returns to bank shareholders and staff. Subsequently, as these risks have materialized, returns to banking have reversed. In this sense, high pre-crisis returns to finance may have been more mirage than miracle. This suggests that better measuring of risk-taking in finance is an important public policy objective—for statisticians and regulators as well as for banks and their investors.

2.1 INTRODUCTION

The financial crisis of the past three years has, on any measure, been extremely costly. As in past financial crises, public-sector debt seems set to double relative to national income in a number of countries (Reinhart and Rogoff 2009). And measures of foregone output, now and in the future, put the net present value cost of the crisis at anywhere between one and five times annual world GDP (Haldane 2010). Either way, the scars from the current crisis seem likely to be felt for a generation.

It is against this backdrop that an intense debate is underway internationally about reform of finance (see chapter 5). Many of the key planks of

We would like to thank Stephen Burgess, Melissa Davey, Rob Elder, Perry Francis, Jen Han, Sam Knott, Nick Oulton, Peter Richardson, Jeremy Rowe, Chris Shadforth, Sally Srinivasan and Iain de Weymarn for comments and discussion on earlier drafts, and Alexander Haywood and Laura Wightman for research assistance. The views expressed are those of the authors and not necessarily those of the Bank of England.

that debate are covered in other chapters in this volume. Some of these reform measures are extensions or elaborations of existing regulatory initiatives—for example, higher buffers of higher quality capital and liquidity. Others propose a reorientation of existing regulatory apparatus—for example, through countercyclical adjustments in prudential policy (Bank of England 2009b; Large 2010). Others still suggest a root-and-branch restructuring of finance—for example, by limiting the size and/or scope of banking (Kay 2009; Kotlikoff 2010).

In evaluating these reform proposals, it is clearly important that the ongoing benefits of finance are properly weighed alongside the costs of crisis. Doing so requires an understanding and measurement of the contribution made by the financial sector to economic well-being. This is important both for making sense of the past (during which time the role of finance has grown) and for shaping the future (during which it is possible the role of finance may shrink).

While simple in principle, this measurement exercise is far from straightforward in practice. Recent experience makes clear the extent of the problem. In September 2008, the collapse of Lehman Brothers precipitated a chain reaction in financial markets. This brought the financial system, and many of the world's largest institutions, close to the point of collapse. During the fourth quarter of 2008, equity prices of the major global banks fell by around 50% on average, a loss of market value of around $640 billion. As a consequence, world GDP and world trade are estimated to have fallen at an annualized rate of about 6% and 25% respectively in 2008 Q4. Banking contributed to a Great Recession on a scale last seen at the time of the Great Depression.

Yet the official statistics on the contribution of the financial sector paint a rather different picture. According to the National Accounts, the nominal gross value added (GVA) of the financial sector in the UK grew at the fastest pace on record in 2008 Q4. As a share of whole-economy output, the direct contribution of the UK financial sector rose to 9% in the last quarter of 2008. Financial corporations' gross operating surplus (GVA less compensation for employees and other taxes on production) increased by £5 billion to £20 billion, also the largest quarterly increase on record. At a time when people believed banks were contributing the least to the economy since the 1930s, the National Accounts indicated that the financial sector was contributing the most since the mid 1980s. How do we begin to square this circle?

That is the purpose of this chapter. It is planned as follows. In section 2.2, we consider conventional measures of financial sector value

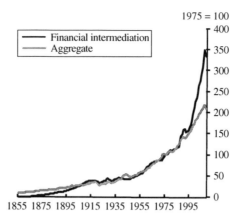

Figure 2.1. UK financial intermediation and aggregate real GVA.
Sources: Feinstein (1972), Mitchell (1988), ONS and Bank of England calculations.

added and how these have evolved over time. In section 2.3, we consider a growth-accounting decomposition of the factor inputs which have driven growth—quantities of labour and capital and the returns to these factors. This suggests that banking has undergone, at least arithmetically, a 'productivity miracle' over the past few decades. Section 2.4 explores in greater detail some of the quantitative drivers of high aggregate returns to banking, while section 2.5 explores some of banks' business activities. Risk illusion, rather than a productivity miracle, appears to have driven high returns to finance. The recent history of banking appears to be as much mirage as miracle. Section 2.6 concludes with some policy implications.

2.2 MEASURING FINANCIAL SECTOR OUTPUT

2.2.1 *Historical Trends in GVA*

The standard way of measuring the contribution of a sector to output in the economy is GVA. This is defined as the value of gross output that a sector or industry produces less the value of intermediate consumption (that is, goods and services used in the process of production). GVA only measures the sector's direct contribution to the economy. The indirect contribution of finance—for example, on productivity growth through the provision of funds for start-up businesses and new investment projects— may also be important. But looking at historical trends in value added is a useful starting point.

Table 2.1. Average annual growth rate of UK financial intermediation.

	Aggregate GVA	Financial intermediation GVA	Difference (pp)
1856–1913	2.0	7.6	5.6
1914–1970	1.9	1.5	−0.4
1971–2008	2.4	3.8	1.4
1856–2008	2.1	4.4	2.3

Sources: Feinstein (1972), Mitchell (1988), ONS and Bank of England calculations.

Figure 2.1[1] plots an index of real GVA of the financial intermediation sector in the UK from the middle of the nineteenth century, alongside an index of whole-economy output. Both series are in constant prices and indexed to 1975 = 100. Table 2.1 breaks down the growth rates of finance and whole-economy output into three subsamples: pre-World War I, from World War I to the early 1970s, and thence to date. The historical trends in GVA for the financial sector are striking.

Over the past 160 years, growth in financial intermediation has out-stripped whole-economy growth by over 2 percentage points per year. Or put differently, growth in financial sector value added has been more than double that of the economy as a whole since 1850. This is unsurprising in some respects. It reflects a trend towards financial deepening which is evident across most developed and developing economies over the past century. This structural trend in finance has been shown to have contributed positively to growth in the whole economy (see chapter 4).

The subsample evidence suggests, however, that this has not been a straight line trend. The pre-World War I period marked a time of very rapid financial deepening, with the emergence of joint stock banks to service the needs of a rapidly growing non-financial economy. Finance grew at almost four times the pace of the real economy during this rapid-growth period (table 2.1).

---

[1] Some of the figures in this chapter refer to the 'LCFIs' (large complex financial institutions) and 'Major UK banks' peer groups. Membership of the major UK banks group is based on the provision of customer services in the UK, regardless of the country of ownership. The following financial groups, in alphabetical order, are currently members: Banco Santander, Bank of Ireland, Barclays, Co-operative Financial Services, HSBC, Lloyds Banking Group, National Australia Bank, Nationwide, Northern Rock and RBS. The LCFIs include the world's largest banks, which carry out a diverse and complex range of activities in major financial centres. The group is currently identified as Bank of America, Barclays, BNP Paribas, Citigroup, Credit Suisse, Deutsche Bank, Goldman Sachs, HSBC, JPMorgan Chase & Co., Morgan Stanley, RBS, Société Générale and UBS. Membership of both peer groups changes over time and these changes are reflected in the charts.

Figure 2.2. Gross operating surplus of UK private financial corporations (as a percentage of the total).
Sources: ONS and Bank of England calculations.

The period which followed, from World War I right through until the start of the 1970s, reversed this trend. The growth in finance fell somewhat short of that in the rest of the economy. This in part reflected the effects of tight quantitative constraints on, and government regulation of, the financial sector.

The period from the early 1970s up until 2007 marked another watershed. Financial liberalization took hold in successive waves. Since then, finance has comfortably outpaced growth in the non-financial economy, by around 1.5 percentage points per year. If anything, this trend accelerated from the early 1980s onwards. Measured real value added of the financial intermediation sector more than trebled between 1980 and 2008, while whole-economy output doubled over the same period.

In 2007, financial intermediation accounted for more than 8% of total GVA, compared with 5% in 1970. The gross operating surpluses of financial intermediaries show an even more dramatic trend. Between 1948 and 1978, intermediation accounted on average for around 1.5% of whole-economy profits. By 2008, that ratio had risen tenfold to about 15% (figure 2.2).

Internationally, a broadly similar pattern is evident. In the US, following a major decline during the Great Depression, the value added of the financial sector has risen steadily since the end of World War II. As a fraction of whole-economy GVA, it has quadrupled over the period, from about 2% of total GDP in the 1950s to about 8% today (figure 2.3). Similar trends are evident in Europe and Asia. According to data from the *Banker*, the largest 1,000 banks in the world reported aggregate pre-tax

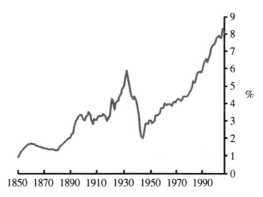

Figure 2.3. Share of the financial industry in US GDP.
Source: Philippon (2008).

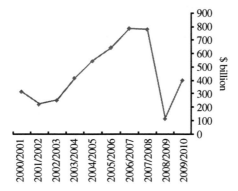

Figure 2.4. Pre-tax profits of the world's 1,000 largest banks.
Source: www.thebankerdatabase.com.

profits of almost $800 billion in fiscal year 2007–8 (figure 2.4), almost 150% higher than in 2000–2001. This equates to annualized returns to banking of almost 15%.

Some of these trends in the value added and profits of the financial sector, and in particular their explosive growth recently, are also discernible in the market valuations of financial firms relative to non-financial firms. Total returns to holders of major banks' equity in the UK, US and Eurozone rose a cumulative 150% between 2002 and 2007 (figure 2.5). This comfortably exceeded the returns to the non-financial economy and even to some of the more risk-seeking parts of the financial sector, such as hedge funds.

To illustrate this rather starkly, consider a hedged bet placed back in 1900, which involved going long by £100 in financial sector equities and

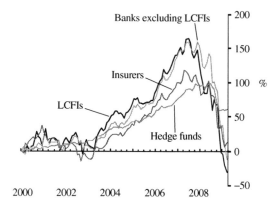

Figure 2.5. Average cumulative total returns of UK, US and Euro area financials. *Sources*: Bloomberg, CreditSuisse/Tremont and Bank of England calculations. *Notes*: market capitalization-weighted average; sample based on banks and insurers in S&P 500, FTSE All Share and DJ EuroSTOXX indices as of March 2009 (excludes firms for which returns are not quoted over entire sample period).

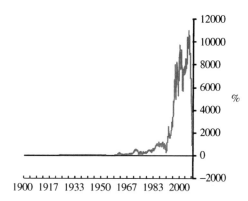

Figure 2.6. Cumulative excess returns from hedged bet in UK equities placed in 1900. *Sources*: Global Financial Data and Bank of England calculations. *Notes*: strategy is long £100 of UK financial equities and short £100 of UK broad equity index established at the start of 1900 and held throughout the period.

short in non-financial equities by the same amount. Figure 2.6 shows cumulative returns to following this hedged strategy. From 1900 up until the end of the 1970s, this bet yielded pretty much nothing, with financial and non-financial returns rising and falling roughly in lockstep. But from then until 2007, cumulative returns to finance took off and exploded in a bubble-like fashion. Only latterly, with the onset of the crisis, has that bubble burst and returned to earth.

2.2.2   Measuring GVA in the Financial Sector

To begin to understand these trends, it is important first to assess how financial sector value added is currently measured and the problems this poses when gauging the sector's contribution to the broader economy.

Most sectors charge explicitly for the products or services they provide and are charged explicitly for the inputs they purchase. This allows the value added of each sector to be measured more or less directly. For example, gross output of a second-hand car dealer can be calculated as the cash value of all cars sold. The value added of that dealer would then be estimated by subtracting its intermediate consumption (the value of cars bought) from gross output.

This is also the case for some of the services provided by the financial sector.[2] For example, investment banks charge explicit fees when they advise clients on a merger or acquisition. Fees or commissions are also levied on underwriting the issuance of securities and for the market-making activities undertaken for clients. But such direct charges account for only part of the financial system's total revenues. Finance—and commercial banking in particular—relies heavily on interest flows as a means of payment for the services they provide. Banks charge an interest rate margin to capture these intermediation services.

To measure the value of financial services embedded in interest rate margins, the concept of FISIM (Financial Intermediation Services Indirectly Measured) has been developed internationally. The concept itself was introduced in the 1993 update of the United Nations System of National Accounts (SNA). The SNA recognizes that financial intermediaries provide services to consumers, businesses, governments and the rest of the world, for which explicit charges are not made. In associated guidelines, a number of such services are identified including

- taking, managing and transferring deposits;
- providing flexible payment mechanisms such as debit cards;
- making loans or other investments; and
- offering financial advice or other business services.

FISIM is estimated for loans and deposits only. The calculation is based on the difference between the effective rates of interest (payable and

---

[2]For further details refer to, for example, Akritidis (2007).

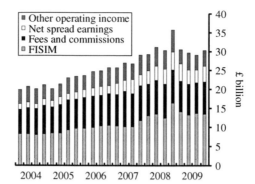

Figure 2.7. Value of gross output of the UK banking sector.
Source: Bank of England.

receivable) and a 'reference' rate of interest, multiplied by the stock of outstanding balances. According to SNA guidelines,[3]

> This reference rate represents the pure cost of borrowing funds—that is, a rate from which the risk premium has been eliminated to the greatest extent possible, and that does not include any intermediation services.

For example, a £1,000 loan with a 9% interest receivable and a 4% reference rate gives current price FISIM on the loan of £1,000×(9%−4%) = £50. And for a £1,000 deposit with a 3% interest payable and a 4% reference rate, this gives current price FISIM on the deposit of £1,000 × (4% − 3%) = £10. Overall, estimated current price FISIM accounts for a significant share of gross output of the banking sector (figure 2.7).

Estimating a real measure of FISIM is fraught with both conceptual and computational difficulties. In the earlier example of the second-hand car dealer, statisticians can use the number of cars sold as an indicator of the volume of gross output. But the conceptual equivalent for financial intermediation is not clear. Would two loans of £50 each to the same customer represent a higher level of activity than one loan of £100 would? Methods for measuring FISIM at constant prices are based on conventions. In the UK, real FISIM is calculated by applying the base-year interest margins to an appropriate volume indicator of loans and deposits. The latter is estimated by deflating the corresponding stocks of loans and deposits using the GDP deflator. This method means that any volatility in the current

---

[3]System of National Accounts, 1993, paragraph 6.128. Available at http://unstats.un.org/unsd/sna1993/toctop2.asp.

price measure of FISIM caused by changes in interest margins does not feed into the real measure.

2.2.3 Refining the Measurement of FISIM

While the introduction of FISIM into the national accounts was an important step forward, it is not difficult to construct scenarios where the contribution of the financial sector to the economy could be mismeasured under this approach. A key issue is the extent to which bearing risk should be measured as a productive service provided by the banking system.

Adjusting FISIM for Risk

Under current FISIM guidelines, which use riskless policy rates to measure the reference rate, banks' compensation for bearing risk constitutes part of their measured nominal output. This can lead to some surprising outcomes. For example, assume there is an economy-wide increase in the expected level of defaults on loans or in liquidity risk, as occurred in October 2008. Banks will rationally respond by increasing interest rates to cover the rise in expected losses. FISIM will score this increased compensation for expected losses on lending as a rise in output. In other words, at times when risk is rising, the contribution of the financial sector to the real economy may be overestimated. This goes some way towards explaining the 2008 Q4 National Accounts paradox of a rapidly rising financial sector contribution to nominal GDP.

Of course, the financial sector does bear the risk of other agents in the economy. Banks take on maturity mismatch or liquidity risk on behalf of households and companies. And banks also make risky loans funded by debt, which exposes them to default or solvency risk. But it is not clear that bearing risk is, in itself, a productive activity. Any household or corporate investing in a risky debt security also bears credit and liquidity risk. The act of investing capital in a risky asset is a fundamental feature of capital markets and is not specific to the activities of banks. Conceptually, therefore, it is not clear that risk-based income flows should represent bank output.

The productive activity provided by an effectively functioning banking system might be better thought of as measuring and pricing credit and liquidity risk. For example, banks screen borrowers' creditworthiness when extending loans, thereby acting as delegated monitor. And they manage liquidity risk through their treasury operations, thereby acting as delegated treasurer. These risk-pricing services are remunerated implicitly through the interest rates banks charge to their customers.

Table 2.2. Current and risk-adjusted FISIM estimates if risk is priced correctly.

Current FISIM	Borrower rate − Riskless rate
	= (7% − 5%) × $100 = $2
Risk-adjusted FISIM	Borrower rate − Market rate of risk (A)
	= [7% − (5% + 1%)] × $100 = $1

Stripping out the compensation for bearing risk to better reflect the service component of the financial sector could be achieved in different ways. One possibility would be to adjust FISIM using provisions as an indicator of expected losses. A broader adjustment for risk would be to move away from the riskless rate as the reference rate within FISIM (Wang *et al.* 2004; Wang 2003; Mink 2008; Colangelo and Inklaar 2010). For example, a paper prepared for the OECD Working Party on National Accounts (Mink 2008) suggested that the FISIM calculation should use reference rates that match the maturity and credit risk of loans and deposits. This would also eliminate an inconsistency within the current National Accounts framework. Measured financial intermediation output increases if a bank bears the risk of lending to a company. But gross output is unchanged if a household holds a bond issued by the same company and thus bears the same risk.

To see how such a mechanism would work, consider the following simple example. A bank lends £100 to a corporate borrower at 7% per annum for one year. The riskless rate is 5%. The bank correctly assesses the credit risk of the corporate to be A-rated. The market spread for A-rated credits at a maturity of one year is 1% over the riskless rate. Current FISIM would estimate the bank's output as £2 (table 2.2). Risk-adjusted FISIM, though, would estimate the bank's output as £1.

An adjustment of FISIM along these lines could potentially be material. According to simulations on the impact of such an approach for the Eurozone countries, aggregate risk-adjusted FISIM would stand at about 60% of current aggregate FISIM for the Eurozone countries over the period 2003–7 (Mink 2008).

Measuring Risk

Adjusting FISIM for risk would better capture the contribution of the financial sector to the economy. The fundamental problem is, however, that risk itself is unobservable *ex ante*. The methodology described above measures risk in a relative way; it effectively assumes that if banks deviate from prevailing market rates, this is to compensate for the services

Table 2.3. Current and risk-adjusted FISIM estimates if risk is priced incorrectly.

Current FISIM	Borrower rate – Riskless rate = (7% – 5%) × $100 = $2
'Measured' risk-adjusted FISIM	Borrower rate – Market rate of risk (A) = [7% – (5% + 1%)] × $100 = $1
'True' risk-adjusted FISIM	Borrower rate – Market rate of risk (BB) = [7% – (5% + 2%)] × $100 = $0

they provide to borrowers and depositors. But at no point is there an assessment of the ability of the financial system to price risk correctly in an absolute sense. This might not be the objective of statisticians when measuring output. But it is essential when gauging the contribution of finance to economic well-being.

To see this more clearly, consider an alternative example (table 2.3). A bank lends £100 to a corporate borrower. But the bank incorrectly assesses the credit risk of the corporate to be A-rated, when the true credit risk is BB-rated. Assume for simplicity that the corporate, knowing that its credit risk is greater than A, is prepared to pay a spread higher than that on an A-rated credit risk (say 2%). The market spreads for A-rated and BB-rated credits are 1% and 2%, respectively. 'Measured' risk-adjusted FISIM is still an improvement on current FISIM. But the value of bank output is still overstated relative to 'true' risk-adjusted FISIM.

This would be equivalent to second-car hand dealers consistently selling lemons. But a dodgy car seller would be quickly found out. Mechanical risk is observable. Dealers that persistently misprice cars would be driven out of the market. Buyers might instead then choose to meet online.

A banking system that does not accurately assess and price risk is not adding much value to the economy. Buyers and sellers of risk could meet instead in capital markets—as they have, to some extent, following the crisis. But unlike the condition of a car, risk is unobservable. So mispricing of risk, and mismeasurement of the services banks provide to the real economy, may persist. This echoes events in the run-up to the crisis when market prices systematically underpriced risk for a number of years. Using the market price of risk would have led statisticians systematically to overstate the potential contribution of the financial sector over this period.

Attempting to adjust the measurement of bank output for risk by changing the reference rate in FISIM is an improvement on current practices. But it would still fall short of assessing whether the financial sector is pricing risk correctly and hence assessing the true value of the services banks provide to the wider economy. Unless the price of risk can be evaluated, it seems unlikely that the contribution of the financial sector to the economy can be measured with accuracy.

2.3 DECOMPOSING THE CONTRIBUTION OF THE FINANCIAL SECTOR: THE 'PRODUCTIVITY MIRACLE'

To that end, an alternative way of looking at the contribution of the financial sector is through inputs to the production process. This might shed more light on the sources of the rapid growth in finance. Was this expansion accompanied by a rising share of resources employed by finance relative to the rest of the economy? Or did it instead reflect unusually high returns to these factors of production? This section considers these questions in turn.

2.3.1 Growth-Accounting Decomposition

The basic growth-accounting framework breaks down the sources of economic growth into the contributions from increases in the inputs to production, capital and labour. This amounts to relating growth in GDP to growth in labour input and in various capital services (from buildings, vehicles, computers and other resources). When these factors have all been accounted for, the remainder is often attributed to technical change—the so-called Solow residual (Solow 1957).

The growth-accounting framework assumes an underlying aggregate production function. In its most basic form, the aggregate production function can be written as

$$Q = f(K, L, t),$$

where Q is output, K and L represent capital and labour units and t appears in f to allow for technical change.

Assuming constant returns to scale, perfect competition (so that factors of production are paid their marginal products) and Hicks-neutral technical change (so that shifts in the production function do not affect marginal rates of substitution between inputs), output growth can be expressed as a weighted sum of the growth rates of inputs and an additional term that captures shifts over time in the production technology. The weights for the input growth rates are the respective shares in total

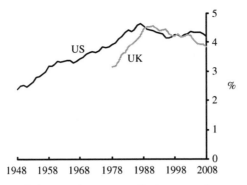

Figure 2.8. Share of financial intermediation employment in UK and US whole-economy employment.

Sources: ONS, Bureau of Economic Analysis and Bank of England calculations. *Notes*: US figures are for full-time and part-time employees in finance and insurance as a percentage of total; UK figures are for employee jobs in financial intermediation as a percentage of total.

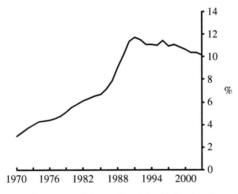

Figure 2.9. UK financial sector physical capital (share of total industry capital).

Source: Bank of England dataset (2003); see also Oulton and Srinivasan (2005). *Notes*: annual data for thirty-four industries across UK economy; capital includes buildings, equipment, vehicles, intangibles, computers, software and communication equipment.

input payments: the labour and capital shares. More specifically,

$$\frac{\dot{Q}}{Q} = \frac{\dot{A}}{A} + \alpha_K \frac{\dot{K}}{K} + \alpha_L \frac{\dot{L}}{L},$$

where $A(t)$ is a multiplicative factor in the production function capturing technical change, and α_K and α_L represent the capital and labour shares of income, respectively.

Figures 2.8 and 2.9 look at the proportion of labour and physical capital employed by the financial intermediation sector in the UK relative to the

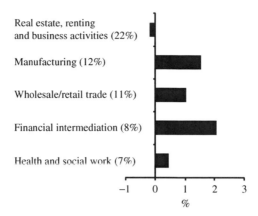

Figure 2.10. Annual TFP growth across the five largest UK industries: average 2000–2007.

Sources: EU KLEMS and Bank of England calculations; see O'Mahony and Timmer (2009). *Notes*: numbers in parentheses denote share of industry GVA in total GVA in 2007; TFP estimated using a value added rather than gross-output based approach (estimates account for changes in both the quantity and quality of labour).

whole economy over the past forty years. They follow a not dissimilar path, with both labour and capital inputs rising as a share of the whole economy for much of the period. The proportion of labour employed by finance rises by around 50% between 1977 and 1990, while the proportion of capital almost trebles from 4% to 12% over the same period. Financial liberalization over the period drew factors of production into finance, both labour and capital, on a fairly dramatic scale.

Perhaps the most striking development, however, is what happens next. These trends have not persisted during this century. If anything, the labour and capital shares of the financial sector have been on a gently declining path over this period. Growth in both labour and capital employed in the financial sector has been modest and has been lower than in the economy as a whole. Since this fall in factor input shares coincides with a period when measured value added of the financial sector was rising sharply, this suggests something dramatic must have been happening to productivity in finance—the Solow residual.

The measured residual, in a growth-accounting sense, reflects improvements in the total factor productivity (TFP) of the inputs. A growth-accounting decomposition suggests that measured TFP growth in the financial sector averaged about 2.2% per year between 1995 and 2007 (figure 2.10). This comfortably exceeds TFP growth at the whole-economy level, estimated at an average of about 0.5–1.0% over the same period. In

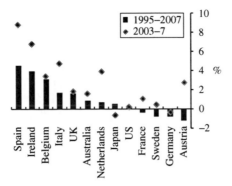

Figure 2.11. Differential in TFP growth between financial intermediation and the whole economy.

Sources: EU KLEMS and Bank of England calculations; see O'Mahony and Timmer (2009).
Notes: TFP estimated using a value added rather than gross-output based approach (estimates account for changes in both the quantity and quality of labour); a positive number implies higher TFP growth in financial intermediation relative to the whole economy.

other words, on the face of it at least, there is evidence of the financial sector having undergone something of a 'productivity miracle' during this century. This pattern has not been specific to the UK. Measured TFP growth in the financial sector exceeded that of the whole economy across many developed countries between 1995 and 2007, a trend that accelerated in the 'bubble' years of 2003–7 (figure 2.11).

2.3.2 *Returns to Factors of Production*

TFP in a growth framework is no more than an accounting residual. It provides no explanation of the measured 'productivity miracle' in finance. A related question is whether the observed productivity miracle was reflected in returns to the factors of production in finance. Figure 2.12 decomposes total GVA of financial corporations into income flowing to labour (defined to include employees only) and income flowing to capital. Broadly speaking, the rise in GVA is equally split between the returns to labour (employee compensation) and to capital (gross operating surplus). The miracle has been reflected in the returns to both labour and capital, if not in the quantities of these factors employed.

For labour, these high returns are evident both in cross-section and time-series data. Figure 2.13 shows average weekly earnings across a range of sectors in the UK in 2007. Financial intermediation is at the top of the table, with weekly average earnings roughly double those of the whole-economy median. This differential widened during this century,

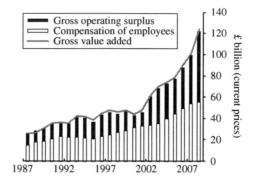

Figure 2.12. Returns to labour and capital in UK financial intermediation.
Sources: ONS and Bank of England calculations. *Notes*: data refer to financial corporations; the implied split between labour and capital is only approximate; compensation of employees underestimates total returns to labour as it excludes income of the self-employed (which is measured as part of gross operating surplus).

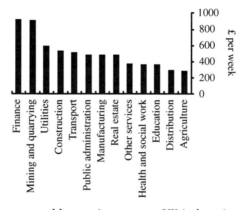

Figure 2.13. Average weekly earnings across UK industries, 2007.
Sources: ONS and Bank of England calculations. *Notes*: 'Utilities' covers electricity, gas and water supply; 'Transport' covers transport, storage and communication; 'Real estate' covers real estate, renting and business activities; 'Distribution' covers distribution, hotels and restaurants; and 'Agriculture' covers agriculture, forestry and fishing.

broadly mirroring the accumulation of leverage within the financial sector (figure 2.14).

The time-series evidence is in some respects even more dramatic. Philippon and Reshef (2009) have undertaken a careful study of 'excess' wages in the US financial industry since the start of the previous century, relative to a benchmark wage. Figure 2.15 plots their measure of excess wages. This shows a dramatic spike upwards which commenced in the early 1980s, but which exploded from the 1990s onwards. The

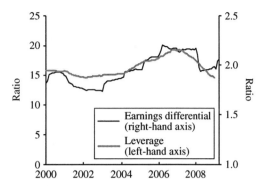

Figure 2.14. Ratio of financial intermediation to economy-wide earnings versus leverage of the UK banking sector.

Sources: ONS, Bank of England and Bank of England calculations.

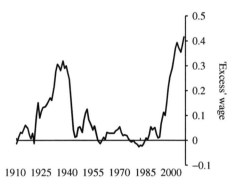

Figure 2.15. Historical 'excess' wage in the US financial sector.

Source: Philippon and Reshef (2009). *Notes*: difference between the actual relative wage in finance and an estimated benchmark series for the relative wage.

only equivalent wage spike was in the run-up to the Great Crash in 1929. Philippon and Reshef attribute both of these wage spikes to financial deregulation.

This picture is broadly mirrored when turning from returns to labour to returns to capital. In the 1950s gross profitability of the financial sector relative to capital employed was broadly in line with the rest of the economy (figure 2.16). But since then, and in particular over the past decade, returns to capital have far outpaced those at an economy-wide level.

Figure 2.17 plots UK banks' return on equity capital (ROE) since 1920 (Alessandri and Haldane 2009). Although conceptually a different measure of returns to capital, the broad message is the same. Trends in ROE are clearly divided into two periods. In the period up until around 1970,

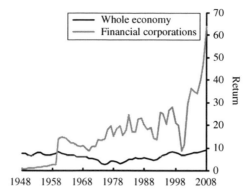

Figure 2.16. Net operating surplus over net capital stock in UK financial inter-mediation and the whole economy.

Sources: ONS and Bank of England calculations. *Notes*: gross operating surplus less cap-ital consumption, divided by net capital stock.

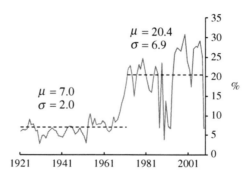

Figure 2.17. Return on equity in UK finance.

Sources: British Bankers' Association, Billings and Capie (2004) and Bank of England calculations. *Notes*: there is a definitional change in the sample in 1967. The latter period has a slightly larger number of banks and returns on equity are calculated somewhat differently, including pre-tax.

ROE in banking was around 7% with a low variance. In other words, returns to finance broadly mimicked those in the economy as whole, in line with the gamble payoffs in figure 2.6. But the 1970s mark a regime shift, with the ROE in banking roughly trebling to over 20%, again in line with gamble payoffs. Excess returns accumulated to capital as well as labour.

These returns were by no means unique to UK banks. Figure 2.18 plots ROEs for major internationally active banks in the US and Europe dur-ing this century. Two features are striking. First, the level of ROEs was consistently at or above 20% and on a rising trend up until the crisis. This is roughly double ROEs in the non-financial sector over the period.

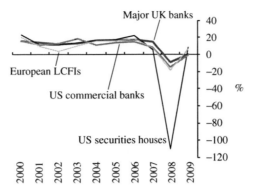

Figure 2.18. Major UK banks' and LCFIs' return on common equity.
Sources: Capital IQ and Bank of England calculations.

Second, the degree of cross-country similarity in these ROE profiles is striking. This, too, is no coincidence. During much of this period, banks internationally were engaged in a highly competitive ROE race. Therein lies part of the explanation for these high returns to labour and capital in banking.

2.4 Explaining Aggregate Returns in Banking: Excess Returns and Risk Illusion

How do we explain these high, but temporary, excess returns to finance which appear to have driven the growing contribution of the financial sector to aggregate economic activity? In this section we discuss potential balance-sheet strategies which may have contributed to these rents. Essentially, high returns to finance may have been driven by banks assuming higher risk. Banks' profits, like their contribution to GDP, may have been flattered by the mismeasurement of risk.

The crisis has subsequently exposed the extent of this increased risk-taking by banks. In particular, three (often related) balance-sheet strategies for boosting risks and returns to banking were dominant in the run-up to the crisis:

- increased leverage, on and off balance sheet;
- increased share of assets held at fair value; and
- writing deep-out-of-the-money options.

What each of these strategies had in common was that they generated a rise in balance-sheet risk, as well as return. Just as importantly, this increase in risk was to some extent hidden by the opacity of accounting

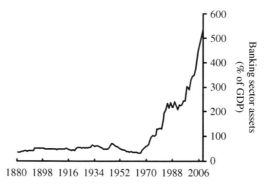

Figure 2.19. Size of the UK banking system.

Sources: Sheppard (1971) and Bank of England. *Notes*: the definition of UK banking sector assets used in the series is broader after 1966, but using a narrower definition throughout gives the same growth profile.

disclosures or the complexity of the products involved. This resulted in a divergence between reported and risk-adjusted returns. In other words, while reported ROEs rose, *risk-adjusted* ROEs did not (Haldane 2009).

To some extent, these strategies and their implications were captured to a degree in performance measures. For example, the rise in reported average ROEs of banks over the past few decades occurred alongside a rise in its variability. At the same time as average ROEs in banking were trebling, so too was their standard deviation (figure 2.17). In that sense, the banking 'productivity miracle' may have been, at least in part, a mirage—a simple, if dramatic, case of risk illusion by banks, investors and regulators.

2.4.1 *Increased Leverage*

Banks' balance sheets have grown dramatically in relation to underlying economic activity over the past century. Figures 2.19 and 2.20 plot this ratio for the UK and the US over the past 130 years. For the US, there has been a secular rise in banks' assets from around 20% to over 100% of GDP. For the UK, a century of flatlining at around 50% of GDP was broken in the early 1970s, since when banks' assets in relation to national income have risen tenfold to over 500% of GDP.

This century has seen an intensification of this growth. According to data compiled by the *Banker*, the balance sheets of the world's largest 1,000 banks increased by around 150% between 2001 and 2009 (figure 2.21). In cross-sectional terms, the scale of assets in the banking system now dwarfs that in other sectors. Looking at the size of the largest

Figure 2.20. Size of the US banking system relative to GDP, 1870–2008.
Source: Schularick and Taylor (2009).

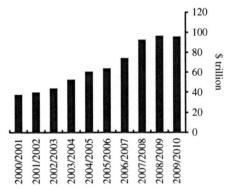

Figure 2.21. Total assets of the world's 1,000 largest banks.
Source: www.thebankerdatabase.com.

firm's assets in relation to GDP across a spectrum of industries, finance is by far the largest (figure 2.22).

The extent of balance-sheet growth was, if anything, understated by banks' reported assets. Accounting and regulatory policies permitted banks to place certain exposures off balance sheet, including special purpose vehicles and contingent credit commitments. Even disclosures of on-balance-sheet positions on derivatives disguised some information about banks' contingent exposures.

This rapid expansion of the balance sheet of the banking system was not accompanied by a commensurate increase in its equity base. Over the same 130-year period, the capital ratios of banks in the US and UK fell from around 15–25% at the start of the twentieth century to around 5% at its end (figure 2.23). In other words, on this metric, measures of balance-sheet leverage rose from around four times equity capital in the

85

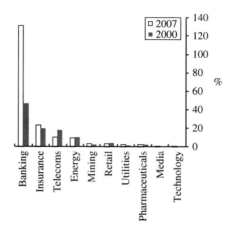

Figure 2.22. Largest companies' assets in each sector relative to annual GDP in the UK.

Sources: Capital IQ, IMF and Bank of England calculations.

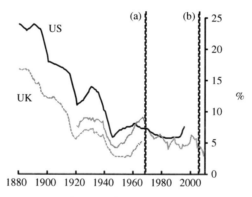

Figure 2.23. Long-run capital ratios for UK and US banks.

Sources: Berger *et al.* (1995) for the US; Sheppard (1971), Billings and Capie (2007), British Bankers' Association, published accounts and Bank of England calculations for the UK. Notes. US data show equity as a percentage of assets (ratio of aggregate dollar value of bank book equity to aggregate dollar value of bank book assets). UK data on the capital ratio show equity and reserves over total assets on a time-varying sample of banks, representing the majority of the UK banking system, in terms of assets. Prior to 1970, published accounts understated the true level of banks' capital because they did not include hidden reserves. The solid grey line adjusts for this. '(a)' denotes a change in UK accounting standards. '(b)' denotes the time when International Financial Reporting Standards (IFRS) were adopted for the end-2005 accounts. The end-2004 accounts were also restated on an IFRS basis. The switch from UK GAAP to IFRS reduced the capital ratio of the UK banks in the sample by approximately one percentage point in 2004.

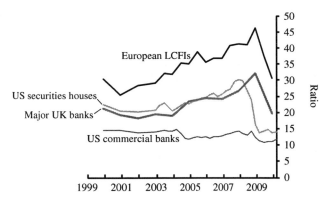

Figure 2.24. Leverage at the LCFIs.

Sources: Bloomberg, published accounts and Bank of England calculations. *Notes*: leverage equals assets over total shareholder equity net of minority interests.

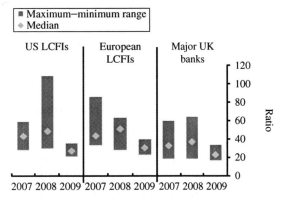

Figure 2.25. The leverage ratios of major UK banks and LCFIs.

Sources: published accounts and Bank of England calculations. *Notes*: assets adjusted on a best-efforts basis to achieve comparability between institutions reporting under US GAAP and IFRS; derivatives netted in line with US GAAP rules; off-balance-sheet vehicles included in line with IFRS rules; assets adjusted for cash items, deferred tax assets, goodwill and intangibles; for some firms, changes in exchange rates have impacted foreign currency assets, but this cannot be adjusted for; capital excludes Tier 2 instruments, preference shares, hybrids, goodwill and intangibles; 'Major UK banks' excludes Northern Rock.

early part of the previous century to around twenty times capital at the end.

If anything, the pressure to raise leverage increased further moving into this century. Measures of gearing rose sharply between 2000 and 2008 among the major global banks, other than US commercial banks which were subject to a leverage ratio constraint (figure 2.24). Once adjustments

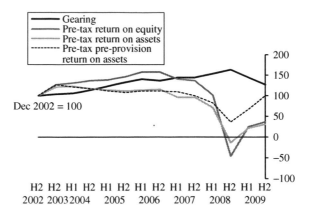

Figure 2.26. Major UK banks' pre-tax return on equity.
Sources: published accounts and Bank of England calculations. *Notes*: based on twelve-month trailing pre-tax revenues and average shareholders equity.

are made to on- and off-balance-sheet assets and capital to give a more comprehensive cross-country picture, levels of gearing are even more striking. Among the major global banks in the world, levels of leverage were on average more than fifty times equity at the peak of the boom (figure 2.25).

For a given return on assets (RoA), higher leverage mechanically boosts a bank's ROE. The decision by many banks to increase leverage appears to have been driven, at least in part, by a desire to maintain ROE relative to competitors, even as RoA fell. For example, as figure 2.26 illustrates, virtually all of the increase in the ROE of the major UK banks during this century appears to have been the result of higher leverage. Banks' return on assets—a more precise measure of their productivity—was flat or even falling over this period.

Between 1997 and 2008, as UK banks increased leverage, they managed to maintain broadly constant capital ratios by, on average, seeking out assets with lower risk weights (figure 2.27). A similar pattern was evident among a number of the Continental European major global banks (figure 2.28). It is possible to further decompose ROE to provide additional insight into how banks increased reported returns as follows:

$$
\begin{aligned}
\text{ROE} &= \frac{\text{Total assets}}{\text{Tier 1 capital}} \times \frac{\text{Tier 1 capital}}{\text{Common equity}} \times \frac{\text{Net income}}{\text{RWAs}} \times \frac{\text{RWAs}}{\text{Total assets}}, \\
\text{ROE} &= \text{Financial leverage} \times \text{Common equity margin} \times \text{RoRWAs} \\
&\qquad\qquad \times \text{Unit risk.}
\end{aligned}
$$

$$(2.1)$$

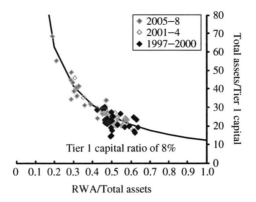

Figure 2.27. Major UK banks' ratios of total assets to Tier 1 capital and risk-weighted assets to total assets, 1997–2008.

Sources: published accounts and Bank of England calculations. *Notes*: see footnote 4 on page 89 for the definition of Tier 1 capital; the Tier 1 capital ratio equals Tier 1 capital over risk-weighed assets.

Banks can boost ROE by acting on any of the terms on the right-hand side of equation (2.1): increasing assets relative to capital (financial leverage), holding a larger proportion of capital[4] other than as common equity (common equity margin), or assuming a greater degree of risk per unit of assets (return on risk-weighted assets (RoRWA))—*leveraging* assets, *leveraging* capital structure or *leveraging* regulation.

Table 2.4 shows two of the elements of this breakdown for the major global banks: leverage and unit risk. For most banks, the story is one of a significant increase in assets relative to capital, with little movement into higher-risk assets (unit risk makes a negative contribution for most banks). Those banks with highest leverage, however, are also the ones which have subsequently reported the largest write-downs. That suggests banks may also have invested in riskier assets, which regulatory risk weights had failed to capture.

Table 2.5 looks at the third component, the common equity margin, of some of the same global banks. Among at least some of these banks, this margin makes a significant contribution to ROE growth, as banks moved into hybrid Tier 1 capital instruments at the expense of core equity. As such hybrid instruments have shown themselves to be largely unable to

---

[4]The term 'Tier 1 capital' refers to the component of banks' regulatory capital comprising common equity and capital instruments close to common equity ('hybrid Tier 1 capital'), as defined by rules set out by regulators. For a discussion of the composition of UK banks' regulatory capital, see Bank of England (2009a).

Table 2.4. Summary of component factors of decomposition of LCFIs' ROE[a].

	Financial leverage		Unit risk		Write-downs	
	2007	Change 2007/04 (%)	2007	Change 2007/04 (%)	End 2010 Q1 (US$ bn)	As % of common equity
Citi	24.5	22.9	0.6	0.0	58.0	51.1
Bank of America	20.6	19.1	0.7	−1.1	20.6	14.5
JPMorgan	17.6	4.4	0.7	−1.5	13.6	11.0
Barclays	37.8	36.4	0.3	−26.0	22.9	56.6
RBS	31.2	22.1	0.4	−21.2	26.5	32.6
HSBC	21.3	11.8	0.5	−15.1	9.4	7.3
Deutsche Bank	58.1	16.6	0.2	12.5	50.8	163.9
SocGen	43.2	49.9	0.3	−14.0	7.8	20.3
BNP Paribas	39.7	18.2	0.4	−3.0	4.6	5.9
Credit Suisse	39.2	−11.6	0.2	25.4	13.8	35.6
Merrill Lynch	35.3	—	0.4	—	58.6	212.6
Morgan Stanley	27.8	—	0.3	—	20.7	68.6
Lehman Brothers	27.6	—	0.3	—	16.3	76.2
Goldman Sachs	25.0	—	0.4	—	10.3	25.8

Sources: published accounts and Bank of England calculations.

[a]Ratios are as at end-year, except for the US securities houses, which are as at end-2008 Q2, and are adjusted for derivatives netting consistent with US GAAP where possible.

Table 2.5. LCFIs' common equity margin.

	2007	Change 2007/04 (%)
Citi	0.8	14.3
Bank of America	0.6	−8.9
JPMorgan	0.7	10.5
Barclays	1.1	9.4
RBS	1.0	48.3
HSBC	0.8	4.1
UBS	1.0	7.7
Deutsche Bank	0.7	3.8
SocGen	0.8	−20.4
BNP Paribas	0.7	−13.8
Credit Suisse	0.8	18.6

Source: published accounts and Bank of England calculations.

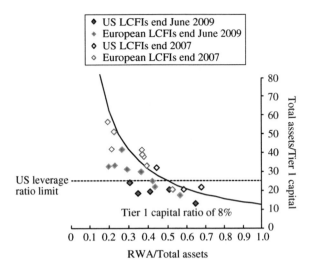

Figure 2.28. LCFIs' ratios of total assets to Tier 1 capital and risk-weighted assets to total assets.

Sources: published accounts and Bank of England calculations. *Notes*: refer to figure 2.25 for details of adjustments made to assets; the 'US leverage ratio limit' is approximated using a ratio of Tier 1 capital to total assets of 4% (the inclusion of qualifying off-balance-sheet assets places some US LCFIs above the leverage ratio proxy); 'US LCFIs end-2007' excludes US securities houses.

absorb losses during the crisis, this boost to ROE is also likely to have been an act of risk illusion.

Taken together, this evidence suggests that much of the 'productivity miracle' of high ROEs in banking appear to have been the result not of productivity gains on the underlying asset pool, but rather a simple leveraging up of the underlying equity in the business.

2.4.2 Larger Trading Books

A second strategy pursued by a number of banks in the run-up to crisis was to increase their assets held at fair value, principally through their trading books, relative to their banking books of underlying loans. Among the major global banks, the share of loans to customers in total assets fell from around 35% in 2000 to 29% by 2007 (figure 2.29). Over the same period, trading-book asset shares almost doubled from 20% to almost 40%. These large trading books were associated with high leverage among the world's largest banks (figure 2.30).

What explains this shift in portfolio shares? Regulatory arbitrage appears to have been a significant factor. Trading-book assets tended

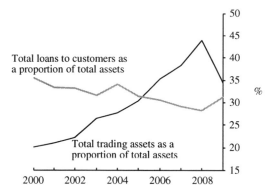

Figure 2.29. LCFIs' trading assets and loans to customers as a proportion of total assets.

Sources: published accounts and Bank of England calculations. *Notes*: excludes US securities houses.

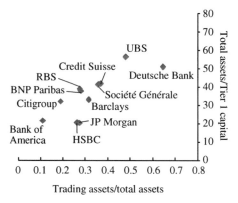

Figure 2.30. LCFIs' ratios of total assets to Tier 1 capital and trading assets to total assets.

Sources: published accounts and Bank of England calculations. *Notes*: refer to figure 2.25 for details of adjustments made to assets; data as at end-2007.

to attract risk weights appropriate for dealing with market risk but not credit risk. This meant that it was capital-efficient for banks to bundle loans into tradable structured credit products for onward sale. Indeed, by securitizing assets in this way, it was hypothetically possible for two banks to swap their underlying claims but for both firms to claim capital relief. The system as a whole would then be left holding less capital, even though its underlying exposures were identical. When the crisis came, losses on structured products were, tellingly, substantial (figure 2.31).

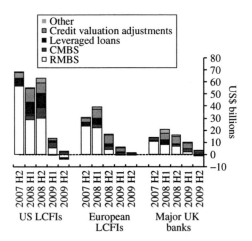

Figure 2.31. The write-downs of major UK banks and LCFIs.

Sources: published accounts and Bank of England calculations. *Notes*: includes write-downs due to mark-to-market adjustments on trading-book positions where details are disclosed by firms; 'Other' includes SIVs and other ABS write-downs; 'Credit valuation adjustments' is on exposures to monolines and others.

A further amplifying factor is that trading books are marked-to-market and any gains or losses are taken through to the profit and loss account. So holding a large trading book is a very good strategy when underlying asset prices in the economy are rising rapidly. This was precisely the set of the circumstances facing banks in the run-up to crisis, with asset prices driven higher by a search for yield among investors. In effect, this rising tide of asset price rises was booked as marked-to-market profits by banks holding assets in their trading book. Everyone, it appeared, was a winner.

But because these gains were driven by a mispricing of risk in the economy at large, trading-book profits were in fact largely illusory. Once asset prices went into reverse during 2008 as risk was repriced, trading-book losses quickly materialized. Write-downs on structured products totalled $210 billion among the major global banks in 2008 alone.

2.4.3 *Writing Deep-Out-of-the-Money Options*

A third strategy, which boosted returns by silently assuming risk, arises from offering tail risk insurance. Banks can in a variety of ways assume tail risk on particular instruments—for example, by investing in high-default loan portfolios, the senior tranches of structured products or writing insurance through credit default swap (CDS) contracts. In each of these cases, the investor earns an above-normal yield or premium from

93

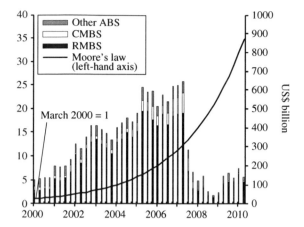

Figure 2.32. Global issuance of asset-backed securities.
Source: Dealogic. *Notes*: 'Other ABS' includes auto, credit card and student loan ABS; bars show publicly placed issuance.

assuming the risk. For as long as the risk does not materialize, returns can look riskless—a case of apparent 'alpha'. Until, that is, tail risk manifests itself, at which point losses can be very large.

There are many examples of banks pursuing essentially these strategies in the run-up to crisis. For example, investing in senior tranches of subprime loan securitizations is, in effect, equivalent to writing deep-out-of-the-money options, with high returns except in those tail states of the world when borrowers default en masse. It is unsurprising that issuance of asset-backed securities, including subprime residential mortgage-backed securities, grew dramatically during the course of this century, easily outpacing Moore's law (the benchmark for the growth in computing power since the invention of the transistor) (figure 2.32).[5]

Tranched structured products, such as collateralized debt obligations (CDOs) and collateralized loan obligations (CLOs), generate a similar payoff profile for investors to subprime loans, yielding a positive return in stable states of the world—apparent alpha—and a large negative return in adverse states. Volumes outstanding of CDOs and CLOs also grew at a rate in excess of Moore's law for much of this century. The resulting systematic mispricing of, in particular, the super-senior tranches of these securities was a significant source of losses to banks during the crisis, with ratings downgrades becoming large and frequent (figure 2.33).

---

[5]Moore's law refers to the observation by Intel cofounder Gordon Moore in 1965 that transistor density on integrated circuits had doubled every year since the integrated circuit was invented and the prediction that this would continue.

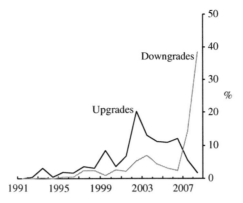

Figure 2.33. Global structured finance ratings changes.
Source: Fitch Ratings. *Notes*: data compares beginning-of-the-year rating with end-of-the-year rating; does not count multiple rating actions throughout the year.

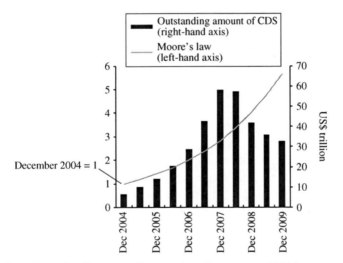

Figure 2.34. Growth of outstanding notional amount of CDSs versus Moore's law.
Sources: BIS and Bank of England calculations.

A similar risk-taking strategy was the writing of explicit insurance contracts against such tail risks, for example through CDSs. These too grew very rapidly ahead of crisis (figure 2.34). Again, the writers of these insurance contracts gathered a steady source of premium income during the good times—apparently 'excess returns'. But this was typically more than offset by losses once bad states materialized. This, famously, was the strategy pursued by some of the monoline insurers and by AIG. For

Figure 2.35. Concentration of US banks, 1935–2008.

Sources: FDIC and Bank of England calculations. *Notes*: top three banks by total assets, as percentage of total banking sector assets; data include only insured depository subsidiaries of banks.

example, AIG's capital market business, which included its ill-fated financial products division, reported total operating income of $2.3 billion in the run-up to crisis from 2003 to 2006, but reported operating losses of around $40 billion in 2008 alone.

What all of these strategies had in common was that they involved banks assuming risk in the hunt for yield—risk that was often disguised because it was parked in the tail of the return distribution. Excess returns—from leverage, trading books and out-of-the-money options—were built on an inability to measure and price risk. The 'productivity miracle' was in fact a risk illusion. In that respect, mismeasurement of the contribution of banking in the National Accounts and the mismeasurement of returns to banking in their own accounts have a common underlying cause.

2.5 EXPLAINING DISAGGREGATED RETURNS TO BANKING

A distinct, but complementary, explanation of high returns to banking is that they reflect structural features of the financial sector. For example, measures of market concentration are often used as a proxy for the degree of market power that producers have over consumers. It is telling that measures of the concentration of the banking sector have increased dramatically over the course of the past decade, coincident with the rise in banking returns. Figure 2.35 plots the share of total bank assets of the largest three banks in the US since the 1930s. Having flatlined up until the 1990s, the top-three share has since roughly tripled. A similar trend

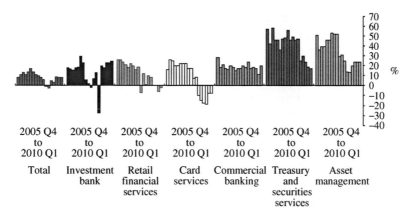

Figure 2.36. JPMorgan Chase business segment return on equity: quarterly 2005 Q4–2010 Q1.

Source: published accounts.

is evident in the UK (where the share of the top three banks currently stands at above 50%) and globally (where the share of the top three has doubled over the past ten years).

At the same time, it is well known that market concentration need not signal a lack of competitiveness or efficiency within an industry or sector (Wood and Kabiri 2010). Highly competitive industries can be concentrated and highly decentralized industries can be uncompetitive. A better arbiter of market power may be measures of market contestability, in particular, the potential for barriers to entry to and exit from the market. Entry and exit rates from banking have, historically, tended to be very modest by comparison with the non-financial sector and other parts of the financial sector, such as hedge funds.

For banks operating in many markets and offering a range of services, aggregate returns may offer a misleading guide to the degree of market contestability. Looking separately at the different activities that financial firms undertake provides a potentially clearer indication of the drivers of performance and the structural factors determining them. In this respect, JPMorgan Chase provides an interesting case study.

JPMorgan Chase is a large universal bank offering a full package of banking services to customers, both retail and wholesale. Its published accounts also provide a fairly detailed decomposition of the returns to these different activities. Figure 2.36 looks at the returns on equity at JPMorgan Chase, broken down by business line and over time. These estimates are based on the firm's economic capital model. So, provided that this model adequately captures risk, these estimates ought to risk-adjust returns across the different business lines, allocating greater amounts of capital to riskier activities.

2.5.1 'Low-Risk/Low-Return' Business Activities

Consider first some of the activities generally perceived to be low risk/low return: asset management and treasury and securities services and retail financial services. All of these seemingly low-risk activities appear to deliver above-average returns on equity, ranging from a high of around 50% on treasury and asset management services to around 20+% on retail financial services.

One potential explanation of these high returns is that the risk associated with these activities, and hence the capital allocated to them, may be underestimated by banks' models. Another is that the demand for these services is highly price inelastic—for example, because of information imperfections on the part of end users of these services. Anecdotally, there is certainly evidence of a high degree of stickiness in the demand for retail financial services. Statistically, an adult is more likely to leave their spouse than their bank.

In a UK context, there have been a number of studies by the authorities on the degree of competition within retail financial services, including by the Competition Commission (2005) and the Office of Fair Trading (OFT) (2008). The OFT market study found a very low rate of switching of personal current accounts between banks—fewer than 6% per year. By itself, however, this low switching rate does not necessarily imply a market failure. For example, it could be the result of a reputational equilibrium in which money gravitates to banks whose brand name is recognized and respected.

A more obvious market friction in the UK retail financial services market derives from 'free in credit' banking. In effect, all retail payment services are charged at a zero up-front fee, except large-value payment transfers through CHAPS[6] (which are typically charged at around £25). This charging schedule is not well aligned with marginal costs. It encourages bundling of payment services and the charging of latent or hidden fees on other transactions services—for example, overdraft fees. Explicit charging for retail financial services would increase transparency and reduce the scope for distortions in the use of these services.

---

[6]CHAPS is the same-day electronic funds transfer system, operated by the bank-owned CHAPS Clearing Company, that is used for high-value/wholesale payments but also for other time-critical lower value payments (such as house purchase).

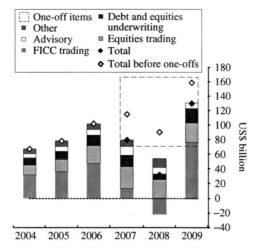

Figure 2.37. A decomposition of the investment banking revenues of US LCFIs. *Sources*: published accounts and Bank of England calculations. *Notes*: 'Other' refers to other activities within the IB business segment, including prime brokerage and securities services; 'FICC trading' includes fixed income, currency and commodities; 'Total before one-offs' is adjusted for write-downs and changes in fair value on FICC and equities trading revenues; revenues are adjusted to reflect the change in reporting cycle for US securities houses.

High returns on treasury management services also present something of a puzzle. These include transactions, information and custodial services to clients. None of these activities is especially expertise-intensive and the market for these services ought in principle to be contestable internationally.

2.5.2 'High-Risk/High-Return' Business Activities

The higher-risk activities associated with finance, such as commercial and investment banking, do not on the face of it appear to yield as high returns on equity. Nonetheless, these returns, at around 20%, are above levels in the non-financial sector.

Investment banking activities are, in risk terms, a mixed bag. They comprise fairly low-risk activities, such as merger and acquisition (M&A) advisory work, with higher-risk activities such as securities underwriting and proprietary trading. To complicate matters, banks' annual accounts data do not differentiate simply between these activities—for example, between market-making and proprietary trading activities in fixed income, currency and commodities (FICC) and equities. Figure 2.37 provides a revenue breakdown of US investment banks' activities.

99

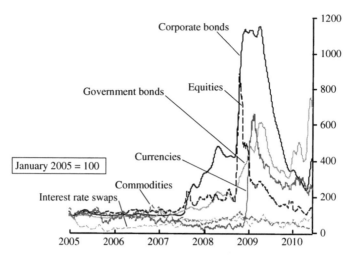

Figure 2.38. Bid–ask spreads on selected assets.

Sources: Bloomberg, UBS Delta and Bank of England calculations. *Notes*: monthly moving averages of daily bid–ask spreads; iBoxx € corporates for corporate bonds; S&P 500 for equities; iBoxx € sovereigns for government bonds; sterling–dollar exchange rate for currencies; gold price for commodities; € five-year swaps for interest rate swaps.

The lack of a breakdown between client and proprietary sources of revenues is problematic when making sense of investment banking activities, both in the run-up to and during the crisis. In the run-up to crisis, FICC and equity-related activity contributed significantly to revenues, partly on the back of proprietary trading in assets whose prices were rising rapidly. Some of these gains then dissolved when asset prices, in particular for FICC, went into reverse during 2008.

The story of 2009–10 is of a strong recovery in FICC and equity revenues. The source of this revenue recovery is, however, different to the boom. Instead of proprietary risk-taking, increased revenues appear instead to have been driven by market-making activities on behalf of clients. These were boosted by a bulge in client activity and wider bid–ask spreads against a backdrop of lower levels of competition (figure 2.38). It is an open question whether these returns to market-making will persist.

In some respects, returns to M&A and advisory activities represent even more of a puzzle. For a start, it is well known that most M&A activity is value-destroying (see, for example, Palia 1995). Advisory fees of 0.5–1.5% are typically taken, even though these activities are essentially riskless. And in total, underwriting fees are often around 3–4% in Europe and higher still in the US, having risen during the course of the crisis. The level and persistence of these fees is also something of a puzzle.

One potential explanation is that high fees on underwriting and advisory activities are sustained as a reputational equilibrium. In effect, clients are willing to pay a premium to have bonds or equity underwritten by a recognized name, as this is a signal of quality to end investors. A similar phenomenon might explain the '2 and 20' fee structure of hedge funds. The OFT has recently announced an investigation into underwriting fees in the UK market.

Another part of the puzzle was banks' approach to managing risk across these business lines. For example, treasury functions are designed to help a firm as a whole manage its balance sheet, with internal transfer pricing for liquidity services to business lines. By acting in that way, the risk-taking incentives of each business unit can be aligned with the business as a whole, thereby complementing firms' internal risk management.

In practice, during the run-up to the crisis, treasury functions were often run as a profit centre. That would tend to encourage two sets of risk-taking behaviour. First, it may have encouraged banks to take risks in balance-sheet management—for example, by seeking out cheaper sources of capital (for example, hybrids over pure equity) or liquidity (shorter-term unsecured borrowing over long-term secured funding). Second, it may have led to the systematic underpricing of liquidity services to banks' business units, fuelling excessive growth and/or risk-taking. Tackling these risks would require banks' treasury operations to cease being profit centres and to execute effective internal transfer pricing.

2.6 CONCLUSION

The financial sector has undergone an astonishing roller-coaster ride in the course of a decade. The ascent to heaven and subsequent descent to hell has been every bit as dramatic as in the 1930s. In seeking to smooth next time's ride, prophylactic public policy has a key role to play. Of the many initiatives that are underway, this chapter has highlighted three which may warrant further attention in the period ahead.

- First, given its ability to both invigorate and incapacitate large parts of the non-financial economy, there is a strong case for seeking improved means of measuring the true value added by the financial sector. As it is rudimentary to its activities, finding a more sophisticated approach to measuring risk, as well as return, within the financial sector would seem to be a priority. The conflation of the two can lead to an overstatement of banks' contribution to the economy and an understatement of the true risk facing banks and the economy at large. Better aggregate statistics and bank-specific performance measures could help better to distinguish miracles and mirages. This might include developing more sophisticated risk adjustments to FISIM and a greater focus on banks' return on assets rather than equity by investors and managers.

- Second, because banks are in the risk business it should be no surprise that the run-up to crisis was hallmarked by imaginative ways of manufacturing this commodity, with a view to boosting returns to labour and capital. Risk illusion is no accident; it is there by design. It is in bank managers' interest to make mirages seem like miracles. Regulatory measures are being put in place to block off last time's risk strategies, including through recalibrated leverage and capital ratios. But risk migrates to where regulation is weakest, so there are natural limits to what regulatory strategies can reasonably achieve. At the height of a boom, both regulators and the regulated are prone to believe in miracles. That is why the debate about potential structural reform of finance is important—to lessen the burden on regulation and reverse its descent into ever-greater intrusiveness and complexity. At the same time, regulators need also to be mindful of risk migrating outside the perimeter of regulation, where it will almost certainly not be measured.

- Third, finance is anything but monolithic. But understanding of these different business lines is complicated by the absence of reliable data on many of these activities. There are several open questions about the some of these activities, not least those for which returns appear to be high. This includes questions about the risks they embody and about the competitive structure of the markets in which they are traded. These are issues for both prudential regulators and the competition authorities, working in tandem. If experience after the Great Depression is any guide, it seems likely that these structural issues will take centre stage in the period ahead.

REFERENCES

Akritidis, L. 2007. Improving the measurement of banking services in the UK National Accounts. *Economic and Labour Market Review* **1**(5), 29–37.

Alessandri, P., and A. G. Haldane. 2009. Banking on the state. Speech. Available at www.bankofengland.co.uk/publications/speeches/2009/speech409.pdf.

Bank of England. 2009a. The changing composition of the major UK banks' regulatory capital. *Bank of England Financial Stability Report* (June), pp. 26-27.

Bank of England. 2009b. The role of macroprudential policy. Discussion Paper. Available at www.bankofengland.co.uk/publications/other/financialstability/roleofmacroprudentialpolicy091121.pdf.

Berger, A., R. Herring and G. Szegö. 1995. The role of capital in financial institutions, *Journal of Banking and Finance* 19(3-4), 393-430.

Billings, M., and F. Capie. 2004. Evidence on competition in English commercial banking, 1920-1970. *Financial History Review* 11, 69-103.

Billings, M., and F. Capie. 2007. Capital in British banking, 1920-1970. *Business History* 49(2), 139-62.

Colangelo, A., and R. Inklaar. 2010. Banking sector output measurement in the Euro area—a modified approach. ECB Working Paper 1204. Available at www.ecb.int/pub/pdf/scpwps/ecbwp1204.pdf.

Competition Commission. 2005. Store cards market inquiry: provisional findings report. Available at www.competition-commission.org.uk/inquiries/completed/2006/storecard/provisional_findings.htm.

Feinstein, C. H. 1972. *National Income, Expenditure and Output of the United Kingdom 1855-1965.* Cambridge University Press.

Haldane, A. G. 2009. Small lessons from a big crisis. Speech. Available at www.bankofengland.co.uk/publications/speeches/2009/speech397.pdf.

Haldane, A. G. 2010. The $100 billion question. Speech. Available at www.bankofengland.co.uk/publications/speeches/2010/speech433.pdf.

Kay, J. 2009. *Narrow Banking: The Reform of Banking Regulation.* London: CSFI.

Large, A. 2010. *Systemic Policy and Financial Stability: A Framework for Delivery.* London: CSFI.

Mink, R. 2008. An enhanced methodology of compiling Financial Intermediation Services Indirectly Measured (FISIM). Paper presented at OECD Working Party on National Accounts, Paris, 14-16 October 2008. Available at www.olis.oecd.org/olis/2008doc.nsf/LinkTo/NT000059AE/$FILE/JT03251258.pdf.

Mitchell, B. R. 1988. *British Historical Statistics.* Cambridge University Press.

OFT. 2008. Personal current accounts in the UK—an OFT market study. Available at www.oft.gov.uk/shared_oft/reports/financial_products/OFT1005.pdf.

O'Mahony, M., and P. T. Marcel. 2009. Output, input and productivity measures at the industry level: the EU KLEMS database. *Economic Journal* 119, 374-403.

Oulton, N., and S. Srinivasan. 2005. Productivity growth in UK industries, 1970-2000: structural change and the role of ICT. Bank of England Working Paper 259.

Philippon, T. 2008. The evolution of the US financial industry from 1860 to 2007: theory and evidence. Available at http://pages.stern.nyu.edu/~tphilipp/papers/finsize.pdf.

Philippon, T., and A. Reshef. 2009. Wages and human capital in the US financial industry: 1909-2006. NBER Working Paper 14644.

Reinhart, C. M., and K. Rogoff. 2009. *This Time Is Different: Eight Centuries of Financial Folly.* Princeton University Press.

Schularick, M., and A. M. Taylor. 2009. Credit booms gone bust: monetary policy, leverage cycles and financial crises, 1870–2008. NBER Working Paper 15512.

Sheppard, D. K. 1971. *The Growth and Role of UK Financial Institutions 1880–1962.* London: Methuen.

Solow, R. M. 1957. Technical change and the aggregate production function. *Review of Economics and Statistics* **39**(3), 312–20.

Wang, J. C. 2003. Loanable funds, risk, and bank service output. Federal Reserve Bank of Boston Working Paper 03-4.

Wang, J. C, A. Basu and J. G. Fernald. 2004. A general-equilibrium asset-pricing approach to the measurement of nominal and real bank output. Invited to appear in *Price Index Concepts and Measurement, Conference on Research on Income and Wealth (CRIW).* Available at www.bos.frb.org/economic/wp/wp2004/wp047.htm.

Wood, G., and A. Kabiri. 2010. Firm stability and system stability: the regulatory delusion. Paper prepared for 'Managing Systemic Risk' conference, University of Warwick, 7–9 April 2010.

CHAPTER THREE

Why Are Financial Markets So Inefficient and Exploitative—And a Suggested Remedy

By Paul Woolley

This chapter offers a new understanding of how financial markets work. The key departure from conventional theory is to recognize that investors do not invest directly in securities but through agents such as fund managers. Agents have better information and different objectives than their customers (principals) and this asymmetry is shown as the source of inefficiency—mispricing, bubbles and crashes. A separate outcome is that agents are in a position to capture for themselves the bulk of the returns from financial innovations. Principal–agent problems do a good job of explaining how the global finance sector has become so bloated, profitable and prone to crisis. Remedial action involves the principals changing the way they contract with, and instruct, agents. The chapter ends with a manifesto of policies that pension funds and other large investors can adopt to mitigate the destructive features of delegation both for their individual benefit and to promote social welfare in the form of a leaner, more efficient and more stable finance sector.

3.1 INTRODUCTION

Much has come to pass in financial markets during the last ten years that has been at odds with the prevailing academic wisdom of how capital markets work. The decade opened with the technology stock bubble that caused large-scale misallocation of capital and was the forerunner of many of the subsequent problems in the global economy. To forestall recession when the bubble burst, central banks countered with a policy of ultra-low interest rates that in turn fuelled the surge in debt, asset prices and risk-taking. These excesses were accompanied by an explosive rise in profits and pay in the banking industry. A sector with the utilitarian role of facilitating transactions, channelling savings into real investment and making secondary markets in financial instruments came, by 2007, to account for 40% of aggregate corporate profits in the US and UK,

I wish to thank Bruno Biais (Toulouse School of Economics), Ron Bird (UTS), Jean-Charles Rochet (University of Zurich) and Dimitri Vayanos (LSE) for their invaluable contributions to the ideas set out here. All the errors are mine.

even after investment banks had paid out salaries and bonuses amounting to 60% of net revenues. The jamboree came to a juddering halt with the collapse of the mortgaged-backed securities markets and the ensuing banking crisis with its calamitous repercussions on the world economy.

Prevailing theory asserts that asset prices are informationally efficient and that capital markets are self-correcting. It also treats the finance sector as an efficient pass-through, ignoring the role played by financial intermediaries in both asset pricing and the macroeconomy. The evidence of the past decade has served to discredit the basic tenets of finance theory. Given that banking and finance are now seen as a source of systemic instability, the wisdom of ignoring the role of financial intermediaries has been called into question.

Some economists still cling to the conviction that recent events have simply been the lively interplay of broadly efficient markets and see no cause to abandon the prevailing theories. Other commentators, including a number of leading economists, have proclaimed the death of mainstream finance theory and all that goes with it, especially the efficient market hypothesis, rational expectations and mathematical modelling. The way forward, they argue, is to understand finance based on behavioural models on the grounds that psychological biases and irrational urges better explain the erratic performance of asset prices and capital markets. The choice seems stark and unsettling, and there is no doubt that the academic interpretation of finance is at a critical juncture.

This chapter advances an alternative paradigm which seems to do a better job of explaining reality. Its key departure from mainstream theory is to incorporate delegation by principals to agents. The principals in this case are the end investors and customers who subcontract financial tasks to agents such as banks, fund managers, brokers and other specialists. Delegation creates an incentive problem insofar as the agents have more and better information than their principals and because the interests of the two are rarely aligned. Asymmetric information has been partially explored in corporate finance and banking but hardly at all in asset pricing, which is arguably the central building block in finance. Incorporating delegation permits the retention of the assumption of rational expectations which, in turn, makes it possible to keep much of the existing formal framework of finance. Introducing agents both transforms the analysis and helps explain many aspects of mispricing and other distortions that have relied until now upon behavioural assumptions of psychological bias.

3.2 OUTLINE OF THE CHAPTER

The chapter opens by showing how the theory of efficient markets has influenced the beliefs and actions of market participants, policymakers and regulators. This is followed by a description of new work showing how asset pricing models based on delegation can explain momentum and reversal, the main source of mispricing which in extreme form causes bubbles and crashes. Any new theory should meet the criteria of relevance, validity and universality. Revising asset pricing theory in this way throws a clearer light on a number of well-known but hard-to-explain pricing anomalies. This alternative paradigm carries important implications for every aspect of finance from investment practice through to regulation and policymaking.

The second key consequence of asymmetric information is the ability of financial intermediaries to capture 'rents', or excess profits. Rent extraction has become one of the defining features of finance and goes a long way to explaining the sector's extraordinary growth in recent years, as well as its fragility and potential for crisis. Mispricing and rent capture are the two main culprits in what might appropriately be described as 'dysfunctional finance'. Each is damaging, but in combination they are devastating. We show how the two effects interact to cause loss of social utility and exploitation on a scale that could ultimately threaten capitalism.

Through a better understanding of the dysfunctionalities of finance, it becomes possible to propose solutions. So far, academics and policymakers have focused on improved regulation as a means to prevent future crises. But regulation is a negative approach based on restrictions, targeted mainly at banks, that bankers will resist and circumvent. This chapter proposes an alternative, though complementary, approach that goes to the source of all the trouble in finance. Since bubbles, crashes and rent capture are caused by principal–agent problems, the solution lies in having the principals change the way they contract and deal with agents. One group of principals with the power and incentive to act are the Giant funds. These are the large pension funds, the sovereign wealth, charitable and endowment funds around the world. They are the principal custodians of social wealth and they have found their assets and returns badly eroded over the last decade or so. Revising the way Giant funds instruct agents is a positive approach in that they have a self-interest in taking such action. If a critical mass of them were to adopt these measures, social benefits would then accrue in the form of more stable and less exploitative capital markets.

3.3 Efficient Markets Theory

Forty years have passed since the principles of classical economics were first applied to finance through the contributions of Eugene Fama (see Fama 1970) and his now renowned fellow economists. Their hypothesis that capital markets are efficient is grounded in the belief that competition among profit-seeking market participants will ensure that asset prices continuously adjust to reflect all publicly available information. Prices will equate to the consensus of investors' expectations about the discounted value of future attributable cash flows. The theory seemed to have common sense on its side: who, it was argued, would pass up the opportunity to profit from exploiting any misvaluations on offer and by doing so, take the price back to fair value? The randomness of prices and the apparent inability of professional managers to achieve returns consistently above those of the benchmark index were taken as validation of the theory. Over the intervening years, capital market theory and the efficient market hypothesis have been extended and modified to form an elegant and comprehensive framework for understanding asset pricing and risk.

A second aspect of competition in financial markets has received more attention from policymakers than academics. It is well known that financial intermediaries can extract rents by exploiting monopoly power through some combination of market share, collusion and barriers to entry. For example, trading in securities has some elements of a natural monopoly. Trading venues with the largest turnover offer the customer the highest levels of liquidity and therefore the best chance of dealing, thereby providing a magnet for business, which the operator of the venue can then exploit through monopolistic pricing. Competition authorities have been alert to blatant instances of monopoly or price-fixing in banking as in any other industry. Apart from collusion or market power, competition has been assumed to work its usual magic and prevent the capture of rents.

Broadly speaking, the finance sector has been viewed as the epitome of competitive perfection. Its scale, profitability and pay therefore went largely unremarked upon by commentators and academics. The logic implied that bankers' rewards reflected their talent and success in offering customers the services they wanted and valued. Theory implied that vast profits were a sign of a job done vastly well. So nobody enquired whether society was being well served by the finance sector.

The efficient market hypothesis also beguiled central bankers into believing that market prices could be trusted and that bubbles either did not exist, were positively beneficial for growth, or could not be spotted. Intervention was therefore unnecessary. Regulators, too, have been faithful disciples of the efficient market, which explains why they were content with light-touch regulation in the years before the crisis. The pressures of competition and self-interest were deemed sufficient to keep banks from pursing strategies that jeopardized their solvency or survival. Regulators were also leaned on by governments keen to maintain each country's international standing in a global industry. Another role of supervision is to approve new products. Here again regulators followed the conventional view that any innovation which enhances liquidity or 'completes' a market by introducing a novel packaging of risk and return is welfare-enhancing and warrants an immediate seal of approval.

Faith in the efficient market has also underpinned many of the practices of investment professionals. The use of security indices as benchmarks for both passive and active investment implies a tacit assumption that indices constitute efficient portfolios. Risk analysis and diversification strategy are based on mean–variance analysis using market prices over the recent past even though these prices may have displayed wide dispersion around fair value. Investors who may have doubted the validity of efficient market theory and enjoyed exploiting the price anomalies for years have nevertheless been using tools and policies based on the theories they disavow or disparage.

3.4 A New Paradigm for Asset Pricing

Once a dominant paradigm is discredited, the search for a replacement becomes urgent. At stake is the need for a science-based, unified theory of finance that is rigorous and tractable; one that retains as much as possible of the existing analytical framework and, at the same time, produces credible explanations and predictions. This is no storm in an academic teacup. The implications for growth, wealth and society could not be greater.

The first step in the search for a new paradigm is to avoid the mistake of jumping from observing that prices are irrational to believing that investors must also be irrational, or that it is impossible to construct a valid theory of asset pricing based on rational behaviour. Finance theory has combined rationality with other assumptions, and it is one of these other assumptions that has proved unfit for purpose. The crucial flaw has been to assume that prices are set by the army of private investors, or the 'representative household' as the jargon has it. Households are assumed to invest directly in equities and bonds and across the spectrum of the derivatives markets. Theory has ignored the real world complication that investors delegate virtually all their involvement in financial matters to professional intermediaries—banks, fund managers, brokers—who therefore dominate the pricing process.

Delegation creates an agency problem. Agents have access to more and better information than the investors who appoint them, and the interests and objectives of agents frequently differ from those of their principals. For their part, principals cannot be certain of the competence or diligence of the agents. Introducing agents brings greater realism to asset-pricing models and, more importantly, gives a far better understanding of how capital markets function. Importantly, this is achieved whilst maintaining the assumption of fully rational behaviour by all participants. Models incorporating agents have more working parts and therefore a higher level of complexity, but the effort is richly rewarded by the scope and relevance of the predictions.

The authors of a recent paper (Vayanos and Woolley 2008) have adopted this approach and are able to explain features of asset price behaviour that have defied explanation using the standard 'representative household' model. The model explains momentum, the commonly observed propensity for trending in prices, which in extreme form produces bubbles and crashes. The existence of momentum has been extensively documented in empirical studies of securities markets, but has proved difficult to explain other than through herding behaviour. The presence of price momentum is incompatible with the efficient market and has been described as the 'premier unexplained anomaly' in asset pricing (Fama and French 1993).

Central to the analysis is that investors have imperfect knowledge of the ability of the fund managers they invest with. They are uncertain whether underperformance against the benchmark arises from the manager's prudent avoidance of overpriced stocks or is a sign of incompetence. As shortfalls grow, investors conclude the reason is incompetence and react by transferring funds to the outperforming managers, thereby amplifying the price changes that led to the initial underperformance and generating momentum.

3.5 HOW MOMENTUM ARISES

The technology bubble ten years ago provides a good illustration of this process at work. Technology stocks received an initial boost from fanciful expectations of future profits from scientific advance. Meanwhile, funds invested in the unglamorous 'value' sectors languished, prompting investors to lose confidence in the ability of their underperforming value managers and to switch funds to the newly successful growth managers, a response that gave a further boost to growth stocks. The same thing happened as value managers themselves began switching from value to growth to avoid being fired.

Through this conceptually simple mechanism, the model explains asset pricing in terms of a battle between fair value and momentum. It shows how rational profit-seeking by agents and the investors who appoint them gives rise to mispricing and volatility. Once momentum becomes embedded in markets, agents then logically respond by adopting strategies that are likely to reinforce the trends. Indeed, one of the unusual features of a momentum strategy is that it is reinforced, rather than exhausted, by widespread adoption, unlike strategies based on convergence to some stable value. There are other sources of momentum as well, such as leverage, portfolio insurance and adherence to guidelines on tracking error, all of which augment the initial effect.

Explaining the formation of asset prices in this way seems to provide a clearer understanding of how and why investors and prices behave as they do. For example, it throws fresh light on why value stocks outperform growth stocks despite offering seemingly poorer earnings prospects. The new approach offers a more convincing interpretation of the way stock prices react to earnings announcements and other news. It shows how short-term incentives, such as annual performance fees, cause fund managers to concentrate on high-turnover, trend-following strategies that add to the distortions in markets, which are then profitably exploited by long-horizon investors. Much of the recent interest in academic finance has been in identifying limits to arbitrage—the forces that prevent mispriced stocks from reverting to fair value. The significance of the model described here is that it shows how prices become thrown off fair value in the first place.

While the model is set in terms of value and momentum in a single equity market, the analysis applies equally to individual stocks, national markets, bonds, currencies, commodities and entire asset classes. Moreover, when the pricing of the primary market is flawed, it follows that the corresponding derivative market will also be mispriced. All the options and futures which are priced by reference to the underlying assets will be subject to the same momentum-based distortions. In short, it will no longer be acceptable to say that competition delivers the right price or that markets exert their own self-discipline.

It seems self-evident that the way forward must be to stop treating the finance sector as a pass-through that has no impact on asset pricing and risk. Incorporating delegation and agency into financial models is bound to lead to a better understanding of phenomena that have so far been poorly understood or unaddressed. Because the new approach maintains the rationality assumption, it is possible to retain much of the economist's existing toolbox, such as mathematical modelling, utility maximization and general equilibrium analysis. The insights, elegance and tractability that these tools provide will be used to study more complex phenomena with very different economic assumptions. Hopefully a new general theory of asset pricing will eventually emerge that should relegate the efficient market hypothesis to the status of a special and limiting case.

Of course, investors may not always behave in a perfectly rational way. But that is beside the point. The test of any theory is whether it does a better job of explaining and predicting than any other. Of course, theories do not have to be mutually exclusive and behavioural finance theories can be helpful in providing supplementary or more detailed insights.

The impact of the new general theory will extend well beyond explaining asset prices.

- Policymakers can only regulate the banking and finance sectors effectively if they have a reasonable idea of how markets work. If regulators believe that capital markets are efficient, they will adopt light-touch regulation with the results we have seen over the past couple of years. On the other hand, if they recognize that markets are imperfect they will regulate accordingly and cause them to become more efficient as a result.

- Macroeconomics has also treated finance as a pass-through and would benefit from changing the economic emphasis and focusing more on the impact of agency and incentives in the savings and investment process. Some macroeconomic models take account of a rudimentary finance sector but more needs to be done in this direction now it is clear that the finance sector can destabilize the real economy. Until now, disruptions were expected to flow the other way, from the overall economy to the banks.

- Corporate finance and banking theory have both been developed under the pro forma assumption of price efficiency and will now need to accommodate mispricing. Corporate managers will now have a better understanding of how equity issuance can be managed to take account of the relative cheapness or dearness of a company's shares. The same applies to bids and deals.

- The fact and scale of mispricing invalidates much of the existing toolbox of fund management. Security market indices no longer constitute efficient portfolios and are no longer seen as appropriate benchmarks for either active or passive investment. Risk analysis based on past prices and used to assess the riskiness of portfolios and the basis for diversification will be seen as flawed. Risk analysis has often failed investors when they needed it most, but now the reason for this can be seen. The risk that is being measured in these models is that based on market prices, which are driven by flows of funds unrelated to fair value. The flows that matter are the underlying cash flows relating to the businesses themselves, for it is on these that a share's value ultimately depends. The distinction between short-horizon and long-horizon investing also becomes critical and this is discussed later. For policymakers, bankers and corporate accountants, the principle of mark-to-market will be recognized as inappropriate and damagingly procyclical in impact.

3.6 RENT CAPTURE BY FINANCIAL INTERMEDIARIES

A second consequence of delegation is the ability of financial agents to capture rents. To understand how this comes about one needs no formal economic model. If a fund manager spots an investment opportunity with a known and certain payoff, he can finance it directly from his own or borrowed funds and enjoy the full gain for himself. His client might like to participate and would be prepared to pay close to the full value of the gain in fees for the privilege. The client would be in pocket so long as the investment, net of fees, gave him a return above the riskless rate. Whether he borrows the funds or raises them from the client, the fund manager captures the bulk of the gain thanks to his superior knowledge of available opportunities. Of course, formal models must take account of risk and learning, but the outcome is similar. A recent paper presents a dynamic rational expectations model showing the evolution of a financial innovation and reveals how competitive agents are able to extract progressively higher rents to the point at which the agent is capturing the bulk of the gain (Biais *et al.* 2009). The key assumption is that of information asymmetry.

3.7 A Description of the Model

First consider the frictionless benchmark case in which principals and agents have access to the same information. The principals are a set of rational, competitive investors and the agents are a set of similarly imbued fund managers. A financial innovation is introduced but there is uncertainty about its viability. As time goes by, investors and managers learn about this by observing the profits that come from adopting the new technique. If it generates a stream of high profits, confidence grows that the innovation is robust. This leads to an increase in the scale of its adoption and therefore the size of the total compensation going to managers. Because of the symmetry of information, these gains are competitively determined at normal levels and the innovation flourishes. Alternatively, profits may deteriorate, market participants come to learn of its fragility and the innovation withers on the vine. In both cases, while learning generates dynamics, with symmetric information there is no crisis. This differs from previous analyses of industry dynamics under symmetric information where the learning model was specified so that certain observations could trigger crises (see Barbarino and Jovanovic 2007; Pastor and Veronesi 2006; Zeira 1987, 1999). As discussed below, in the framework of this model, it is information asymmetries and the corresponding rents earned by agents which precipitate the crisis.

In practice, innovative sectors are plagued by information asymmetry. It is hard for the outsider to understand everything the insiders are doing and difficult to monitor their actions. The implications of the lack of transparency and oversight are explored using optimal contracting theory. The model assumes that managers have a choice. They can exert effort to reduce the probability that the project will fail, even though such effort is costly. Alternatively they can cut corners and 'shirk'—the term used by economists and familiar to every schoolboy. When agents shirk they fail to evaluate carefully and to control the risks associated with the project. The handling of portfolios of CDOs in the run-up to the recent crisis illustrates this well. Fund managers could either scrutinize diligently the quality of the underlying paper or they could shirk by relying on a rating agency assessment and pass the unopened parcel on to the investor. Securitization is a potentially valuable innovation but requires costly effort to implement properly.

The second assumption is that managers have limited liability, either in the legal sense or because the pattern of payoffs enables them to participate in gains but to suffer no losses. The inability to punish gives rise to the moral hazard that characterizes finance at every level from individual traders to the banks that employ them (the simple model of moral hazard used by Biais *et al.* is in line with that of Holmstrom and Tirole (1997)).

The combination of opacity and moral hazard is the nub of the agency problem. Investors have to pay handsomely to provide managers with sufficient incentive to exert effort, and the greater the moral hazard, the larger the rents are likely to be. The model shows that the probability of shirking is higher when the innovation is strong than when it is weak. After a period of consistently high profits, managers become increasingly confident that the innovation is robust. They are tempted to shirk and it becomes correspondingly harder to induce them to exert continuing effort. As the need for incentives grow, the point is reached where agents are capturing most of the gains from the innovation.

The analysis does not end there. Investors become frustrated at the rents being earned by the agents and at their own poor return and withdraw their participation. The dynamics are such that when confidence in the innovation reaches a critical threshold, there is a shift from equilibrium effort to equilibrium shirking. The innovation implodes as managers cease to undertake the necessary risk assessment to maintain the viability of the innovation. In the end, an otherwise robust innovation is brought down by the weight of rents being captured.

3.8 RELATING THE MODEL TO THE REAL WORLD

If this model bears any relation to the way that finance functions in practice, the implications are profound. The innovations in question occur mainly in investment banking and fund management rather than in the more prosaic activities of utility banking. The past decade has seen a surge of new products and strategies, such as hedge funds, securitization, private equity, structured finance, CDOs and credit default swaps. Each came to be regarded as a worthwhile addition that helped to 'complete' markets and spread risk-bearing by offering investors and borrowers new ways of packaging risk and return.

Ominously in light of the model described above, most of these innovations have been accompanied by increased opacity, creating the scope for elevated moral hazard. Hedge funds shroud themselves in mystery with regard to strategies, holdings, turnover, costs and leverage. It is hard to monitor the diligence and competence of their managers in the absence of information on the sources of performance. The growth of structured finance and CDSs has meant greater reliance on over-the-counter trades that circumvent the discipline of open markets and regulation.

The theoretical results are consistent with the empirical findings of Philippon and Reshef (2008). They observe a burst of financial innovation in the first half of this decade, with rapid growth in the size of the finance sector accompanied by an increase in the pay of managers. They estimate that rents accounted for 30–50% of the wage differential between the finance sector and the rest of the economy during this period. They point out that the last time this happened on a similar scale was in the late 1920s bubble—also with calamitous consequences. It is significant that a high proportion of the net revenues of banks and other finance firms goes to the staff rather than shareholders. In terms of the model, this implies that rent extraction is occurring at all operating levels within the institutions.

The model's second prediction is that innovations under asymmetric information are vulnerable to implosion. The current crisis seems to validate this prediction since structured credit, CDOs and CDSs were the immediate cause of the global financial crisis.

3.9 POLICY PRESCRIPTIONS

The policy imperatives are to reduce opacity both in the functioning of capital markets and in the actions of individual institutions. Trades should be conducted in transparent markets so that investors can use price, trades and quotes information to monitor and discipline agents. Transactions should be cleared in open markets with clearing houses requiring call margins and security deposits. This would enable principals and regulators to monitor the risky positions of agents and prevent excessive risk-taking. Risky positions and portfolio structure should also be disclosed to investors and regulators. Hedge funds and private equity need to be less secretive about what they are doing and why.

Moral hazard can also be reduced by extending the period over which performance of portfolios and individual traders is measured and compensation determined—three or four years would be a reasonable horizon.

Policymakers are always looking for ways to anticipate trouble in time. The model shows how a combination of high confidence in finance sector innovations and high rents for finance managers might act as a lead indicator of crisis. If warning signs are showing, policymakers should demand an increase in transparency.

3.10 TOGETHER, MISPRICING AND RENT CAPTURE CREATE THE PERFECT STORM

To summarize so far, asymmetric information is responsible for creating the twin social bads of mispricing and rent capture. Mispricing gives incorrect signals for resource allocation and, at worst, causes stock market booms and busts that lead to macroeconomic instability. Rent capture causes the misallocation of labour and capital, transfers substantial wealth to bankers and financiers and, at worst, induces systemic failure. Both impose social costs on their own, but in combination they create a perfect storm of wealth destruction.

3.11 IMPACT OF MISPRICING ON THE DEMAND FOR FINANCIAL SERVICES

It seems trite to observe that the demand for most goods and services is limited by the physical capacity of consumers to consume. Yet the unique feature of finance is that demand for financial services has no such boundaries. Take the case of a pension fund seeking to meet its long-run objectives expressed in terms of risk and return. The trustees observe a market subject to significant price distortion. They eschew passive investment on the grounds that the market portfolio is inefficient, and instead hire active managers to exploit the mispricing. Because of agency problems, active investing does nothing to resolve the mispricing. The cycle of hiring, firing and price distortion therefore continues unabated.

Active management is not confined to the stock and bond markets but blossoms and thrives in the derivatives markets as well. Given the interdependence of pricing between the two, the pricing flaws in the underlying securities are carried over into the derivatives markets. The field of battle for excess return is thus extended and subject only to the creativity of agents in finding new instruments to trade. Much of asset management takes place in this virtual world of derivatives, which has grown exponentially in the last decade with aggregate outstanding positions reaching $600 trillion at one point last year.

Investors' attempts to control risk have similar results. Observing volatile conditions, the investor decides to reduce his downside risk by buying a put option on his portfolio. The seller of the put seeks to neutralize his own risk by shorting the underlying stock, thereby triggering the decline from which the investor sought protection in the first place. The sequence continues because volatility has now increased and the original investor reacts rationally by raising further his level of protection.

There is a similar effect where principals specify tracking error con-straints on the divergence of the portfolio return in relation to the bench-mark return. The agent is obliged to close down risk by buying stocks that are rising and selling those that are falling, thereby amplifying the initial price moves. In an inefficient market, fund flows put prices in a constant state of flux which leads in turn to an ever-expanding demand for asset management services.

The analysis has implications for the social utility of derivatives, and of finance generally. The creation of new instruments, coupled with the development of option-pricing models in the 1980s, has been applauded as value-creating. Investors will trade these instruments, so the argument goes, only if they derive utility from using them. On this logic, the scale of the derivatives markets is perceived as a measure of their social utility. This would be true in an efficient market, but is not true in an inefficient one. If the theory of mispricing is accepted, the scale of the finance sector becomes testimony to its malfunctioning, not—as the pundits would have it—its efficiency.

The size of the finance sector is also significant because the larger it is, the more damaging the impact on the real economy when it fails. As in the boxing analogy, 'the bigger they are, the harder they fall'. In light of the latest crisis, the idea that banking crises are contained within the realm of money is no longer possible to sustain.

3.12   THE SHORTENING OF INVESTMENT HORIZONS

The shortening of investment horizons has been a feature of capital mar-kets over the past two decades. The best indicator of short-termism is the length of time investors hold securities. Turnover on the major equity exchanges is now running at 150% per annum of aggregate market cap-italization which implies average holding periods of eight months. The growth in trading of derivatives, most of which have maturities of less than a year, is also symptomatic of shortening horizons.

Markets that display trending patterns encourage short-termism. In most equity markets the optimal momentum strategy is to buy stocks that have risen most in the preceding 6–12 months and to hold them for a further 6–12 months. Fund managers have a choice between investing based on fair value, momentum investing or some combination of the two. Those who are impatient for results or who have no ability or desire to undertake the hard work of fundamental analysis to find cheap stocks will use momentum. In fact, in the short run, momentum investing is usually the best bet. There is a self-fulfilling element here because the more investors use momentum strategies, the more likely it is to work.

The design of the contract between principal and agent influences how agents manage money. Fee structures based on short-term performance encourage short horizons and momentum trading and are the reason this is the dominant strategy among hedge funds. Transaction costs also have a bearing on turnover levels. The move from fixed to competitive broker-age commissions in the US and UK in the late 1970s was a watershed in this respect and the relentless expansion of turnover dates from this period.

Momentum trading, and the distortions to which it gives rise, are part and parcel of the trend towards the increasing short-termism and high trading volumes in finance. Both have their origins in principal–agent problems and both contribute to the loss of social utility. There is one justification that is always wheeled out to support the case for increased trading. It is that trading raises liquidity and liquidity is an unalloyed ben-efit because it enables investors to move in and out of assets readily and at low cost. That is true as far as it goes, but it ignores a crucial point. Liq-uidity is undeniably welcome in an efficient market, but the case becomes more problematic in one subject to mispricing. Lowering the frictional costs of trading opens the door to short-termism and momentum trad-ing which distort prices. Under these conditions liquidity often comes and goes depending on the price swings that are occurring at any moment. The investor is happy to know he can always trade, but the ability to trade may have come at the cost of increased volatility. In an inefficient mar-ket, therefore, liquidity should never be assessed in isolation from the volatility of the asset.

High turnover comes at a heavy cost to long-term investors. Active management fees and its associated trading costs based on 100% annual turnover erode the value of a pension fund by around 1.0% per annum. Pension funds are having their assets exchanged with other pension funds twenty-five times during the life of the average liability for no col-lective advantage but at a cost that reduces the end-value of the pension by around 30%.

3.13 HEDGE FUNDS: A MICROCOSM OF FINANCE

The hedge fund industry provides a clear and unflattering insight into the problems of modern-day finance. Hedge funds have the veneer of a worthwhile innovation in several respects. They enjoy the freedom to implement negative views through short selling and to target absolute return instead of return relative to an index benchmark. They are also able to use derivatives and borrowing to leverage fund performance. All this should work to the advantage of their investors and help make markets more efficient. But the bad features of their behaviour outweigh the apparent merits.

First, their fee structures encourage short-termism and momentum-type trading. Hedge funds charge a base fee, usually 2% per annum of the value of assets, and a performance fee, typically 20% of any positive return each year. This makes for a classic case of moral hazard; the hedge fund gains on the upside, but receives no penalty for underperformance and even keeps the base fee. To make the most of the lopsided payoff, the manager plays the momentum game because that gives him the best chance of winning quickly and then moving on to the next momentum play. High charges also make investors impatient for success and the performance fees make the manager more so.

Hedge funds' use of momentum contaminates pricing in the various asset classes they occupy. In recent years they have accounted for around one-third of daily trading volume in equity markets and are often the marginal investors driving the direction of prices. Their investors receive patterns of return that reflect the risky strategies associated with situations of moral hazard—erratic performance with frequent blow-ups and redemption blocks at times of liquidity stress. Some hedge funds sell volatility instead of buying it, but this can be as risky as momentum strategies since it involves receiving a steady premium in return for crippling payouts in the event of crisis.

As discussed in an earlier section, hedge funds display all the features that contribute to a high level of rent extraction. To put this in context requires information on performance. A number of recent studies have sought to calculate the return on indices of hedge funds, making appropriate allowance for the high failure rate among funds. They conclude that the long-run returns have been no better than a passive investment in the S&P or FT indices (see Ibbotson *et al.* 2010; Bird *et al.* 2010). These returns are calculated using the conventional time-weighted returns which represent the return per dollar invested. Once allowance is made for investors buying into funds *after* they have done well and moving out *after* they have done badly—which a money-weighted return does—investors are shown to have fared worse still. This disappointing performance is largely explained by the high fees charged—all the alpha, or excess returns, that hedge funds achieve from investing the funds is absorbed in fees, leaving the principals with the residual of indexed performance at best. The successful funds are in effect making more in fee revenue than the customers derive in cash returns from their investments.

An unremarked feature of hedge funds is how much alpha they capture from the market. Even to deliver index-like returns net of fees, they have to extract sufficient alpha from the zero-sum game to meet both their fees and their costs. We can observe the investors' returns and we can estimate the managers' fees, but we can only hazard a guess at the costs of the complex trading they undertake with prime brokers, the borrowing costs incurred through leveraging, and investment bank fees in general. Altogether hedge funds probably need to capture three times the return they report simply to meet these overheads. Traditional asset management has to be making losses equal to hedge funds' gross winnings in order to satisfy the identities of the zero-sum game. Hedge funds are far from the innocuous sideshow they often purport to be.

3.14 THE NEED FOR A RESOLUTION

One tangible measure of the impact of all this on the end investor is the declining trend in pension fund returns. The annual inflation-adjusted return on UK pension funds for the period 1963–2009 averaged 4.1% (IFSL 2010, chart B9). For the most recent ten years, 2000–2009, the average real return collapsed to 1.1% per annum with high year-to-year volatility. These poor results have exposed massive pension fund deficits, necessitating subventions from sponsoring companies, reductions in benefits and scheme closures. The performance of pension funds in the US and of Giant funds globally reveal a similar decline.

In their attempts to make capital markets safer and more socially constructive, policymakers are focusing on bank levies and tighter regulation. Bankers will resist and circumvent taxes and restrictions and there are bound to be unintended consequences. Governments also need to agree collective actions because no country will be prepared to disadvantage itself by taking unilateral action. This will take time and have limited chance of success so it would be far better if the private sector could deal with the problem.

This chapter has shown how principal–agent problems lie at the heart of mispricing and rent extraction. The solution lies in having the principals recognize the nature and extent of the problems and then change the way they contract and deal with agents. The group of principals best placed to act in this way are the world's biggest public, pension and charitable funds. They constitute a distinct class of end investor insofar as they are charged with representing the interests of their beneficiaries and, unlike mutual funds, do not sell their services commercially. Sadly these Giant funds have been failing to act in ways that advance and protect their beneficiaries and have instead been acting more like another tier of agents.

3.15   MANIFESTO FOR GIANT FUNDS

Set out below is a manifesto of ten policies that Giant funds are urged to introduce to improve their long-run returns and help stabilize markets. Each fund that adopted these changes could expect an increase in annual return of around 1–1.5%, as well as lower volatility of return. The improvement would come from lower levels of trading and brokerage, lower management charges and, importantly, from focusing on fair value investing and not engaging in trend-following strategies. The gains would accrue regardless of what other funds were doing. These are the private benefits that funds could capture as price-takers by revising their approach to investment and changing the way they delegate to agents.

Once these policies became widely adopted, there would be collective benefits enjoyed by all funds in the form of more stable capital markets, faster economic growth, less exploitation by agents and lower propensity for crisis. The ultimate reward achievable from both private and collective gains could be an increase of around 2–3% in the real annual return of each fund.

1. Adopt a long-term approach to investing based on long-term dividend flows rather than momentum-based strategies that rely on short-term price changes.   Investing on the basis of estimated future earnings and dividends wins out in the long run. Investing on the basis of short-term price changes, which is synonymous with momentum investing, may win over short periods but not in the long run. It is rather like the hare and the tortoise. The hare is boastful and flashy (rather like hedge funds) and has bursts of success. The tortoise plods steadily on concentrating on real value and wins the race in the end.

The return on equities ultimately depends on dividends. Historically, the real return on equities in the US and UK has comprised the dividend yield, which grows in line with local inflation, plus a small increment of dividend growth. Real price changes have more to do with revaluation effects (changing price–earnings ratios) than with any long-term shareholder gain.

This has been forgotten in the brash new world of finance. The trend towards short-horizon investing has thrust short-term price changes to the fore and placed dividends in the background in the thinking of most investors. Such has been the shift in emphasis that a third of companies no longer bother to pay dividends but have substituted periodic share buy-backs as an opaque (though tax-efficient) substitute.

2. Cap annual turnover of portfolios at 30% per annum. There is no better way of forcing fund managers to focus on long-run value than to restrict turnover. Capping annual turnover at 30% implies an average holding period of just over three years. Turnover is measured as the lesser of sales or purchases so this limit is not as constricting as it seems, because new cash flows also permit adjustment to portfolio composition.

3. Understand that all the tools currently used to determine policy objectives and implementation are based on the discredited theory of efficient markets. Most investors accept that markets are, to greater or lesser degree, inefficient and devote themselves to exploiting the opportunities on offer. But by a nice irony, they have continued to use tools and adopt policies constructed on the assumptions of efficiency. It is a costly mistake.

The volatility and distortions that come with inefficient pricing mean that equity indices do not represent optimal portfolios and are therefore inappropriate benchmarks for passive tracking or active management. Recall that Japan accounted for 55% of the global equity index in 1990 and, ten years later, tech stocks represented 45% of the S&P index.

Risk analysis based on market prices is similarly flawed. Prices are much more volatile than the streams of attributable cash flows and earnings, meaning that risk estimates using short-run price data will overstate risk for investors such as pension funds with long-term liabilities. In consequence, they will be purchasing unnecessary levels of risk protection. The correct approach is to measure risk using dividends or smoothed earnings as inputs, rather than prices.

Endless effort is devoted by funds to discovering how best to reduce risk by diversification. The analysis is always undertaken using correlations based on asset prices. But correlations using prices will vary in response to changing patterns of fund flows and are unlikely to provide a suitable basis for spreading risk. This is best illustrated when investors move en masse into a new asset class to take advantage of low or negative correlation with their existing assets. The correlations become more highly positive and invalidate the analysis. The answer is again to use correlations based on the underlying cash flows coming from the various asset classes.

4. Adopt stable benchmarks for fund performance. The ideal benchmark for performance is one that follows a relatively stable path over time, reflects the characteristics of the liabilities and is grounded in long-term cash flows. Giant funds target long-term performance and, in the case of pension funds, have explicit liability streams that depend on wage and salary growth. Wages and salaries grow in line with the productivity of the economy and this points to the growth of GDP as the ideal benchmark for the performance of pension assets. Giant funds will be able to beat the GDP growth, which averages around 2.5–3.0% after inflation for the advanced economies, by taking some credit risk and investing in equities. Equities offer a leveraged exposure to economic growth, through commercial and financial leverage, so the funds should set a target of GDP growth plus a risk premium.

5. Do not pay performance fees. Trying to assess whether a manager's performance is due to skill, market moves or luck is near impossible. Also performance fees encourage gambling and therefore moral hazard. If funds cannot resist paying them, performance should be measured over periods of several years and with high water marks so that performance following a decline has to recover to its previous best before the managers are eligible for further fees.

6. Do not engage in any form of 'alternative investing'. Alternative investing offers little or no long-run return advantage over traditional forms of investing, carries greater risk, and the lauded diversification benefits largely disappear once they are widely adopted. Currently the most popular categories of alternative investing are hedge funds, private equity and commodities.

Any greater levels of manager skill they enjoy, or any advantages conferred by innovation, are swallowed up in higher management fees. Most alternative investing is leveraged which increases the asymmetry of pay-offs to investors and therefore moral hazard. Hedge funds mostly emphasize short-term investing, typically momentum strategies, which have a lower return expectation than fair value investing and contribute to market destabilization. Fund blow-ups, suspended redemptions and performance volatility are the result.

Hedge funds and private equity both carry high unseen costs from financing charges, advisory fees and trading costs which mean they have to withdraw large helpings of alpha from the zero-sum public markets before delivering the published returns to investors. Private equity is also plagued by opacity, resorts to quick-fix commercial strategies and expropriates gains that should have gone to public shareholders.

Commodity investment should be especially shunned. Commodities as a general asset class offer a long-run return no better than 0% after inflation, and less after fees. The cost of holding commodity positions is bedevilled by the herding of portfolio investors all seeking to roll over their futures positions at quarterly expiry dates. Commodity indices that act as the benchmark for performance can also be gamed by the investment banks that maintain them. The flood of portfolio investment going into commodities in the past few years has turned their hitherto negative correlation with equities into a high and positive correlation.

Before the middle of the last decade the prices of individual commodities could be explained by the supply and demand from producers and consumers. With the flood of passive and active investment funds going into commodities from 2005 onwards, prices have been increasingly driven by fund inflows rather than fundamental factors. Prices no longer provide a reliable signal to producers or consumers. More damagingly, commodity prices have a direct impact on consumer price indices and the role of central banks in controlling inflation is made doubly difficult now that commodity prices are subject to volatile fund flows from investors.

7. Insist on total transparency by managers with respect to their strategies, costs, leverage and trading.

8. Do not sanction the purchase of 'structured', untraded or synthetic products. Everything in the portfolio should be traded and quoted on a public market. Allowing managers to buy over-the-counter securities opens another door for agents to capture rent and should be denied. This would rule out the use of Dark Pools and other forms of opaque trading. It would also ensure that Giant funds did not hold CDOs or CDSs unless such transactions were publicly traded and recorded.

9. Work with other shareholders and policymakers to secure full transparency of banking and financial service costs borne by companies in which the Giant funds invest. Earnings of companies are struck after deductions of banking charges incurred by companies. Principal–agent problems are alive and well here too. Underwriting fees have doubled over the past few years for an activity that incurs minimal risk for banks. It is a cosy arrangement among bankers and corporate managements that keeps the bankers' tills ringing happily. The OFT in the UK has just announced its intention to investigate underwriting fees.

The scope of bank services to companies is very wide and includes advisory fees for mergers and acquisitions, initial public offerings, everyday financial transactions, insurance, charges relating to loans and the purchase of pension liabilities. It is a grey, undocumented area and agents are in a position to extract in fees amounts that equate to the benefit the service confers to their customers. This is the counterpart in corporate finance of what is happening in the asset management industry.

Corporate earnings could probably be raised by a further 1.0% per annum after inflation if shareholders were successful in persuading corporate management to recognize the principal–agent problems at this level and to challenge the agents' rents.

10. Provide full disclosure to all stakeholders and allow public scrutiny of each fund's compliance with these policies.

3.16   WHY THE GIANT FUNDS HAVE NOT ACTED ALREADY

Those in charge of the Giant funds have been concerned at the poor performance of their funds, but have felt safe from criticism because their funds were suffering the same fate as their peers. The stakeholders, who have been the ultimate victims, mostly fail to grasp what is happening and see themselves without franchise and powerless.

The Giant funds seem oblivious to the depredations caused by principal–agent problems. They have been acting like another tier of agent rather than the principals they should be. This is hardly surprising given that they are advised by agents and that their trustees and staff are drawn from the investment industry or aspire to win lucrative jobs in it. They have also failed to understand the damage done to performance from following benchmarks and using risk analysis based on a defunct theory.

Another problem has been that the early success of the Harvard/Yale model of investing won a large following, especially among charitable funds and endowments in recent years. Both funds were pioneers in alternative investing, building up their exposure to hedge funds, private equity and forestry over the past two decades. They enjoyed the early success that typically accompanies innovation and enjoyed returns head and shoulders above the comparator universe. All worked well in the early stages when they could dictate terms to their agents and while returns from alternative investments remained uncorrelated and uncontaminated by what was happening in other asset classes. But the flow of new money going into alternatives undermined their diversification attractions and the financial crisis revealed other vulnerabilities of the Harvard/Yale model with the result that the value of their funds collapsed by 25% or more in 2008. These events showed that the model was neither resilient nor scalable and Giant funds have lost what they thought to be the new paradigm of investing.

There may be reservations about adopting the policies set out here even though there are long-run return advantages to any fund that acts. The fear will be that in the early years a bubble may form that causes the rash hare to overtake the prudent tortoise. That being so, policymakers may have to step in to ensure the changes occur.

3.17 Supportive Actions Available to Policymakers

Policymakers and regulators worldwide can provide back-up to encourage adoption of the manifesto by funds located nationally. There need be no prior agreement among governments since the measures are privately beneficial to those adopting them and since there is every advantage to countries and funds from acting promptly.

1. Encourage adoption by all public funds. The ideal start would be for the IMF to apply these policies to its new $12 billion endowment fund created from the sale of the IMF's holdings of gold. The next step would be to try to encourage Sovereign Wealth Funds around the world to adopt these policies. The means to bring this about might also involve the IMF, which two years ago convened a meeting of Sovereign Wealth Funds to agree the 'Santiago Principles' setting out best practice for the management of their assets. Governments could also encourage public funds within their jurisdiction to take action.

2. Withdraw tax-exemption rights for all funds that fail to cap turnover. Giant funds worldwide enjoy exemption from taxes in one form or another. Funds should lose these rights, first on any sub-portfolio where the 30% turnover limit is breached and then across the entire portfolio if no corrective action is taken. For over thirty years the UK tax statutes have contained a clause withdrawing tax exemption for any fund deemed to be 'trading' rather than 'investing'. It has rarely been implemented, but this is the model to follow and the time to start.

3. National governments to issue GDP bonds. Issuance of GDP-linked bonds by sovereign governments would encourage the adoption of GDP as a performance benchmark for funds, as well as being an attractive proposition for investors and issuers alike. Bonds delivering a return equal to the annual growth of a country's GDP offer investors the three features that everyone wants from their investments: growth, inflation protection and relative stability of price. The last feature would be ensured by the issuance of bonds in a range of maturities. There currently exists no single instrument that offers all three characteristics and part of the volatility in asset class returns arises from investors lurching between equities, bonds and cash in their attempt to have their portfolios combine these objectives. Issuers would also find growth-related bonds appealing because of the positive correlation of tax revenue and debt service costs.

Trading in GDP bonds would contribute usefully toward greater stability of equity prices. Investors would be able to switch out of equities into GDP bonds when equity prices became over-valued. Similarly, they could switch out of the bonds into equities when shares were depressed. The existence of GDP bonds would also help anchor expectations about the realistic level of future corporate earnings.

4. Recognize that mark-to-market accounting is inappropriate when pricing is inefficient.

5. Regulators should not automatically approve financial products on the grounds that they enhance liquidity or complete markets. This manifesto and the associated policy proposals derive directly from the new and more realistic paradigm for understanding the way capital markets function outlined in this chapter. Recognizing that markets are inefficient, and doing so in a rational framework, makes it possible to construct policy measures that directly address the problems. This is no intellectual game; the stakes are high since it is doubtful that capitalism could survive a fresh calamity on the scale of the last.

REFERENCES

Biais, B., J. C. Rochet and P. Woolley. 2009. Rents, learning and risk in the financial sector and other innovative industries. PWC London School of Economics Working Paper. Available at www.lse.ac.uk/collections/PaulWoolleyCentre/pdf/NewsFiles/BRW_Sept_15_2009webcopy.pdf.

Bird, R., H. Liam and S. Thorp. 2010. Hedge fund excess returns under time varying beta. Paul Woolley Centre Working Paper, University of Technology, Sydney.

Buiter, W. 2009. The unfortunate uselessness of most 'state of the art' academic monetary economics. VoxEU.org (6 March). Available at www.voxeu.org/index.php?q=node/3210.

Fama, E. F. 1970. Efficient capital markets, a review of theory and empirical work. *The Journal of Finance* **25**(2), 383–417.

Fama, E. F., and K. R. French. 1993. Common risk factors in the returns on stocks and bonds. *Journal of Financial Economics* **33**, 3–56.

Ibbotson, R., P. Chen and K. Zhu. 2010. The ABCs of hedge funds: alphas, betas and costs. Ibbotson Associates Working Paper.

Kirman, A. 2009. Economic theory and the crisis. VoxEU.org (14 November). Available at www.voxeu.org/index.php?q=node/4208.

Kobayashi, K. 2009. Why this new crisis needs a new paradigm of economic thought. VoxEU.org (24 August). Available at www.voxeu.org/index.php?q=node/3897.

Holmstrom, B., and J. Tirole. 1997. Financial intermediation, loanable funds, and the real sector. *Quarterly Journal of Economics* **112**(3), 663–91.

IFSL. 2010. *Pension Markets 2010.* International Financial Services London.

Pástor, L., and P. Veronesi. 2006. Was there a Nasdaq bubble in the late 1990s? *Journal of Financial Economics* **81**, 61–100.

Philippon, T., and A. Reshef. 2008. Skill biased financial development: education, wages and occupations in the US financial sector. NBER Working Paper 13437.

Vayanos, D., and P. Woolley. 2008. An institutional theory of momentum and reversal. The Paul Woolley Centre for the Study of Capital Market Dysfunctionality Working Paper 1.

Zeira, J. 1987. Investment as a process of search. *Journal of Political Economy* **95**, 204–10.

Zeira, J. 1999. Informational overshooting, booms, and crashes. *Journal of Monetary Economics* **43**(1), 237–57.

CHAPTER FOUR

What Mix of Monetary Policy and Regulation Is Best for Stabilizing the Economy?

By Sushil B. Wadhwani

We argue that the attempts to exonerate the conduct of monetary policy from a role in the crisis are unconvincing. We offer several reasons why macroprudential policy may be less effective than monetary policy and suggest that the two policies need to be set jointly. Hence, the proposed plan to separate them in the UK should be revisited.

In contemplating regulatory change, it is also important to recognize that financial innovation has played a central role in economic growth over time, and also to be aware that mistakes made by regulators contributed to the crisis.

A more appropriate macroeconomic stabilization framework may help reduce output volatility by more than regulatory micro-meddling. The latter may hurt growth or not work in any case. Indeed, in some countries (e.g. China, India), more financial liberalization would stimulate growth and help reduce global imbalances.

4.1 INTRODUCTION

Since the 2007–8 crisis, we have seen a plethora of proposals to change how we regulate the financial sector. Yet we have seen surprisingly little change in beliefs about how we should run monetary policy.

For example, senior figures at the US Federal Reserve have continued to resist changes in how monetary policy should respond to asset price misalignments. In the UK, the incoming chancellor has said he would create a new Financial Policy Committee (FPC) but also appears to have said that there was nothing the Bank could have done with interest rates to reduce the magnitude of the crisis.

In section 4.2.1, I discuss the respective roles of 'macroprudential' and monetary policy. I discuss several reasons why the use of monetary policy to 'lean against the wind' is critically important in its own right and to the success of the 'macroprudential' policy to be adopted by the FPC.

I am extremely grateful to Richard Layard for his helpful comments and to Roy Cromb and Rohan Sakhrani for their help and advice.

130

I turn next (in section 4.2.2) to discussing some of the inadequacies of the arguments expressed by those who assert that inappropriate monetary policy did not contribute to the crisis.

Since there has been so much emphasis on changes in regulation and structure in the public debate after the crisis, I discuss in section 4.3.1 some of the mistakes made by regulators. At least some of our difficulties could have been avoided if these errors had not been made, and one should not neglect the possibility of 'policymaker/regulator failure' when designing a structure to deal with 'market failure'.

I then turn my attention to the voluminous literature showing that financial innovation and development have been important to economic growth (section 4.3.2), and argue that we ignore this at our peril. Contrary to the oft-expressed view that recent financial innovation has not helped, I specifically cite evidence showing the contrary. It is important to recall that the bursting of the South Sea Bubble in 1720 was followed by a ban on joint stock companies! Hence, we should not throw out the baby with the bathwater now.

Indeed, I assert that some countries (e.g. China) need more financial liberalization, not less (section 4.3.3). Moreover, such deregulation is likely to make the global economy less unbalanced and thereby reduce the risk of future crises.

As I witness the post-crisis debate, I worry that too many of the proposed regulatory measures will hurt growth. Moreover, unless they are accompanied by changes in how we run monetary policy, they may not even work.

Long ago, Keynes recognized that macroeconomic policy could deal with some of the very bad outcomes that can occur in capitalist economies. He argued that the use of such appropriate macro policy could help us preserve some of the considerable microeconomic advantages of capitalist economies. Similarly, with an appropriate monetary and fiscal policy framework, we should be able to deal better with the volatility associated with credit cycles, and this should reduce the need for changes in regulatory policy and structure that may be inimical to growth, or might not work in any case.

4.2 SHOULD THE WAY WE SET MONETARY POLICY CHANGE AFTER THE CRISIS?

Over the last decade or so, we have seen vigorous debate about how monetary policy should respond to asset price bubbles (see, for example, Bean

2003; Bernanke and Gertler 1999; Borio and Lowe 2002; Cecchetti *et al.* 2000; Wadhwani 2008).

I have long believed that monetary policy should react to asset price misalignments over and above fixed-horizon inflation forecasts (that is, it should 'lean against the wind' (LATW)) and that one should not rely, as per the Greenspan (1999) 'mopping up' doctrine, on dealing with the fallout of the bursting of the asset price bubble.

Since this crisis has amply illustrated the difficulties with 'mopping up', one might have expected a widespread change of heart regarding the use of monetary policy to LATW preemptively. To my surprise, this has not occurred. Hence, for example, Don Kohn (2008) argues that

> In sum, I am not convinced that the events of the past few years and the current crisis demonstrate that central banks should switch to trying to check speculative activity through tight monetary policy... We must thoroughly review the regulatory structure of the US and the global financial systems, with the objective of both identifying and implementing the comprehensive changes needed to reduce the odds of future bubbles arising.

Similarly, Bernanke (2010) echoes this by asserting that we primarily need to look at strengthening the regulatory system to prevent a recurrence of the crisis, though he concedes that monetary policy may be used as a supplementary tool if regulatory policy fails.

Turning to the UK, the Bank of England, in arguing for so-called macroprudential tools, is also rather dismissive of the role of monetary policy in reacting to financial imbalances (see, for example, the discussion in box 3 in Bank of England (2009)).

The government that came to power in the UK in May 2010 also appears to have accepted this line of argument. Hence, in his Mansion House speech, Chancellor Osborne (2010), discussing the pre-existing monetary policy framework, argued that

> the very design of the policy framework meant that responding to the explosion in balance sheets, asset prices and macro imbalances was impossible. The Bank of England was mandated to focus on consumer price inflation to the exclusion of other things.

He then used this argument to justify setting up the new Financial Policy Committee (FPC) at the Bank.

It is important to recognize that Chancellor Osborne's assertion that the policy framework implied that the Bank of England could not respond to the explosion of asset prices and macro imbalances is wrong. As has long been recognized (see, for example, Cecchetti *et al.* 2000; Bean 2003), the Bank of England's remit has required it to aim to meet the inflation target *at all times*. Since asset price misalignments were likely to jeopardize the central bank's attempt to do so because, say, the bursting of a bubble might threaten deflation at a later date, Cecchetti *et al.* (2000) argued a decade ago that the practical process of setting monetary policy on the basis of fixed-horizon inflation forecasts needed to be amended so that interest rates could 'lean against the wind'. Many others also argued along similar lines, most notably the Bank for International Settlements (BIS) (see, for example, Borio and Lowe 2002; White 2006).

Furthermore, some other inflation targeting central banks (e.g in Australia and Sweden) did actually 'lean against the wind' (see, for example, Heikensten (2009) for a discussion of the Swedish experience). Similarly, in the UK and US, an LATW-style monetary policy would have helped as the house price bubbles were emerging because it would have implied that policy rates would have been set higher than they were.

Unfortunately, the Bank of England and the Treasury argued against the need for such a change. For example, when Stephen Cecchetti, Hans Genberg, John Lipsky and I presented our report in 2000 recommending LATW, a representative of Her Majesty's Treasury (see O'Donnell 2000), who was a discussant at the conference, vigorously defended the status quo. Subsequently, at the Treasury Select Committee, several MPC colleagues distanced themselves from the LATW proposal. In moving forward, it is important to recognize that it is not the framework that failed, but the failure to use the policy flexibility already implied by the framework.[1]

4.2.1 The Respective Roles of Macroprudential Policy and Monetary Policy

It now appears that the new FPC will be empowered to vary capital requirements over the cycle in order to deal with future asset price misalignments.

In some ways this is a welcome development as it is useful to have an additional policy instrument to help the Bank of England to hit the twin targets of price and financial stability that it has always had. However, it is odd that the authorities have chosen to separate the FPC from the MPC. After all, standard economic theory suggests that when one has

---

[1] See also Wadhwani (2009) for a discussion of some of the issues here.

two instruments and two targets, it is, in general, more efficient to set the instruments simultaneously to achieve the two targets than to have specific assignments.

Taking an example where these decisions were separated, recall that in Spain dynamic provisioning did not prevent a housing market bubble as interest rates (set by the European Central Bank) were inappropriate to Spain's needs. We discuss other difficulties with the separation of the FPC from the MPC below.

Furthermore, it is plausible that banks will attempt to find ways round the capital requirements. After all, regulatory arbitrage has, over the years, been a significant part of the financial sector's activities. It is less easy to avoid the effects of higher policy rates. There is a more general difficulty here. Diamond and Rajan (2008) point out that, in good times, because the costs of illiquidity seem remote, short-term debt appears 'cheap' compared with longer-term debt, and the markets appear to favour a bank capital structure that is heavier with respect to short-term leverage. Hence, in the good times, one would expect the 'market capital requirement' to prompt banks to engage in regulatory arbitrage.

In bad times, as the costs of illiquidity seem more salient, the markets are likely to hold bankers to higher capital norms than may be imposed by the FPC. Therefore, countercyclical capital requirements may prove to be relatively ineffective. In addition, it is widely recognized that in order to be effective capital requirements will have to be coordinated internationally. This is not easy to achieve. An advantage of moving interest rates is that, given flexible exchange rates, each central bank has policy autonomy.

Setting time-varying capital requirements (TVCRs) appropriately will require detailed knowledge of their impact on the economy. We do not have this, as has been amply illustrated by the recent debate about the impact of the new Basel capital and liquidity rules on the economy. For example, Barrell (2010) of the National Institute has argued that equilibrium output would fall by 0.1% for each 1% increase in capital requirements. By contrast, there is other work he cites that points to an effect that is about ten times as big!

Moreover, there is disagreement about the shorter-term impact on output too. While Barrell argues that a rapid introduction 'could induce a new banking crisis and cause a sharp reduction of output', the chief economist of the BIS has been cited in the *Financial Times* as suggesting a much smaller effect.[2] Given our ignorance, the FPC could set the level of capital

---

[2] See Cecchetti as quoted in Giles (2010).

requirements at the wrong level entirely. We have been here before. Romer (2009) reminds us that the 1937 recession in the US was, in part, precipitated by an accidental switch to contractionary monetary policy that was brought about by the doubling of reserve requirements for banks.

It behoves us to recall that the Bank of England did struggle with estimating the required capital (in terms of both quantity and quality) during the crisis. As late as August 2007, and therefore *after* a number of financial organizations had already succumbed to the subprime crisis, the governor was still postulating that securitization had made the global banking system a safer place (see Bank of England 2007). In September 2007 the governor was still asserting that British banks were more than adequately capitalized (see Treasury Select Committee 2007). Recall that, by then, the bank sector index of the FTSE All-Share index had, since early 2006, already underperformed the total index by over 20%, so the markets were scenting problems.

A significant advantage of using interest rates instead of TVCRs to achieve greater macroeconomic stability is that we have years of experience of doing it and have a much better sense of the relevant elasticities. By contrast, remember that the main Bank of England macro model (the Bank of England Quarterly Model) has no explicit role for bankruptcy and its core implicitly assumes the Modigliani–Miller theorem whereby capital requirements do not even matter. Starting with those kinds of assumption is a sure recipe for a significant policy mistake.

A common argument against using interest rates to respond to asset price misalignments is that, to quote Bank of England (2009),

> monetary policy would probably have needed to slow materially money spending in the economy below that consistent with meeting the inflation target... This would have generated lower output relative to trend.

Others go even further: for example, Goodhart and Persaud (2008) say that 'the level of interest required to prick a bubble might eviscerate the rest of the economy'.

However, I believe that this argument only applies to those who are actually using monetary policy actively to prick bubbles. As already discussed, this is not what an LATW-tilt to monetary policy involves. Such a tilt is directed towards improving macroeconomic stability, not towards pricking bubbles per se.

Though a bubble may be damped if monetary policy reacts to it, the argument for LATW does not depend on this. LATW can help reduce volatility in output and inflation through the normal effects of monetary policy on demand by partially offsetting the macroeconomic impacts of the bubble. The simulation results in Cecchetti *et al.* (2000) suggested that the LATW tilt helped stabilize output and inflation relative to the no-tilt scenario even when monetary policy does not directly affect the bubble. The degree of tilt applied to monetary policy is designed to optimize macroeconomic stability and is most unlikely to involve creating a recession to prick the bubble.

In any case, note that increasing capital requirements will primarily operate through changing the spread between the lending rate and the central bank's policy rate. Hence, it will have a significant macroeconomic impact on output and inflation. If TVCRs are to make bubbles less likely, they must impose some short-term macroeconomic costs that are similar to those imposed by higher interest rates (albeit somewhat more targeted). There is no 'free lunch' that comes with using TVCRs.

The Bank of England (2009) has also repeated another commonly expressed argument against LATW: that using interest rates to LATW might de-anchor the private sector's expectations of inflation. In my opinion, this risk is easily exaggerated as it is not difficult to explain that one is, say, temporarily undershooting the consumer price inflation target because house prices are booming. Also, Carney (2009) argues that one can avoid threatening the monetary policy objective by ensuring that these deviations can be recovered over time in order to keep the economy on a predetermined path for the price level (i.e. so-called price-level targeting). However, the Bank asserts that one should use macroprudential tools to target financial imbalances directly given the risks of de-anchoring inflation expectations. This appears to imply that the Bank believes that the FPC can use its tool(s) (e.g. capital requirements) to affect a housing price boom without perturbing consumer price inflation because the MPC would set interest rates appropriately.

Is that credible? Let's suppose that we have a house price bubble and that the FPC increases capital requirements, which leads banks to widen lending margins *in general*. The rise in actual borrowing rates then slows the economy and leads the MPC to forecast that consumer price inflation will undershoot the target. The MPC then lowers the policy rate to push inflation back to target. Can we be confident that the lowering of the policy rate accompanying the widening in lending margins will not keep the house price boom going? In this regard, Davies and Green (2010) are surely correct in warning that with the separate FPC and MPC, we have 'a risk of "push-me, pull-you" policies within the Bank'.

When considering regulatory change it is important to recall that we have had financial crises associated with bursting asset price bubbles in many countries at many times throughout history. These episodes have occurred under different types of regulatory structures and banking systems. It would be unrealistic to expect that any regulatory or structural change would prevent a future crisis. It is therefore important to use monetary and fiscal policy to, at least, attempt to improve macroeconomic stability.

4.2.2   The Role of Monetary Policy in the Recent Crisis

It is unlikely that the recent crisis had a single cause. Therefore, if we are to attempt to reduce the amplitude of the next crisis, it is important that we work on improving performance in a number of areas. This is why it is disappointing that many central bankers have not been willing to accept responsibility for their errors. One can, therefore, have considerable sympathy for critics like Plender (2010), who notes that

> central bankers are escaping very lightly in the post crisis bust-up. For while incentive structures in banking exacerbated the credit bubble, they were a much less potent cause of trouble than central bank behaviour across the world.

In his defence of the Federal Reserve's monetary policy record, Bernanke (2010) argued that interest rates had not seemed too low during the 2002–6 period. He did so by modifying a version of the so-called Taylor rule. Using Bernanke's preferred inputs, the Taylor rule prescribes a path for policy that is close to what actually occurred. However, this, to me, is to entirely miss the point. Many of us who had argued for LATW monetary policy (see, for example, Cecchetti *et al.* 2000, 2002) had explicitly asserted that the Taylor rule was not an appropriate benchmark for monetary policy, but that it needed to be modified to include an additional term for asset price misalignments. Specifically, if, say, house prices were significantly above their equilibrium value, then interest rates needed to be set above the conventional Taylor rule benchmark. Consequently, I would argue that, even using Bernanke's preferred inputs into the Taylor rule, he would have to concede that interest rates were set lower than would have been implied by a Cecchetti *et al.* style interest rate setting rule that had incorporated a role for asset price misalignments.

Bernanke (2010) also argues that only a small portion of the increase in house prices during the decade could be attributed to the stance of

US monetary policy. Instead, he asserts that the availability of alternative, exotic mortgage products is a key explanation for the housing bubble. Therefore, he concludes that regulatory and supervisory policies, rather than monetary policies, would have been a more effective means of addressing the run-up in house prices. One wonders whether the analysis upon which Bernanke relies is sufficiently robust. Econometric models of house prices have not fared particularly well in recent years and one should, therefore, be suspicious of any conclusions based on them.

Moreover, as Chancellor (2010) convincingly argues, the role of these exotic mortgage products is easily overstated. After all, home prices soared in many other countries where monetary policy was also too easy, even though they did not have those new exotic mortgage products (e.g. Spain). Moreover, it would be a mistake to assert that the evolution of these exotic mortgage products in the US were, somehow, unrelated to the loose monetary policy regime. Diamond and Rajan (2009) provide a persuasive argument that the so-called Greenspan put, whereby the authorities cut interest rates rapidly and deeply in 'bad times' but were reluctant to raise interest rates above conventional benchmarks in 'good times', may well have contributed to the illiquidity of assets and the excessive leverage of banks. Furthermore, research at the BIS using a dataset for banks in sixteen countries does suggest support for the notion that lower interest rates lead banks to take more risks (see, for example, Altumbas *et al.* 2010).

Some have also argued that domestic monetary policy did not lead to house price bubbles. Instead, they blame the excess savings in other countries leading to low long-term real interest rates. Specifically, Bernanke (2010), in line with his global savings glut hypothesis, shows that, in a cross-section, countries in which current accounts worsened and capital inflows rose also appear to have had greater house price appreciation. He then asserts that more accommodative monetary policies generally reduce capital inflows and that, therefore, the apparent relationship between capital flows and house price appreciation appears to be inconsistent with the existence of a strong link between monetary policy and house price appreciation.

However, Laibson and Mollerstrom (2010) suggest that it is the asset price bubbles that may have drawn in the capital flows. To the extent that accommodative monetary policy led to a house price bubble, it may actually have increased capital inflows, which contradicts Bernanke's assumption. Therefore, more research is needed with respect to the global savings glut hypothesis.

While many central bankers (current and former) have tried hard to minimize the role of monetary policy in contributing to the house price bubbles we have seen, one has to conclude that their attempts have, at best, been unconvincing.

4.3 CHANGING THE REGULATORY FRAMEWORK TO REDUCE THE PROBABILITY OF FUTURE CRISES

While I have argued that changing the way we set monetary policy is important if we are to reduce the probability of future crises, we need to revisit the design and operation of our regulatory framework too. This crisis has many causes—it is important that we modify a variety of things. However, amidst the current popular clamour to 'hang the bankers' it is also important that we do not neglect the possibility that future growth may be hurt by inappropriate regulatory reform.

4.3.1 *The Regulators Made Mistakes Too*

Private-sector bankers have got much of the blame for the crisis and it is striking that regulators have attracted much less attention. However, it is critically important that they absorb the lessons of the crisis too.

A sad aspect of this crisis is that there were many policymakers who understood what was going on and voiced concerns, and yet our regulators did not respond. For example, a former governor of the Riksbank, Lars Heikensten (2009), writes of chairing a G10 working group which discussed provisioning in banks and measures to deal with the emerging housing price bubble. He reveals that political opposition from the US and Britain led to the report of this group not even being published as a G10 report! Heikensten also laments that public pleas for the Riksbank to amend European supervisory and crisis management practices were ignored.

Levine (2010) also resists the popular notion that, somehow, the crisis was an unpredictable accident—a view, for example, advanced by luminaries such as Alan Greenspan, Robert Rubin and Charles Prince in their testimonies to the Financial Crisis Inquiry Commission. Instead, Levine asserts: 'The crisis did not just happen. Policymakers and regulators, along with private-sector co-conspirators, helped cause it.'

He argues that, in a variety of areas, US regulators incentivized financial institutions to engage in activities that generated enormous short-run profits but dramatically increased long-run fragility. Levine also claims that, in some cases, the regulatory agencies were aware of the risks associated with their policies but chose not to modify them.

It is therefore unfortunate that in the 'blame game' that has been played out in the last two years, central bankers and regulators have typically attempted to pin all the blame on the private sector without always admitting the need for them to learn their own lessons from the crisis.

Taking a more parochial view, the Bank of England and the overall regulatory system in the UK had a poor crisis. Little was done to deal with the bubble, despite public concerns about excessive risk-taking, while the response to the crisis was slow. (This is something that was made most visible by the Northern Rock debacle.) Yet the absence of contrition from the Bank has been surprising. The Bank's mistakes stemmed in large part from the prevailing doctrine that financial markets were efficient. Any attempt to question that was strongly resisted.[3]

In my time at the MPC at the Bank, I was surprised by the lack of interest in issues relating to financial markets. Indeed, there seemed to be a deliberate policy to run down resources in the financial stability wing.

It is therefore odd that the new regulatory structure makes an unrepentant Bank of England even more powerful with respect to regulatory matters.

4.3.2 Some Proposals for Reforming the Financial Sector May Hurt Growth

Since the 2007–8 crisis we have seen a bewildering variety of proposals for reforming the financial sector, including structural reform (e.g. 'narrow banking'), changes in capital and liquidity requirements, and modifying the remuneration framework. Some of these proposals will be discussed in other chapters.

Given that the crisis had a huge negative impact on global welfare, the temptation to reform the financial sector is easily understood. Indeed, after financial crises it is not uncommon to blame recent financial innovations. Recall that the bursting of the South Sea Bubble in 1720 was followed by a ban on joint stock companies in 1720 and by the Barnard Act in 1734 that banned option trading (see, for example, Stulz 2009). Clearly, not all post-crisis reform is sensible!

---

[3]Even an attempt to amend the main macroeconomic model to incorporate the well-documented empirical finding that the so-called uncovered interest parity hypothesis did not hold encountered significant resistance, on the ostensible grounds that we should not assume such a departure from market efficiency (see, for example, Wadhwani 1999).

I have no difficulty with the notion that financial markets failed this time, as they have done before. For much of my professional career I have been sceptical about the efficient markets hypothesis (EMH). Much of my early research as an academic (see, for example, Wadhwani 1988) questioned the notion of market efficiency at a time when the consensus view amongst policymakers and academics alike was strongly pro-EMH. However, economists have long understood that 'market failure' does not, of itself, justify government intervention. Specifically, certain forms of intervention may not be justifiable in terms of standard cost–benefit analysis because, for example, we may end up depressing growth significantly and/or 'policymaker failure' may be an important consideration.

The current understandable obsession with 'bashing the bankers' neglects the theoretical and empirical literature documenting the highly significant contribution of the financial sector to growth (see, for example, the masterly summary by Levine (2004)). For example, financial market development has allowed us to deal with liquidity risk, by facilitating the financing of some high-return projects that require a long-run commitment of capital even though individual savers do not like to relinquish control of their savings for long periods. Financial market development enabled savers to hold liquid assets (e.g. equities, bonds or bank deposits) while capital markets transformed these into longer-term capital investments.

The eminent economist Sir John Hicks asserted that the products that were manufactured during the first decade of the Industrial Revolution had been invented much earlier, but in his view the critical innovation that had ignited growth in eighteenth-century England was capital market liquidity (Hicks 1969). It is important that we do not lose sight of this important consideration when discussing proposals that may impede the maturity transformation undertaken by banks.

Historically, financial systems that are more effective at pooling savings are regarded as helping growth. Indeed, Bagehot (1873) argued that a major difference between England and other countries was that England had a financial system that could mobilize resources for 'immense works' more effectively than other countries.

In a widely cited study, King and Levine (1993) showed that the initial level of financial intermediation and its growth had highly beneficial effects on economic growth over the 1960–89 period. More recently, Aghion *et al.* (2005) contended that financial development helped explain whether or not growth convergence occurred and, if so, the rate at which it did. Over a longer time period, Rousseau and Sylla (2001) studied seventeen countries over the 1850–1997 period, and concluded that financial development stimulated growth in these economies. Furthermore, Jayaratne and Strahan (1996) compared thirty-five US states that relaxed restrictions on branch banking versus those who did not, and showed that bank reform was associated with accelerating real per capita growth rates. In another widely cited study, Rajan and Zingales (1990) found that industries that were naturally heavier users of external finance grew faster in economies with better developed financial systems. Hence, using a variety of different types of statistical tests, the finance–growth nexus appears to be an important and robust result. It is, therefore, critically important that we take the potential growth-retarding effects into account when recommending any reform of the financial sector.

In some circles, though, it has become fashionable to dismiss the voluminous academic literature documenting a significant link between financial innovation and economic growth. The argument advanced is that, while it is accepted that financial innovation helped us during the Industrial Revolution or may help countries with less well-developed financial systems like India, it is asserted that the financial innovation over the last thirty years have *not* helped us.[4]

However, this scepticism about the value of recent financial innovation is almost certainly unwarranted. Firstly, Greenwood et al. (2010) show that during the period 1974–2004 about 30% of US growth can be accounted for by technological improvement in financial intermediation.

Secondly, using data for the 1973–95 period, Michalopoulos et al. (2010) show that financial innovation is an important determinant of the rate of growth convergence. They conclude that 'institutions, laws, regulations, and policies that impede financial innovation slow technological change and economic growth'.

Thirdly, in terms of anecdotal evidence, many who have succeeded in the information and communication technologies sector point to innovation within the venture capital sector as contributing to their success. One hears similar things about the biotech sector.

Fourthly, anecdotal evidence also points to a highly significant reduction in bid–offer spreads associated with a variety of instruments used by the corporate sector (e.g. interest rate swaps). Note that Greenwood

---

[4]Turner (2010) cites Schularick and Taylor (2009) as providing evidence suggesting that innovation had no effect on trend growth. However, a more recent version of the latter paper distances itself from such a claim, which had, though, been made in an earlier version that Turner cites.

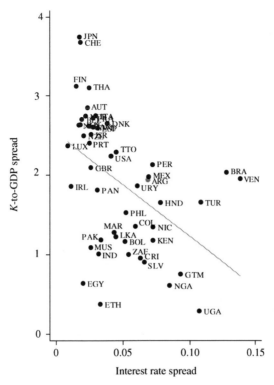

Figure 4.1. The cross-country relationship between interest rate spreads and capital-to-output ratios.

et al. showed that, on a cross-country basis, lower interest rate spreads go hand in hand with higher capital-to-output ratios and also higher TFP (see figures 4.1 and 4.2, respectively).

Increasing micro-intervention in our financial markets could plausibly retard financial innovation and hurt economic growth. Moreover, there is a substantial literature about how policymakers hurt growth through, for example, diverting resources for political or other non-economic reasons. This is another reason I believe that monetary (and macro) policy should play a more important role with respect to financial stability. Thereby, we can preserve the microeconomic advantages of financial innovation while simultaneously curbing the overexuberance of the financial sector by using macroeconomic tools like interest rates. The latter has the advantage that it does not require the degree of detailed knowledge that would be necessary for successful microeconomic intervention.

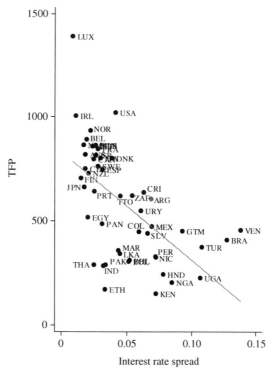

Figure 4.2. The cross-country relationship between interest rate spreads and TFP.

4.3.3 We Need More, Not Less, Financial Liberalization in Some Countries to Reduce the Probability of Future Crises

It is widely accepted that it will be difficult to achieve *sustained* growth in the US unless there is a significant 'rebalancing' towards Asia. Of course, greater financial liberalization in Asia would make such rebalancing more likely.

This is best illustrated by considering the Chinese case more carefully. Note that the Chinese current-account surplus shot up from around 1.6% of GDP early in the decade to as high as 11% of GDP in 2007. The increased saving which went hand in hand with the rise in the current-account surplus was the rise in gross *corporate* savings, which went from about 15% of GDP in 2000 to around 26% of GDP by 2007.

According to conventional economic theory, in a world with perfect capital markets and no tax distortions, the level of total private savings should be invariant to corporate saving. However, figure 3.7 in IMF (2009) shows (see our figure 4.3) that while this theoretically predicted

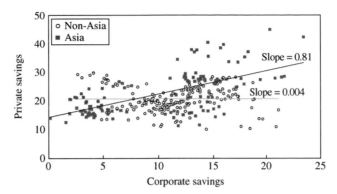

Figure 4.3. Private and corporate savings (as percentages of GDP).

relationship holds outside Asia, it definitively does not hold in Asia. Recall that, in China, corporates are often state owned or local government led. The state does not usually receive dividends, and large companies either reinvest their profits or simply accumulate assets.

What China needs is financial liberalization. With a more market-driven system, firms are less likely to need to retain earnings (less reliance on self-financing). The IMF estimates that achieving the average level of financial liberalization in the G7 would reduce corporate savings by 5% of GDP. Similarly, improvements in corporate governance would help, as it would make it more likely that corporates would pay dividends.

There is an internal debate with respect to the merits of financial liberalization within China. The louder the critics of the finance sector within the G7 shout the more they undermine those who would push financial reform in China.

4.3.4 Financial Liberalization, Crises and Growth

In an intriguing paper that may have some applicability to the current conjuncture, Tornell *et al.* (2004) show that

(i) financial liberalization leads to a greater incidence of crises, but

(ii) financial liberalization also leads to higher GDP growth, and

(iii) there is a positive link between GDP growth and the *negative skewness* of credit growth (which is a correlate of crises).

They conclude that 'occasional crises need not forestall growth and may even be a necessary component of a developing country's growth and experience'.

They illustrate their argument by comparing Thailand and India. India followed 'slow and steady' growth—GDP per capita grew by 114% between 1980 and 2002. In contrast, Thailand experienced lending booms and crisis, but GDP per capita grew by 162% despite the effects of a major crisis.

With regards to the conjuncture, it *may* be that countries with more developed financial systems do have more 'negative skewness', but also higher growth. (We don't know if their work carries over to the more developed countries. Also, as Professor Layard has reminded us,[5] if happiness is an objective of growth, the stability of that growth matters too, as unemployment and fear of unemployment have been found to be more important determinants of happiness than income.)

Therefore, the recent crisis in the developed world might not, by itself, be a reason to 'destroy the financial industry'. Indeed, I wonder whether we need to secure the microeconomic advantages of financial liberalization while using macroeconomic policy to deal with the overexuberance that precedes the financial crises that do so much harm.

4.4 CONCLUSIONS

I have six *key* conclusions.

- Monetary policy mistakes played a key role in the run-up to this crisis, and the arguments made in defence of the policy actually followed are unconvincing.
- Monetary policy needs to work 'hand in hand' with TVCRs in responding to asset price misalignments. Moreover, monetary policy is likely to be more effective than TVCRs and less likely to result in policy mistakes. This may imply that the current redesign of the policymaking structure in the UK is inappropriate and there may well be a case for merging the MPC and the FPC.
- The regulators made many mistakes before and during the crisis. We need to be acutely aware of this before giving them even more power, and we need to ensure that lessons are learnt.
- Financial innovations, including some of the improvements in recent years, have played a central and important role in economic growth. While the current feeling of revulsion towards the financial sector is not uncommon after a crisis, we must be careful that we do not harm growth.

---

[5] See, for example, Layard (2005). This is an important topic on which more research is needed.

- Some countries (e.g. China) need more, not less, financial liberalization. This would help rebalance the global economy, which might reduce the probability of future crises. Anti-finance rhetoric in the developed markets weakens those who are arguing for financial reform in China and India.

- Macroeconomic policy (including monetary policy) needs to 'lean against the wind' so that we can deliver greater macroeconomic and financial stability without having to resort to a lot of micro-meddling that may hurt growth significantly.

REFERENCES

Aghion, P., P. Howitt and D. Mayer-Foulkes. 2005. The effect of financial development on convergence: theory and evidence. *Quarterly Journal of Economics* **120**(1), 173–222.

Altunbas, Y., L. Gambacorta and D. Marquez-Ibanez. 2010. Does monetary policy affect bank risk-taking?. BIS Working Paper 298 (March).

Bagehot, W. 1873. *Lombard Street*. Homewood, IL: Richard D. Irwin.

Bank of England. 2007. Inflation Report press conference (August). Transcript available at www.bankofengland.co.uk.

Bank of England. 2009. The role of macroprudential policy. Discussion Paper (November).

Barrell, R. 2010. Should we shut the stable door before the horse bolts again? Paper presented at the NIESR Westminster Economics Forum (June).

Bean, C. 2003. Asset prices, financial imbalances and monetary policy: are inflation targets enough?. BIS Working Paper 140.

Bernanke, B. 2010. Monetary policy and the housing bubble. Speech at the American Economic Association (3 January).

Bernanke, B., and M. Gertler. 1999. Monetary policy and asset price volatility. In *New Challenges for Monetary Policy: A Symposium Sponsored by the Federal Reserve Bank of Kansas City*, pp. 77–128. Federal Reserve Bank of Kansas City.

Borio, C., and P. Lowe. 2002. Asset prices, financial and monetary stability: exploring the nexus. BIS Working Paper 114.

Carney, M. 2009. Some considerations on using monetary policy to stabilize economic activity. Speech at a symposium sponsored by the Federal Reserve Bank of Kansas City, Jackson Hole, Wyoming (22 August).

Cecchetti, S. G., H. Genberg, J. Lipsky and S. Wadhwani. 2000. *Asset Prices and Central Bank Policy*. Geneva Reports on the World Economy, volume 2. Geneva/London: CEPR/ICMB.

Cecchetti, S. G., H. Genberg and S. Wadhwani. 2002. Asset prices in a flexible inflation targeting framework. In *Asset Price Bubbles: The Implications for Monetary, Regulatory and International Policies* (ed. W. C. Hunter, G. G. Kaufman and M. Pomerleano), pp. 427–44. Cambridge, MA: MIT Press.

Chancellor, E. 2010. Ben Bernanke has learnt so little. *Financial Times* (10 January).

Diamond, D., and R. Rajan. 2009a. Illiquidity and interest rate policy. University of Chicago Mimeo.

Diamond, D., and R. Rajan. 2009b. The credit crisis: conjectures about causes and remedies. University of Chicago Mimeo.

Davies, H., and D. Green. 2010. Final touches for sensible regulatory reform. *Financial Times* (20 May).

Giles, C. 2010. Bankers' 'doomsday scenarios' under fire. *Financial Times* (30 May).

Goodhart, C. A. E., and A. Persaud. 2008. A party pooper's guide to financial stability. *Financial Times* (4 June).

Greenspan, A. 1999. Testimony to the Committee on Banking and Financial Services, US House of Representatives (22 July).

Greenwood, J., J. M. Sanchez and C. Wang. 2010. Quantifying the impact on financial development on economic development. NBER Working Paper 15893.

Heikensten, L. 2009. Inflation targeting 20 years on. Presentation at Norges Bank Conference, Oslo, 12 June.

Hicks, J. 1969. *A Theory of Economic History.* Oxford: Clarendon.

IMF. 2009. *Regional Economic Outlook: Asia* (October).

Jayaratne, J., and P. E. Strahan. 1996. The finance–growth nexus: evidence from bank branch deregulation. *Quarterly Journal of Economics* **111**, 639–70.

King, I. R. G., and R. Levine. 1993. Finance and growth: Schumpeter might be right. *Quarterly Journal of Economics* **108**, 717–38.

Kohn, D. L. 2008. Monetary policy and asset prices revisited. Cato's Institute's 26th Annual Monetary Policy Conference, 19 November.

Laibson, D., and J. Mollerstrom. 2010. Capital flows, consumption booms and asset bubbles: a behavioural alternative to the savings glut hypothesis. NBER Working Paper 15759.

Layard, R. 2005. *Happiness: Lessons from a New Science.* London: Penguin.

Levine, R. 2004. Finance and growth: theory and evidence. In *Handbook of Economic Growth* (ed. P. Aghion and S. Durlauf), volume 1, pp. 865–934. Elsevier.

Levine, R. 2010. An autopsy of the US financial system. NBER Working Paper 15956.

Michalopoulos, S., L. Laeven and R. Levine. 2010. Financial innovation and endogenous growth. Brown University Mimeo.

O'Donnell, G. 2000. How can monetary policy deal with asset price inflation. In Cecchetti *et al.* (2000).

Osborne, G. 2010. Speech at the Lord Mayor's Dinner at Mansion House (16 June).

Plender, J. 2010. Blame the central bankers more than the private bankers. *Financial Times* (13 June).

Rajan, R. G., and L. Zingales. 1998. Financial dependence and growth. *American Economic Review* **88**, 559–86.

Romer, C. 2009. The lessons of 1937. *The Economist* (20 June).

Rousseau, P., and R. Sylla. 2001. Financial system, economic growth and globalization. NBER Working Paper 8323 (June).

Schularick, M., and A. M. Taylor. 2009. Credit booms gone bust: monetary policy, leveraged cycles and financial crises 1870 to 2008. NBER Working Paper 15512 (November).

Stulz, R. 2009. Credit default swaps and the credit crisis. Fisher College of Business Working Paper Series, The Ohio State University.

Treasury Select Committee. 2007. Transcript (20 September).

Tornell, W., F. Westermann and L. Martinez. 2004. The positive link between financial liberalization, growth and crises. NBER Working Paper 10293.

Turner, A. 2010. After the crises: assessing the costs and benefits of financial liberalization. Fourteenth Deshmukh Memorial Lecture, Reserve Bank of India, Mumbai (15 February).

Wadhwani, S. B. 1998. On the inefficiency of financial markets. *LSE Quarterly* (March).

Wadhwani, S. B. 1999. Currency puzzles. Speech delivered at the London School of Economics (16 September).

Wadhwani, S. B. 2008. Should monetary policy respond to asset price bubbles? Revisiting the debate. *National Institute Economic Review* **206**, 25–34.

Wadhwani, S. B. 2009. Inflation targeting, capital requirements and leaning against the wind. Presentation at the Norges Bank 'Inflation Targeting 20 Years On' conference, Oslo (12 June).

White, W. R. 2006. Procyclicality in the financial system: do we need a new macro financial stabilization framework?. BIS Working Paper 193.

PART 2
WAYS FORWARD

How Should We Regulate the Financial Sector?

By Charles Goodhart

Financial regulation is normally imposed in reaction to some prior crisis, rather than founded on theoretical principle. In the past, regulation has been deployed to improve risk management practices in individual banks. This was misguided. Instead, regulation should focus first on systemic externalities (contagion) and second on consumer protection (asymmetric information). The quantification of systemic externalities is difficult. Since the costs of financial breakdown are high, a natural response is to pile extra regulation onto a set of regulated intermediaries, but this can impair their capacity to intermediate and leads to border problems between regulated and unregulated systems and also between different national regulatory systems.

5.1 INTRODUCTION

Financial regulation has always been atheoretical: a pragmatic response by practical officials, and concerned politicians, to immediate problems, following the dictum that 'we must not let that happen again'. When the Basel Committee on Banking Supervision (BCBS) was established in 1974–75 to handle some of the emerging problems of global finance and cross-border banking, the modus operandi then developed was to hold a round-table discussion of current practice in each member state with the objective of reaching an agreement on which practice was 'best', and then to harmonize on that. Little, or no, attempt was made to go back to first principles, and to start by asking why there should be a call for regulation on banking, whether purely domestic or cross-border, in the first place.

Thus Basel I, the Accord on Capital Regulation of 1988, was propelled by concern that many of the major international banks, especially in the US, would have been made insolvent, under a mark-to-market accounting procedure, by the MAB (Mexico, Argentina, Brazil) default crisis of 1982. Congress wanted to impose higher capital regulations on US banks, but was deterred by the 'level playing field' argument that any unilateral move would just shift business to foreign, especially Japanese, banks. Hence the appeal to the BCBS. Again, little or no attempt was made to explore what the fundamental need for holding capital was, or what its optimal level might be (see Hellwig 1996, 2008). The target of 8% was the outcome of a balance between a desire to prevent, and if possible to reverse, the prior long decline in that ratio counteracted by a concern that any sharp rise in the required ratio above pre-existing levels could force banks into deleveraging and a slowdown on bank lending, which would be bad for the economy. It was a thoroughly practical compromise.

Basel I was hammered out by central bank officials behind closed doors, with little input from the commercial banks, the regulated. When those same central bank practitioners sought to move on from attention to credit risk (the sole focus of Basel I) to a wider range of risks (most notably market risk) in the mid 1990s, however, their initial *de haut en bas* 'building block' approach to such risks was rejected by the commercial banks on the grounds that it was technically antediluvian, and that the banks had a much more up-to-date methodology of risk assessment, notably Value at Risk (VaR) (note that VaR was itself derived from earlier developments in finance theory by economists such as Markowitz and Sharpe). The officials seized on this eagerly. It enabled regulation to be based on the precept that each individual bank's own risk management should be brought up to the level of, and harmonized with, those of the 'best' banks, and had the added bonus that the methodology of regulation could be rooted in the (best) practices of the most technically advanced individual banks. The implicit idea was that if you made all banks copy the principles of the best, then the system as a whole would be safe. Hardly anyone critically examined this proposition, and it turned out to be wrong.

It was wrong for two main associated reasons. First, the risk management concerns of individual banks are, and indeed should be, quite different from those of regulators. A banker wants to know what his/her individual risk is under normal circumstances, 99% of the time. If an extreme shock occurs, it will, the banker may assume, be for the authorities to respond. The VaR measure is well designed for normal conditions but it does not handle tail risk adequately (see Danielsson 2002). It is the tail risk of such extreme shocks that should worry the regulator.

Next, the whole process focused on the individual bank, but what should matter to the regulator is systemic risk, not individual risk. Under most measures of individual risks, each individual bank had never seemed stronger, as measured by Basel II and mark-to-market accounting, than in July 2007, on the eve of the crisis; Adair Turner emphasizes that CDS spreads on banks generally reached their all-time minimum then.

5.2 THE RATIONALE FOR REGULATION

Bankers are professionals. It should not be for the government, or for delegated regulators, to try to determine how much risk they take on board, nor to set out the particular way that they assess such risks, so long as any adverse fallout from adverse outcomes is internalized amongst themselves and their professional investors, debt or equity holders. Under these circumstances the authorities have no locus for any intervention, however risky the bank's business plan may seem.

This immediately indicates two of the three theoretical reasons for regulation/supervision, which are externalities and the protection of non-professional consumers of banking services (asymmetric information). There is a third reason for regulation, i.e. the control of monopoly power, but, with a few minor exceptions, e.g. access to clearing houses, this is not a relevant concern in the financial system. All this is set out at greater length in Brunnermeier *et al.* (2009). Although externalities are the more important concern, in terms of the potential loss to society from lack of, or inappropriate, regulation/supervision, it is perhaps easiest to begin with customer protection (asymmetric information).

5.2.1 *Asymmetric Information*

The expertise of professionals, whether doctors, lawyers, independent financial advisors or bankers, lies in their presumed greater knowledge. Since obtaining such knowledge is time consuming and costly, the client is, by definition, at a disadvantage. In most cases we do not need professional help, but when we do need it it is vital, so repetition is not a safeguard. Schleifer (2010) asks why a Coaseian appeal to the courts could not replace regulation in such circumstances and answers that the legal process is too time consuming, costly and uncertain. Again, while disclosure and enforced dual capacity (i.e. the separation of advice from execution) can be partial safeguards, the former depends on the customer having the time/intelligence to interpret what is disclosed and the latter adds greatly to the expense.

Moreover, when some shock makes depositors realize (eventually) that their bank may be in trouble, a run ensues, and once a run is perceived it is always rational to join it. With a fractional reserve banking system, any such run is likely to cause the bank involved to fail, unless supported by the central bank. If the losses from such a failure were entirely internalized, that would only matter to that one bank's clients, and, apart from customer protection, would not matter (much) to the wider economy.

However, in many (but not all) cases there are serious externalities arising from such a bank failure.

So there are two reasons to adopt deposit insurance, at least for non-professional retail depositors: to protect customers and to prevent bank runs. Insurance is both costly and creates moral hazard. So the regulators/supervisors, who should themselves also be professionals, should, in principle, like any other professional investor, be in a position to assess the relative risk of the provision of such insurance and charge an appropriate levy or premium for so doing. In practice, this has not happened in the past. No one can measure risk accurately in an uncertain (non-ergodic) world, so any attempt to do so has been put in the 'too difficult' category. Instead, insurance premia have usually been related, on a flat-rate basis, to total insured deposits at a low, historically related, level. Following the recent crisis and the Obama (January 2010) initiative proposing a tax on banks, that may now change. Thus there may be a, possibly widespread, introduction of bank taxes in many countries. I would hope that such a tax would be imposed *ex ante* rather than *ex post*, and risk-related rather than flat rate, or related to transactions (Tobin tax). We will see.

Some commentators have argued that the introduction of a risk-related bank levy is all that is needed to provide incentives for bankers to be appropriately prudent, and to provide a fund to support financial intermediaries that are too big to fail, so that otherwise, and apart from other consumer protection measures, all other regulation/supervision could be removed. This is not so, since it ignores the role and importance of externalities, to which we now turn.

5.2.2 *Externalities*

Any market action taken by one player in a market is always likely to affect the economic position of all the other players in that market. If I buy (sell) an asset, its price will tend to rise (fall) and the current wealth of all players, as measured by current market prices tends to increase (fall). If I am more defensive (aggressive) in my lending practices by seeking more (less) collateral from my prospective borrowers, they in turn can purchase and hold fewer (more) assets, thereby lowering (raising) asset prices more generally. If I want to hold safer (riskier) assets, the risk spreads, and often the volatility, of riskier assets rises (falls), making such assets appear even riskier (less risky) in the market. Such pecuniary effects of market adjustments do not in themselves represent social externalities, nor are they causes of systemic contagion, but they can become so, particularly when extreme losses result in bankruptcies and liquidation, as described subsequently.

There are many such self-amplifying spirals in our financial system (see, for example, Adrian and Shin 2008; Brunnermeier and Pedersen 2005; Brunnermeier *et al.* 2009). Such inherent procyclicality becomes more immediately apparent when accounting is done on a fair value, mark-to-market basis. This is not, however, a knockdown argument against the adoption of such a measuring rod, since many partially informed (wholesale) counterparties, who are the most likely to run, can imagine the effect of current market price changes on underlying wealth, and, given the uncertainty, their imagination may lead to a picture worse than the reality. Anyhow, if accounting is not to be at a 'fair' value, what 'unfair' value would be preferable? The conclusion from such considerations must surely be that a better way to handle procyclicality is to introduce contracyclicality into our macroprudential regulations, a theme taken further in the chapters by Large (chapter 7) and Smithers (chapter 6).

Such self-amplifying market spirals would not matter in themselves, except to those directly involved, if all such losses/gains were internalized. There would then be no social externalities. This would be the case if all such losses/gains fell on shareholders, which would be so if all assets were backed by equity capital, or if the equity holders had unlimited liability (and the wealth to meet all debts). Indeed, in the early days of banking, until about 1850 in many countries, this was the intention of policy towards banks. As the scale of industry increased, however, relative to the size and the willingness and ability of the small, unlimited-liability, private partnership banks to extend sufficient medium-term credit to such enterprises, a conscious choice was made to move towards limited-liability joint stock banks, whose resulting greater riskiness was to be held in check by more transparency in their accounts and by external regulation.

The insiders—the executives—of any business know far more about it than anyone else does, and they are liable to use that information to extract rents from outsiders. This fact of life is the ultimate reason both for the existence of banks, who (should) have a comparative advantage in obtaining information about borrowers, and for the existence of certain contracts, e.g. fixed-interest debt (and fixed nominal wage), the purpose of which is to economize on information by imposing legal penalties on the borrower (employer) when she fails to meet the terms of the contract, in the guise of bankruptcy (and/or renegotiation under duress).[1] Unfortunately, the societal costs of such bankruptcies are generally enormous in the case of large, interconnected financial intermediaries, so much so that, following the bankruptcy of Lehman Brothers in September 2008, it has been accepted by most governments that such intermediaries are indeed too big to close in bankruptcy (that is, they are too big to fail (TBTF)). What are these costs? There are, perhaps, five such sets of costs.

(i) The direct costs of using legal/accounting resources to wind down the enterprise. These can be sizeable.

(ii) The potential dislocation of financial markets and settlement/payment systems.

(iii) The loss of the specialized skills/information of those working in the bankrupt institution. Many will be deployed in similar jobs elsewhere after a time but, even so, the loss could be considerable.

(iv) The immediate uncertainty, and ultimate potential loss, for all counterparty creditors of the financial intermediary. This will not only include bank depositors and those with insurance claims, but also those with uncompleted transactions, pledged or custodian assets, other forms of secured or unsecured debt, etc. Even when the ultimate loss may be quite small (as, for example, in the case of Continental Illinois), the interim inability to use the frozen assets and the uncertainty both about the ultimate timing of, and the valuation at, their release can be severe.

(v) Besides creditors of the failing financial intermediary, potential debtors generally have an explicit or implicit agreement with the intermediary to borrow more, i.e. unused credit facilities. These disappear instantaneously on bankruptcy. While these may or may not be capable of replication elsewhere, this would take time, effort and perhaps extra cost. In the meantime, potential access to money is lost.

Some of our colleagues, notably John Kay in his accompanying chapter (see chapter 8 as well as Kay (2010) and House of Commons, Treasury Select Committee (2010)), focus on the bankruptcy costs falling on bank depositors and payments systems, and argue that, once these are protected, no other financial intermediary need be regulated or protected

---

[1] This is essentially the reason why the proposals by Kotlikoff with various colleagues to transform all banking into mutual-fund, equity-based banking is a non-starter (see Chamley and Kotlikoff 2009; Ferguson and Kotlikoff 2009; Goodman and Kotlikoff 2009; Kotlikoff and Leamer 2009).

from bankruptcy. In my view, that is to take far too narrow a view of the costs of bankruptcy. Lehman Brothers was a 'casino' bank with few, if any, retail deposits and few links with the payment system. In the crisis of 2007–9, hardly any bank depositor lost a cent and, following government guarantees, none need now expect to do so. In contrast, the crisis both generated, and was in turn deepened by, a sharp reduction in access to credit and a tightening in the terms on which credit might be obtained. A capitalist economy is a credit-based economy, and anything which severely restricts the continuing flow of such credit damages that economy. A sole focus on (retail) depositor protection is not enough.

One of the purposes of this section is to demonstrate that the social externalities that provide a rationale (beyond consumer protection) for financial regulation are intimately related to the governance structure of financial intermediaries, to which we now turn, and to the form, structure and costs of bankruptcy, to which we shall turn later.

5.3   THE GOVERNANCE STRUCTURE OF BANKS

There is no call for a generalized reversion to unlimited liability for the shareholders of banks, though there is a degree of regret about the earlier switch of the large investment houses (broker/dealers) in the US from a partnership status to incorporation as a public company. Especially in view of the recent crisis, it would be impossible to raise sufficient equity funding to finance our financial intermediaries on an unlimited-liability basis. In view, moreover, of the nature of a limited-liability shareholding, equivalent to a call option on the assets of the bank, shareholders will tend to encourage bank executives to take on riskier activities, particularly in boom times. Northern Rock was a favourite of the London Stock Exchange until just a few months before it collapsed. It is, therefore, a mistake to try to align the interests of bank executives, who take the decisions, with those of shareholders (Bebchuk and Fried 2009; Bebchuk and Spamann 2010). Indeed as Beltratti and Stulz (2009) have shown, it was banks with the most shareholder-friendly governance structures that tended to do worst in the recent crisis.

The payment structures for those in Wall Street and the City have been, arguably, more appropriate for a partnership structure than for limited liability. The wrath of the public was related more to the continuation of high remuneration following widespread disaster than to the massive bonus rewards in good times. This raises the question of whether more could be done to make (at least part of) the remuneration of bank executives once again more akin to unlimited liability: for example, by some extended clawback system (Squam Lake Working Group 2010), by making bonus payments subject to unlimited liability (Record 2010), or by requiring such executives' pensions to be invested wholly in the equity of their own bank (a suggestion once made by Geoffrey Wood). The case for doing so, however, rests, for the time being, in some large part on public perception of what would be ethically appropriate, rather than on much empirical evidence that existing payment structures for bank executives led them consciously to take risks in the expectation that their bank would be bailed out by the taxpayer (Fahlenbrach and Stulz 2009). The evidence is, instead, that top management were generally simply unaware of the risks that they were taking (but maybe in some cases they just did not want to know; the warnings of risk managers can get brushed aside during booms).

If there are limits to the extent that it is possible to lessen the social cost of bankruptcy by a reversion to unlimited liability, for shareholders or bank executives, then it may be possible to do so by increasing the ratio of equity to debt, i.e. reducing leverage, thereby allowing a larger proportion of any loss to be internalized. Moreover, the understandably famous Modigliani–Miller theorem (Modigliani and Miller 1958) states that, under some carefully structured assumptions, the value of a firm should be independent of its capital (liability) structure. The basic intuition is that, as equity capital increases proportionality, the risk premium on debt should fall away *pari passu*.

One reason why this does not happen is that debt is deductible for tax, so a shift from debt to equity gives up a tax wedge. While the tax advantages of debt are occasionally reconsidered—it was once mooted that the UK shadow chancellor was thinking along these lines—the international disadvantages of doing so unilaterally would be overwhelming, and there is no likelihood of this being enacted at an international level. The other main reasons for debt to be seen as more advantageous are that the benefits of avoiding bankruptcy costs are social (external) rather than internalized *and* that the implicit, or explicit, provision of safety nets for TBTF intermediaries, e.g. in the guise of liquidity and solvency support, guarantees and outright insurance, are not yet priced.

This leads on to three (at least), not mutually exclusive, considerations. First, since the benefits of greater equity, in avoiding bankruptcies in TBTF intermediaries, are mostly social while the costs are private, society has the right to impose regulations, e.g. on capital, liquidity and margins, that should make the possibility of bankruptcy more remote. Such regulation is reviewed in the next section. Second, since part of the problem is that the generalized insurance provided to TBTF intermediaries is not priced, a (partial) solution would be to price the risk of such insurance having to be provided, by having a specific risk premium levied. Such a response took a giant step forward when President Obama proposed a specific tax on banks in January 2010. To be sure this was only in small part risk-related, and was to be levied on an *ex post*, not an *ex ante*, basis and so was incapable of affecting behavioural incentives. Even so, it opened the door to a consideration of how a more careful assessment of how a risk-related *ex ante* tax/levy might be designed.

A major objection to this line of attack is that bureaucrats and regulators will *never* be able to price risk appropriately, so TBTF intermediaries will always engage in regulatory arbitrage. A suggestion put forward by Acharya *et al.* (2009, 2010) is to require the private sector to price the insurance, but who would then insure the insurers? Acharya *et al.* respond by suggesting that the private sector only provide a small percentage of such insurance, say 5%: large enough to get them to do the exercise carefully but small enough for them to absorb any resulting loss without domino contagion. Meanwhile the public sector would provide the bulk of the insurance, but at a price determined by the private sector.

The third approach is to require, or to encourage, more equity to be obtained by TBTF intermediaries—not all the time but at times of impending distress. The main version of this is the proposal to require banks to issue debt convertible into equity at times of distress, i.e. conditional convertible debt, or CoCos (Squam Lake Working Group 2009). While there has been some enthusiasm for this in principle, the details of its operation (e.g. triggers, pricing and market dynamics) still need to be worked out, and the relative advantages of CoCos compared with countercyclical macroprudential capital requirements need to be considered in more detail.

Another version of this general approach has been put forward by Hart and Zingales (2009), who suggest that, whenever a TBTF intermediary's CDS spread rises above a certain level, it should then be required to raise more equity in the market or it should be closed. This can be viewed both as another version of prompt corrective action (trying to deal with a failing TBTF intermediary *before* it runs into insolvency), the general idea of which is dealt with further in the final section of this chapter, and also as a way to require banks to obtain more capital at times of distress. The problem with this particular proposal is that, in my view, the resulting market dynamics would be disastrous. A bank breaking the trigger would be required to issue new equity at a moment when the

161

new issue market would be likely to be unreceptive, driving down equity values. That example would lower equity values, and raise CDS spreads, on all associated banks. It would, in my view, lead almost immediately to the temporary public ownership (nationalization) of almost all banks in a country.

What is surprising, to me, is the enthusiasm of so many economists to conjure up quite complex financial engineering schemes to deal with such problems when simpler and/or older remedies exist. Why not just stipulate that no TBTF intermediary can pay a dividend or raise executive compensation (on a per capita basis) when disastrous conditions prevail (Goodhart *et al.* 2010)? One problem with this is that if distress conditions are defined on an individual bank basis, it would provide even more incentive for manipulating accounting data, while, if done on an overall national basis, it would both have a differential impact on foreign vis-à-vis domestic banks *and* unfairly penalize the relatively prudent and successful banks. Perhaps an answer would be to make the requirement effective only when both of these conditions are triggered at the same time.

Another older proposal was to make the equity holder liable for a call for additional capital up to some amount, usually the par value of the share. While commonly adopted in the US in earlier years, this fell into disuse after the 1930s, having failed to avert bank failures then. Moreover, it can lead to the net present value of a share becoming negative, leading not only to a collapse in equity values but also to such equities being unloaded onto the ignorant.

What I observe (Goodhart 2010) is that Europeans tend to focus more on the first of these mechanisms for reducing the frequency and costs of TBTF and bankruptcy in the guise of financial regulations. In contrast, Americans tend to put more emphasis on the second and third mechanism, i.e. introducing and pricing insurance via some kind of market mechanism. This reflects the greater scepticism of Americans about the efficacy of bureaucratic regulation, and the greater scepticism of Europeans about the efficiency of market mechanisms.

However sceptical one may be about the efficacy of financial regulation, it is certain that one response of the recent crisis will be to tighten and to extend such regulation, and it is to this that we now turn.

5.4   TIGHTER REGULATION

Any fool can make banks safer. All that has to be done is to raise capital requirements (on risk-weighted assets) and introduce (or constrict)

Table 5.1. Annual summary statistics by period.

	Pre-World War II			Post-World War II		
	N	Mean	SD	N	Mean	SD
Δ log Money	729	0.0357	0.0566	825	0.0861	0.0552
Δ log Loans	638	0.0396	0.0880	825	0.1092	0.0738
Δ log Assets	594	0.0411	0.0648	825	0.1048	0.0678
Δ log Loans/Money	614	0.0011	0.0724	819	0.0219	0.0641
Δ log Assets/Money	562	0.0040	0.0449	817	0.0182	0.0595

'Money' denotes broad money. 'Loans' denotes total bank loans. 'Assets' denotes total bank assets. The sample runs from 1870 to 2008. War and aftermath periods are excluded (1914–19 and 1939–47), as is the post-World War I German crisis (1920–25). The fourteen countries in the sample are the US, Canada, Australia, Denmark, France, Germany, Italy, Japan, the Netherlands, Norway, Spain, Sweden and the UK.

leverage ratios, reestablish appropriate liquidity ratios and apply higher margins to leveraged transactions, such as mortgage borrowing (i.e. loan-to-value (LTV) and/or loan-to-income (LTI) ratios). Why, then, have our banks and other systemic financial intermediaries not been made safer already? Is this just foolish oversight? The problem is that there is a cost to regulation; it puts banks into a less profitable, less preferred position in their activities as intermediaries. Their previous preferred position may well have been partially due to receiving rents from the underpricing of social insurance to TBTF intermediaries. But even so, if such rents are removed, either by regulation or by pricing such risks, bank intermediation will become less profitable. If so, such intermediation will become considerably more expensive, i.e. higher bid–ask spreads, and less of it will be done. Moreover, bank lending will continue to contract and a creditless recovery then becomes more likely, as the IMF has warned (Cardarelli *et al.* 2009).

Many of the problems in our financial system have arisen because the trend growth of lending (credit expansion) has decisively exceeded the trend growth in retail bank deposits in recent decades (see table 1 of Schularick and Taylor (2009, p. 6), part of which is reproduced in our table 5.1).

This has induced banks to respond in three main ways.

(i) By replacing safe public-sector debt with riskier private-sector assets.

(ii) By augmenting retail deposits with wholesale funding, with the latter often at a very short maturity because it is both cheaper and easier to obtain whenever markets get nervous.

    (iii) By originating to distribute, thereby securitizing an increasing proportion of new lending.

The danger posed to leveraged intermediaries from illiquidity is becoming increasingly well understood. Failure then arises from a combination of concern about ultimate solvency, which prevents other ways of raising new funds in the market, *and* illiquidity, the inability to pay bills coming due, which finally pushes institutions that are at risk over the edge. In a comparison of failing and more successful banks over the course of the recent crisis (IMF 2009), capital ratios, in the period immediately preceding the crisis, did *not* show any significant difference! This suggests, but certainly does not prove, that the older (pre-1970s and pre-global finance) penchant for putting much more weight on liquidity ratios, and perhaps slightly less on capital ratios, might be sensible.

There is a counterargument, advanced by Willem Buiter (2008). This is that any asset is liquid if the central bank will lend against it. But the central bank can lend against anything. So long as the central bank takes an expansive approach to its own role as Lender of Last Resort, there should be no need for specific liquidity requirements. Interestingly, Buiter (2009) more recently came up with an entirely contrary argument, following Marvin Goodfriend (2009), that the central bank should restrict its operations to dealing in public-sector debt because of the quasi-fiscal implications of dealing in private-sector assets. I do not endorse this view either, but it does raise the point that operations (whether outright purchases or lending against collateral) in private-sector debt with narrower and more volatile markets, and hence less certain valuation, do raise the question of what price and terms should be offered by the central bank. Terms that are too generous provide a subsidy to the banks, and a potential cost and danger to both the central bank and the taxpayer. Terms that are too onerous would not help the banks or encourage much additional liquidity injection. The advantage of having banks hold a larger buffer of public-sector debt is that it both finesses the problem for the central bank of pricing its liquidity support *and* provides all concerned with more time to plan their recovery strategy.

A liquidity *requirement* is an oxymoron. If you have to continue to hold an asset to meet a requirement, it is not liquid. What is needed is a buffer, not a minimum requirement. There is a story of a traveller arriving at a station late at night, who is overjoyed to see one taxi remaining. She hails it, only for the taxi driver to respond that he cannot help her, since local by-laws require one taxi to be present at the station at all times! If the approach towards making banks safer is primarily through some form of insurance premium, a pricing mechanism (Perotti and Suarez 2009), then the levy imposed on the TBTF intermediary can be an inverse function of its liquidity ratio (possibly amongst other determinants). If the mechanism is to be external regulation, then the objective should be to ensure that it acts as a buffer, not a minimum. That should involve quite a high 'fully satisfactory' level with a carefully considered ladder of sanctions as the liquidity ratio becomes increasingly impaired. Devising a ladder of sanctions is essential and much more critical than the arbitrary choice of a satisfactory level at which to aim. It was the prior failure of the BCBS to appreciate this crucial point that vitiated much of their earlier work.

To recapitulate, there is a trade-off between the extent and degree of regulation on banks, to make them safer, and their capacity to intermediate between lenders and borrowers, particularly their ability to generate credit flows on acceptable terms to potential borrowers. One possible way to combine a smaller/safer banking system with a larger flow of credit is to restart securitization: the practice of originating to distribute. A problem with this latter is that it largely depended on trust that credit qualities were guaranteed by the ratings agencies, by due diligence undertaken by the originators and by the liquidity enhancement and support of the parent bank. Without that trust, the duplication of information can be horrendously expensive. The attempt to restore trust, notably in due diligence, by requiring banks to hold a (vertical) share of all tranches in a securitized product can make the whole exercise less attractive to potential originators. So, the market for securitization remains becalmed.

Thus, the ability of our financial system to generate credit growth well in excess of deposit growth may be at an end, at a time when deposit growth itself may slow. Phasing the new regulation in gradually over some transitional period may do little more than prolong the adjustment. Quite how the financial system, and the broader economy, will adjust to this is far from clear. What is more worrying is that in the rush to re-regulate and to 'bash the bankers', far too few participants are thinking about such structural problems.

Such structural problems are not, alas, the only ones facing regulators. We turn to some of these next.

5.5 THE BORDER PROBLEMS

There are several generic problems connected with financial regulation. Amongst them, two perennial problems are connected with the existence of important, but porous, borders or boundaries. The first such boundary is that between regulated and non-regulated (or less regulated) entities, where the latter can provide a (partial) substitute for the services of the former. The second, key, border is that between states, where the legal system and regulatory system differs from state to state.

I have dealt with the first boundary problem at some length in Goodhart (2008) and in an appendix to Brunnermeier *et al.* (2009). Forgive me for reproducing a few paragraphs of this here.

> In particular if regulation is effective, it will constrain the regulated from achieving their preferred, unrestricted, position, often by lowering their profitability and their return on capital. So the returns achievable within the regulated sector are likely to fall relative to those available on substitutes outside. There will be a switch of business from the regulated to the non-regulated sector. In order to protect their own businesses, those in the regulated sector will seek to open up connected operations in the non-regulated sector, in order to catch the better opportunities there. The example of commercial banks setting up associated conduits, SIVs [structured investment vehicles] and hedge funds in the last credit bubble is a case in point.
>
> But this condition is quite general. One of the more common proposals, at least in the past, for dealing with the various problems of financial regulation has been to try to limit deposit insurance and the safety net to a set of 'narrow banks', which would be constrained to hold only liquid and 'safe' assets. The idea is that this would provide safe deposits for the orphans and widows. Moreover, these narrow banks would run a clearing-house and keep the payments' system in operation, whatever happened elsewhere. For all other financial institutions outside the narrow banking system, it would be a case of 'caveat emptor'. They should be allowed to fail, without official support or taxpayer recapitalization.
>
> In fact, in the UK something akin to a narrow banking system *was* put in place in the 19th century with the Post Office Savings Bank [POSB] and the Trustee Savings Bank [TSB]. But the idea that the official safety net should have been restricted to POSB and TSB was never seriously entertained. Nor could it have been. When a 'narrow bank' is constrained to holding liquid, safe assets, it is simultaneously prevented from earning higher returns, and thus from offering as high interest rates, or other valuable services (such as overdrafts), to its depositors. Nor could the authorities in good conscience prevent the broader banks from setting up their own clearing house. Thus the banking system outside the narrow banks would grow much faster under normal circumstances; it would provide most of the credit to the private sector, and participate in the key clearing and settlement processes in the economy.
>
> This might be prevented by law, taking legal steps to prohibit broader banks from providing means of payment or establishing clearing and

settlement systems of their own. There are, at least, four problems with such a move. First, it runs afoul of political economy consider-ations. As soon as a significant body of voters has an interest in the preservation of a class of financial intermediaries, they will demand, and receive, protection. Witness money market funds and 'breaking the buck' [i.e. not being able to repay at par, or better; so involving a net loss to deposit funds] in the US. Second, it is intrinsically illiberal. Third, it is often possible to get around such legal constraints, e.g. by having the broad bank pass all payment orders through an associated narrow bank. Fourth, the reasons for the authorities' concern with financial intermediaries, for better or worse, go well beyond insuring the maintenance of the basic payment system and the protection of small depositors. Neither Bear Stearns nor Fannie Mae had small depositors, or played an integral role in the basic payment system.

When a financial crisis does occur, it, usually, first attacks the unprotected sector, as occurred with SIVs and conduits in 2007. But the existence of the differential between the protected and unprotected sector then has the capacity to make the crisis worse. When panic and extreme risk aversion take hold, the depositors in, and creditors to, the unprotected, or weaker, sector seek to withdraw their funds, and place these in the protected, or stronger, sector, thereby redoubling the pressures on the weak and unprotected sectors, who are then forced into fire sales of assets, etc. The combination of a boundary between the protected and the unprotected, with greater constraints on the business of the regulated sector, almost guarantees a cycle of flows into the unregulated part of the system during cyclical expansions with sudden and dislocating reversals during crises.

Insofar as regulation is effective in forcing the regulated to shift from a preferred to a less desired position, it is likely to set up a boundary prob-lem. It is, therefore, a common occurrence, or response, to almost *any* regulatory imposition. A current example is the proposal to introduce additional regulatory controls on systemically important financial inter-mediaries (SIFIs). If SIFIs are to be penalized, there needs, on grounds of equity and fairness, to be some definition, some criteria, of what consti-tutes an SIFI—an exercise with considerable complication. But once such a definition is made and a clear boundary established, there will be an incentive for institutions to position themselves on one side or another of that boundary, whichever may seem more advantageous. Suppose that we started in a small country with three banks, say, each of which had a third of total deposits and each of which was regarded as TBTF, and that the definition of an SIFI was a bank with over 20% of total deposits. If each bank then split itself into two identical clones of itself, to avoid the tougher regulation, with similar portfolios and interbank linkages, would there have been much progress? Similarity implies contagion. Indeed, regulation tends to encourage and to foster similarity in behaviour. Does it then follow that regulation thereby enhances the dangers of systemic collapse that its purpose should be to prevent? Does the desire to encourage all the regulated to adopt, and to harmonize on, the behaviour of the 'best' actually endanger the resilience of the system as a whole?

The second boundary of critical importance to the conduct of regulation is the border between states, each with their own legal and regulatory structures: the cross-border problem. In a global financial system with (relatively) free movement of capital across borders, most financial transactions that are originated in one country can be executed in another. This means that any constraint, or tax, that is imposed on a financial transaction in a country can often be (easily) avoided by transferring that same transaction to take place under the legal, tax and accounting jurisdiction of another country, sometimes, indeed often, under the aegis of a subsidiary, or branch, of exactly the same bank/intermediary as was involved in the initial country.

This tends to generate a race for the bottom, though not always since the parties to a contract will prize legal certainty and contract reliability. Another aspect of this same syndrome is the call for 'a level playing field'. Any state which seeks to impose, unilaterally, tougher regulation than that in operation in some other country will face the accusation that the effect of the regulation will just be to benefit foreign competition with little, or no, restraining effect on the underlying transactions.

Moreover, the cross-border concern may constrain the application of countercyclical regulation. Financial cycles—booms and busts—differ in their intensity from country to country. Housing prices rose much more in Australia, Ireland, Spain, the UK and the US than in Canada, Germany and Japan in the period 2002–7. Bank credit expansion also differed considerably between countries. But if regulation becomes countercyclically tightened in the boom countries, will that not, in a global financial system, just lead to a transfer of such transactions offshore. Indeed, London has been at the centre of arranging such cross-border financial operations.

5.6 ARE THERE SOLUTIONS?

Perhaps the greatest need is for a fundamental change in the way that we all, but especially regulators and supervisors, *think* about the purposes and operation of financial regulation, i.e. a paradigm shift. The old idea was that the purpose of regulation was to stop individual institutions assuming excessive risk, and that the way to do this was to encourage, or force, all institutions (banks) to harmonize on 'best practices' by *requiring* them to hold the appropriate ratios of capital, or liquidity, or whatever.

It is the thesis of this chapter that this approach has been fundamentally misguided along several dimensions. First, it should *not* be the role of the regulator/supervisor to seek to limit the risks taken by the individual institution, so long as those risks are properly internalized. The concern instead should be on externalities, i.e. limiting the extent to which adverse developments facing one actor in the financial system can lead to greater problems for other actors. Various methodologies for measuring, and then counteracting, such externalities—such as CoVar, expected shortfall, CIMDO—are being developed, but much more needs to be done.[2]

Second, the attempt to limit such externalities should not be done by a process of setting minimum required ratios, whether for capital, liquidity or even, perhaps, for margins more generally. There are two main reasons why not. First, that process sterilizes, and makes unusable, the intra-marginal capital or liquidity. Second, no one can ever correctly determine what the 'correct' level of such a safeguard should be, and effort and time gets wasted in trying to do so. Instead, much more thought needs to be put into devising a (preferably continuous) ladder of penalties, whether pecuniary, e.g. in the form of a tax, or non-pecuniary, in the form of prohibitions of increasing severity on the freedom of action of an intermediary as its capital, liquidity and margins decrease and its leverage increases.

One purpose of having a more continuous function of sanctions is that it might be possible to apply the regulation over a wider range of intermediaries, and thus avoid the boundary problem between the regulated and non-regulated. Thus, all (leveraged) financial intermediaries would fall under the regulations—small as well as large banks, and hedge funds and money markets mutual funds as well as banks—but so long as the leveraged institution was small, with few counterparties amongst other financial intermediaries (i.e. not interconnected), with low leverage and satisfactory liquidity, it should not suffer any penalties. The more that a leveraged institution became a risky 'shadow bank', the greater the penalty (against the risk of externalities and thus imposing costs on society) that should be applied. It will involve a considerable effort to try to

---

[2] This branch of analysis includes the 'CoVaR' of Brunnermeier and Pedersen (2009) and Adrian and Brunnermeier (2009); the 'systemic expected shortfall' of Acharya *et al.* (2010); and the 'CIMDO' of Segoviano (2006, 2010) and Segoviano and Goodhart (2009). See also IMF (2009, chapter 3).

recast regulation along such lines, but it could be one way of overcoming the boundary problem between the regulated and the non-regulated.

Incidentally, John Kay's 'narrow banks' and Larry Kotlikoff's all-equity-based financial intermediaries would, under this rubric, face no, or very few, penalties or sanctions, whereas there would be increasing penalties/sanctions as intermediaries took on increasingly risky strategies, where the ladder of penalties/sanctions should be calibrated to relate to the additional risk to society. While such calibration is surely hard to do, this would be preferable to leaving all such 'risky' intermediation either completely unregulated or banned entirely. Neither of these approaches would be sensible, or desirable.

In order to limit and control systemic risk, supervisors have to be able to identify it. That requires greater transparency. That is one reason, but not the only one, for requiring standardized derivative deals to be put through a centralized counterparty, and for requiring that remaining over-the-counter (OTC) transactions be reported to, and recorded by, a centralized data repository. Similarly, it would be desirable to simplify and increase the transparency of securitizations. Reliance on credit ratings was a means for enabling buyers in the past to disregard much (legal) detail. In this field, the credit rating agencies have, for the time being, lost their reputation, even if in the exercise of sovereign debt rating their clout now seems stronger than ever!

However many incentives may be provided for more prudent behaviour, failures and insolvencies will still occur. As noted earlier, the occasions of such a bankruptcy is the main source of social risk and reliance on taxpayers. So the need is to try, first to limit and to prevent bankruptcy, and second to lessen its social ramifications should it occur, e.g. by internalizing losses.

In addition to the objective of controlling externalities, social risk and the need for reliance on taxpayers, there is also, as already noted in section 5.2, a rationale for some additional regulation based on asymmetric information and customer protection. It is largely, though not entirely, under this latter rubric that proposals such as 'product regulation' and 'deposit insurance' take their place. We will not discuss these further here, since both the difficulties of applying such regulation and the overall costs of regulatory failure are much less severe than in the case of macroprudential regulation.

Considerable weight had been placed by many economists on the concept of prompt corrective action (PCA) as a means of lessening the costs of failure. This had been incorporated into the FDIC Improvement Act of 1991, whereby any bank that was severely undercapitalized, under 2% (i.e. a leverage ratio greater than fifty), either had to raise more equity rapidly or be closed, with the aim of doing so before there was a burden of losses to be somehow shared.

Yet this did not prevent the crisis in the US—though the main initial failures (Fannie Mae, Lehman, AIG) occurred in intermediaries to which such PCA was not applicable. Even so, PCA was less effective than had been hoped. In crises the estimated residual value of equity can erode fast; and, prior to the final collapse, may be manipulated by accounting dodges (such as the Repo 105 used by Lehman Brothers). *In extremis*, liquidity may be a better, or even more desirable supplementary, trigger than capital.

A widespread complaint has been that too little of the losses suffered have been internalized amongst bond holders and transferred to taxpayers instead, thereby increasing externalities and social cost. But we need to remind ourselves why this was done. This was because many such bondholders were either themselves leveraged intermediaries—such as the Reserve Primary Fund, whose 'breaking of the buck' unleashed the run on money-market mutual funds—or had sufficient power (the Chinese?) to threaten to withdraw funds massively from this market, thereby unleashing an even worse disaster. Contagion was therefore as much an issue amongst bondholders as it was amongst depositors.

One conclusion is that if losses cannot, in the event of a financial crisis, be internalized amongst either bondholders or depositors, then banks should be induced and encouraged (note: by a continuous ladder of penalties, not by a required minimum) to hold more tangible core equity. Another approach is to precommit, e.g. by contract, to make bond holders face equity-type losses in a crisis. This is one of the purposes of the proposed conditional contingent bonds (CoCos) which are to be forcibly transmuted into equity format under certain triggers of distress. As with ordinary bank bonds, this could lead to contagion if such CoCos were held by other levered financial intermediaries. Even without such contagion, the relative cost and the market dynamics of such CoCos in a crisis have yet to be clearly observed. Moreover, the extent to which their use would be preferable to the simpler procedure of encouraging more equity holding, perhaps in countercyclical format, has yet to be fully worked out.

One important way of diminishing both the probability and the cost of failure is to get the levered institution and its supervisor(s) to plan for such adverse eventualities in advance. This is the purpose of the concept of the 'living will', or special resolution regime (SRR), which has obtained (and rightly so) much traction recently as a desirable initiative in the field of financial regulation. Such a living will has two parts (see Huertas 2010a,b,c). The first part consists of a recovery plan, which outlines how, in the face of a real crisis, a leveraged institution could bolster its liquidity and its capital, for example by disposing of non-core assets, so as to remain an ongoing business. This could be agreed between an institution and its lead (home) supervisor, though there would be implications for host supervisors.

The second part of a living will involves planning for the resolution of a failing financial institution should the recovery plan be insufficient. In this case the supervisor(s) may *require* the financial institution to take certain preparatory actions, for example to maintain a data room (that would enable an outside liquidator/administrator to have sufficient knowledge of the current condition of a financial intermediary to wind it down) and, perhaps, to simplify its legal structure, for the same purpose. But the agreement on how to resolve the intermediary, and to share out residual losses, would need to be amongst its regulators/supervisors.

Even within a single country, many intermediaries, particularly large 'universal' ones, may have several supervisors, and each should know their role in advance. But almost all SIFIs have significant cross-border activities, and, while they may be international in life, they become national in death. Indeed, some of the worst complications and outcomes following bankruptcy arose from the difficulties of international resolution, notably in the cases of Lehman, the Icelandic banks, Fortis and Dexia.

Avgouleas *et al.* (2010) have suggested building on the concept of living wills in order to develop an internationally agreed legal bankruptcy procedure for SIFIs, but, given the entrenched preferences in each country for their historically determined legal traditions and customs, this may well be utopian. Instead Hüpkes (2009a,b) has proposed that, for each SIFI, an international resolution procedure be adopted on a case-by-case basis.

Such a procedure might, or might not, also include an *ex ante* burden-sharing agreement (Goodhart and Schoenmaker 2006). Apart from the difficulty of doing so, arguments against are that attempts would be made, *ex post*, to renegotiate; that the prior agreement might seem unfair or inappropriate in unforeseeable circumstances, and that it might involve moral hazard. While this last claim is often made—so long as the executives, who actually take the decision, are sacked whether or not the entity is kept as a going concern—it can be overstated. The arguments for such an *ex ante* exercise is that, without it, uncoordinated and costly failure and closures will be much more likely (Freixas 2003).

More generally, financial globalization in general, and the cross-border activities of SIFIs in particular, mean that the level-playing-field argument is advanced to oppose almost any unilateral regulatory initiative. The main response to this, of course, is to try to reach international agreement, and a whole structure of institutions and procedures has been established to try to take this forward with varying degrees of success. Inevitably, and perhaps properly, this is a slow process. Those who claimed that we were losing the potential momentum of the crisis for reforming financial regulation simply had no feel for the mechanics of the process. Moreover, any of the major financial countries, perhaps some three or four countries, can effectively veto any proposal that they do not like, so again the agreements will tend to represent the lowest common denominator, again perhaps desirably so.

Finally, there can be circumstances and instances when a regulator can take on the level-playing-field argument and still be effective. An example can be enforcing a margin for housing LTVs by making lending for the required down payment unsecured in a court of law. Another example is when the purpose of the additional constraint is to prevent excessive leverage and risk-taking by domestic banks, rather than trying to control credit expansion more widely (as financed by foreign banks).

5.7 CONCLUSION

The current crisis has forced a fundamental reconsideration of financial regulation, and rightly so, since much of the focus, and of the effects, of the existing system were badly designed, with its concentration on individual, rather than systemic, risk and its procyclicality. In response we now have a ferment of new ideas, many of which we have touched on here. A great deal of further work needs to be done to discern which of these ideas are good and which are less so.

REFERENCES

Acharya, V., L. H. Pedersen, T. Philippon and M. Richardson. 2009. Measuring systemic risk. Stern School of Business, New York University Working Paper.
Acharya, V., L. H. Pedersen, T. Philippon and M. Richardson. 2010. A tax on systemic risk. Stern School of Business, New York University Working Paper.
Acharya, V., and M. Richardson (eds). 2009. *Restoring Financial Stability: How to Repair a Failed System.* John Wiley & Sons.

Adrian, T., and M. K. Brunnermeier. 2009. CoVaR. Federal Reserve Bank of New York Staff Report 348 (August).

Adrian, T., and H. S. Shin. 2008. Liquidity, monetary policy, and financial cycles. *Current Issues in Economics and Finance* **14**(1), 1–7.

Avgouleas, E., C. Goodhart and D. Schoenmaker. 2010. Living wills as a catalyst for action. In preparation.

Bebchuk, L. A., and H. Spamann. 2010. Regulating bankers' pay. *Georgetown Law Journal* **98**(2), 247–87.

Bebchuk, L. A., and J. M. Fried. 2009. Paying for long-term performance. Harvard Law and Economics Discussion Paper 658 (1 December).

Beltratti, A., and R. M. Stulz. 2009. Why did some banks perform better during the credit crisis? A cross-country study of the impact of governance and regulation. Fisher College of Business Working Paper 2009-03-012 (13 July).

Brunnermeier, M. K., and L. H. Pedersen. 2005. Predatory trading. *Journal of Finance* **60**(4), 1825–63.

Brunnermeier, M. K., A. Crockett, C. A. E. Goodhart, A. Persaud and H. S. Shin. 2009. *The Fundamental Principles of Financial Regulation.* Geneva Reports on the World Economy, volume 11. Geneva/London: ICMB/CEPR.

Brunnermeier, M. K., and L. H. Pedersen. 2009. Market liquidity and funding liquidity. *Review of Financial Studies,* **22**(6), 2201–38.

Buiter, W. 2008. Central banks and financial crises. Financial Markets Group (LSE) Discussion Paper 619.

Buiter, W. 2009. Reversing unconventional monetary policy: technical and political considerations. Centre for Economic Policy Research Discussion Paper 7605 (December).

Cardarelli, R., S. Elekdag and S. Lall. 2009. Financial stress, downturns, and recoveries. IMF Working Paper 09/100 (May).

Chamley, C., and L. Kotlikoff. 2009. Toolbox: limited purpose banking. *American Interest Online* (1 April).

Danielsson, J. 2002. The emperor has no clothes: limits to risk modelling. *Journal of Banking and Finance* **26**, 1252–72.

Fahlenbrach, R., and R. M. Stulz. 2009. Bank CEO incentives and the credit crisis. National Bureau of Economic Research Working Paper 15212.

Ferguson, N., and L. Kotlikoff. 2009. Reducing banking's moral hazard. *Financial Times* (2 December).

Freixas, X. 2003. Crisis management in Europe. In *Financial Supervision in Europe* (ed. J. Kremers, D. Schoenmaker and P. Wierts), pp. 102–19. Cheltenham: Edward Elgar.

IMF. 2009. Responding to the financial crisis and measuring systemic risks. In *Global Financial Stability Report* (April).

Goodfriend, M. 2009. Central banking in the credit turmoil: an assessment of Federal Reserve practice. Paper presented at the 'Monetary–Fiscal Policy Interactions, Expectations, and Dynamics in the Current Economic Crisis' conference, 22–23 May, Princeton University, Princeton, NJ.

Goodhart, C. A. E. 2008. The boundary problem in financial regulation. *National Institute Economic Review* **206**(1), 48–55.

Goodhart, C. A. E. 2010. The role of macro-prudential supervision. Paper presented at the 'Up From the Ashes: The Financial System after the Crisis' conference of the Federal Reserve Bank of Atlanta, 11–12 May.

Goodhart, C. A. E., M. U. Peiris, D. P. Tsomocos and A. P. Vardoulakis. 2010. On dividend restrictions and the collapse of the interbank market. *Annals of Finance*, in press.

Goodhart, C. A. E., and D. Schoenmaker. 2006. Burden sharing in a banking crisis in Europe. *Sveriges Riksbank Economic Review* **2**, 34–57.

Goodman, J. C., and L. Kotlikoff. 2009. The only way Obama can fix the economy is by changing the way banks do business. *The New Republic* (14 May).

Hart, O. D., and L. Zingales. 2009. A new capital regulation for large financial institutions. Centre for Economic Policy Research Discussion Paper DP7298.

Hellwig, M. 1996. Adequacy rules as instruments for the regulation of banks. *Swiss Journal of Economics and Statistics* **132**(4), 609–12.

Hellwig, M. 2008. Systemic risk in the financial sector: an analysis of the subprime-mortgage financial crisis. Max Planck Institute for Research on Collective Goods (November). (Also published in *De Economist* **157**(2), 129–207 (June 2009).)

House of Commons, Treasury Select Committee. 2010. Too important to fail—too important to ignore. Ninth Report of Session 2009–10, volume 1, HC 261-1 (29 March).

Huertas, T. F. 2010a. Improving bank capital structures. Speech at London School of Economics (18 January).

Huertas, T. F. 2010b. Living wills: how can the concept be implemented? Remarks at the 'Cross-Border Issues in Resolving Systemically Important Financial Institutions' conference, Wharton School of Management, University of Pennsylvania, 12 February.

Huertas, T. F. 2010c. Resolution and contagion. Remarks at the 'Sources of Contagion' conference, Centre for Central Banking Studies/Financial Markets Group, 26 February.

Hüpkes, E. 2009a. Bank insolvency: the last frontier. In *Towards a New Framework for Financial Stability* (ed. D. Mayes, R. Pringle and M. Taylor). London: Risk Books.

Hüpkes, E. 2009b. Complicity in complexity: what to do about the 'too-big-to-fail' problem. *Journal of International Banking and Financial Law* **24**(9), 515–18.

IMF. 2009. Detecting systemic risk. In *Global Financial Stability Report: Responding to the Financial Crisis and Measuring Systemic Risks*, chapter 3 (April).

Kay, J. 2010. Narrow banking. *World Economics* **11**(1), 1–10.

Kotlikoff, L., and E. Leamer. 2009. A banking system we can trust. *Forbes* (23 April).

Modigliani, F., and M. Miller. 1958. The cost of capital, corporation finance and the theory of investment. *American Economic Review* **48**(3), 261–97.

Perotti, E., and J. Suarez. 2009. Liquidity insurance for systemic crises. Centre for Economic Policy Research Policy Insight 31.

Record, N. 2010. How to make the bankers share the losses. *Financial Times* (6 January).

Schularick, M., and A. M. Taylor. 2009. Credit booms gone bust: monetary policy, leverage cycles and financial crises, 1870–2008. National Bureau of Economic Research Working Paper 15512 (November).

Segoviano, M. 2006. Consistent information multivariate density optimizing methodology. Financial Markets Group (LSE) Discussion Paper 557.

Segoviano, M. 2010. The CIMDO-copula. Robust estimation of default dependence under data restrictions. IMF Working Paper.

Segoviano, M., and C. Goodhart. 2009. Banking stability measures. IMF Working Paper 09/04.

Shleifer, A. 2010. Efficient regulation. National Bureau of Economic Research Working Paper w15651 (January).

Squam Lake Working Group. 2009. An expedited resolution mechanism for distressed financial firms: regulatory hybrid securities. Squam Lake Working Group on Financial Regulation Paper.

Squam Lake Working Group. 2010. Regulation of executive compensation in financial services. Squam Lake Working Group on Financial Regulation Paper.

CHAPTER SIX

Can We Identify Bubbles and Stabilize the System?

By Andrew Smithers

In addition to low inflation, central banks must aim to avoid major recessions. They must therefore seek to moderate bubbles, because asset prices are an important transmission mechanism whereby changes in interest rates affect demand in the real economy. Interest rate changes move the prices of assets away from fair value, but their impact is ephemeral. If bubbles are allowed to form, they will break and asset prices will continue to fall even if interest rates decline sharply. Central banks are then unable to stimulate demand. The severe recessions that result require, as we have recently seen, large fiscal stimuli. The recessions are damaging and the deficits reduce our ability to cope with future crises. At present there is no adequate institutional structure for monitoring the asset bubbles and financial excesses and for taking action to moderate them. The government's proposed creation of such a structure is thus essential and welcome.

6.1 THE GREAT MODERATION—THE LIGHT THAT FAILED

We must avoid recurrent crises. To do this we must focus on asset prices as well as on the prices of goods and services. In the years leading up to the recent financial crisis, the mandates and attention of central bankers have largely concentrated on policies designed to achieve low and stable inflation. Two important assumptions widely embraced then are seldom held today. The first was that macroeconomic and financial stability were expected to follow simply from the actions of central banks in maintaining low and stable consumer price inflation through changes in short-term interest rates. The second assumption was that demand weakness resulting from a collapse in asset prices could be readily offset by easing monetary policy. Asset prices were, therefore, not thought to be a matter of concern to central bankers[1] and this complacent view was probably

---

[1] As an example of the view widely held at the time that central bankers should focus solely on the narrow aim of targeting inflation, see Bernanke and Gertler (1999).

encouraged by the thought that both asset prices and economic stability were being seen as 'someone else's problem' (SEP).[2]

Given this background it is not surprising that it has been the usual practice that neither central banks, nor any other body, have had specific responsibility for systemic stability.[3] The attitudes and beliefs that lay behind this lacuna included an economic theory (the efficient market hypothesis), which attributed an efficiency to financial markets far in excess of that assumed for the real economy; a confusion between possible systemic risks in finance with the individual ones, which were the concern of microprudential bodies such as the Federal Deposit Insurance Corporation, the Office of the Comptroller of the Currency and the Securities and Exchange Commission in the US and the Financial Services Authorities in Japan and the UK, and the usual human instinct to avoid raising difficult issues over dormant problems.

Before our recent troubles, both the view that central banks should not be concerned with asset prices and the economic theories that backed it was probably the majority view among economists, as Stephen Wright and I acknowledged when proposing the opposite (Smithers and Wright 2002). Seven years later, however, it seemed reasonable to write that it was then quite hard to find economists who disagreed with the view that central banks needed to be concerned with asset prices, though I attributed the change of heart to events rather than advocacy (Smithers 2009).

6.2 THE CONSEQUENCES OF DISILLUSION

We are now moving into the next stage of the debate. Macroeconomic stability has become a major concern and it is generally accepted that it will not be ensured simply by maintaining low and stable inflation. If central banks, or another policy body, are to 'lean rather than clean' (see White 2009), the existing policy framework must be changed with new and clear mandates given to those responsible. Even if the terms of reference for central banks already include duties beyond attempts to target consumer prices, they will lack legitimacy without new specific legislation to refine their tasks and possibly to add new policy weapons to their armoury. In addition to the need for enlarged responsibilities

---

[2]In *The Hitchhiker's Guide to the Galaxy* by Douglas Adams the presence of a large spaceship occupying Lord's cricket ground during a test match was not observed by the spectators because it was surrounded by a strong SEP field.

[3]For example, the Bank of England Act of 1998 did not include macroeconomic or financial stability among the central bank's concerns.

for central banks, it is necessary to consider whether other steps need to be taken which would reduce the threat to the real economy and to taxpayers which are currently posed by financial turmoil.

We now see signs of an emerging consensus, which holds that

(i) consumer price stability is not enough to achieve macroeconomic or financial stability;

(ii) but it remains of vital importance for their achievement;

(iii) additional steps are therefore needed to mitigate the risks of major recessions;

(iv) these often follow from asset bubbles and financial crashes;

(v) a new policy framework is needed to resolve these issues.

Underlying this marked change in the consensus has been a change in its intellectual backing, away from theory to a more pragmatic foundation. Because of real and perceived weaknesses, economics is held in less respect than formerly. In part this arises from a paradigm shift. The efficient market hypothesis has had a dominant influence, particularly in financial economics. While it has never been universally embraced and its critics are now in the ascendant, no generally accepted alternative has yet been put in its place. We are therefore in the middle of a paradigm shift, with a consequent lack of an agreed theoretical framework for much of the discussion.

The pragmatic issues are, nonetheless, reasonably clear. Drawing on our recent experience and from previous major financial crises, it is vital that steps are taken to mitigate the incidence and severity of future crises.

(i) We should seek to reduce the risks of major recessions, such as that from which we are currently recovering.

(ii) We should seek to reduce the risks of prolonged sub-optimal growth, which has been the legacy of Japan's 1990 bubble.

(iii) We should seek to reduce the costs of financial crises to future taxpayers, such as those that have been imposed by the dramatic rise in national debt/GDP and fiscal deficits since 2000, or in Japan since 1990. These have placed a far greater burden on future taxpayers than the costs involved with bailing out bankrupt institutions.

The fundamental aim boils down to the standard economic objective of improving welfare. It does not necessarily imply faster growth. Welfare should rise through the reduction in the volatility of output, with its associated uncertainty. This will be achieved if the long-term growth in output is maintained with less volatility. On *a priori* grounds the reduction in uncertainty, with the lower required returns on capital that should follow, suggests that lower volatility is more likely to contribute to growth than impede it. Furthermore, a more detailed and less aggregated view of economic welfare, which involved such issues as the pain involved in long-term unemployment, would also add weight to the benefits to be derived from lower economic volatility. Avoiding large swings in output is therefore a sensible objective. Long periods of uninterrupted growth may well increase the risks of major recessions, so it should be recognized that avoiding them probably has the minor cost of requiring more frequent small recessions.

There are a wide variety of measures which could contribute to avoiding, or at least mitigating, major crises. Several of these are the subject of other chapters, such as encouraging safer and smaller financial institutions, perhaps through higher equity ratios escalating with size; others which are potentially important but outside the scope of our discussion include tax[4] and legal reforms. This chapter concentrates on using macroeconomic policy to dampen asset and credit bubbles.

6.3 THE BLAME GAME

Suggesting that macroeconomic policy can be used to moderate future crises implies that poor policy has made a significant contribution to past ones and immediately raises the question, 'Who is to blame?' Those in the dock include commercial bankers, regulators and central bankers. My conclusion is that, while central bankers have made serious policy errors, their blame for these is mitigated by the lack of an appropriate structure for managing policy.

I also consider that far too much attention has been placed on ways to improve behaviour. While it is undesirable that bankers should have an incentive to behave in ways which are detrimental for the economy, it should be recognized that bankers have at least one quality in common with burglars, which is that they both make money by taking risks, not all of which contribute to social welfare. Sudden sharp rises in the incidence of risk-taking cannot sensibly be ascribed to sudden declines in the moral standards of either group, though of late this appears to have been a popular pastime with regard to bankers. Technical advances, such

---

[4]Leverage increases the risk of crises and in every major economy the corporation tax system encourages leverage by effectively subsidizing the cost of debt compared with equity finance.

as new safe-blowing equipment for burglars and new ways of avoiding regulations for bankers, are possible contributors to increased costs for the economy, but increased opportunities will invariably lead to greater activity. In my view, excess liquidity represents for bankers the not-to-be-resisted temptation that open doors and windows provide for burglars.

When seeking to avoid future crises, it is important to consider the recurring problems of major recessions and financial crises. While these have many similarities, they are not identical. Concentrating solely on the latest crisis draws excessive attention to such particular issues as international imbalances and financial innovation, which may have amplified the current problems, but which cannot explain earlier ones.[5] There may be more than one cause of crises and more than one danger signal.

6.4 ASSET PRICES

Historically, asset prices have warned of rises in systemic risk. They affect the real economy and are also an important part of the transmission process, whereby central banks influence demand. They are therefore important as signals and, when they fall sharply, they hinder the ability of central banks to support the economy. A close watch on assets' prices is thus a necessary part of any credible policy for reducing systemic risk. Three sets of prices in particular need to be monitored closely—share prices, house and land prices, and those which measure fluctuations in risk aversion by holders of debt assets.

6.5 WHY THE STOCK MARKET MATTERS

Changes in the level of share prices affect demand in the real economy. Rises reduce the cost of equity capital and are therefore likely to encourage investment, though this impact may be hard to distinguish from the psychological effect on business confidence. By raising the value of past savings, the need for additional savings for retirement at least appears to diminish. 'Why bother to save if the stock market does it for you?' As illustrated in figure 6.1,[6] this relationship is readily demonstrated for the

---

[5]It would be foolish not to ban smoking in petrol station forecourts on the grounds that this has not been the cause of the most recent disaster. We are not seeking to prevent the last crisis, but the next one.

[6]A clarification of some of the sources for figures in this chapter: 'NIPA' is the National Income and Product Accounts, which are published by the US Bureau of Economic Analysis, and 'Z1' is the Flow of Funds Accounts of the US, which are published by the Federal Reserve.

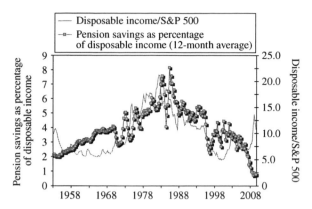

Figure 6.1. Pension savings and the stock market in the US. Correlation coefficient 0.66.

Sources: NIPA (table 2.1); Z1 (table F.100); S&P 500.

US. Pension savings have contributed on average around 50% of the total savings of the household sector and have risen when the stock market has fallen and then fallen again when it has risen.

It has been shown that stock prices respond in an ephemeral way to changes in interest rates, but that there is no long-term relationship between interest rates and share prices.[7] I show that equity prices are mean reverting around fair value and the more they exceed it, the greater is the risk that they will fall whether or not interest rates are also declining. Collapsing equity asset bubbles thus disrupt the transmission mechanism, whereby central banks affect the real economy

The value of the stock market can be measured either by q (market value/net worth of non-financials adjusted for inflation), or by the cyclically adjusted price/earnings ratio ('CAPE'). These metrics are testable and agree. Figure 6.3 illustrates both the agreement and the ability to satisfy one test—that of mean reversion. Figure 6.4 illustrates their ability to satisfy another test, which is that they are able to forecast, albeit weakly, future returns. When we have enough data, such as the next thirty years of returns, we can rank years in the past by the average returns they gave to investors over the next one to thirty years. Years which gave good returns were clearly those in which the market was relatively cheap and vice versa. We can then compare these 'hindsight values' with the value measured by q and CAPE. Figure 6.4 shows how well these hindsight values, derived

---

[7]Figure 6.2 illustrates the ephemeral nature of the relationship between interest rates and share prices. For a fuller explanation, see the third appendix in Smithers (2009), which was written by James Mitchell.

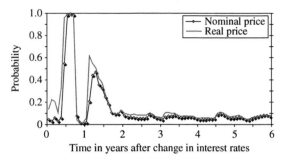

Figure 6.2. The probability that interest rate changes affect share price changes in the US. Data 1871–2007.

Source: Smithers & Co. calculations.

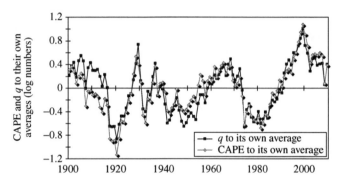

Figure 6.3. US stock market value.

Sources: Shiller, Wright and Fed Z1 (table B.102).

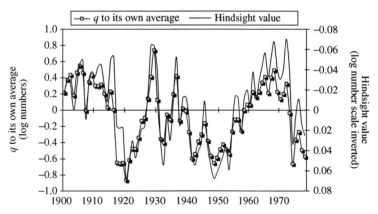

Figure 6.4. Testing: US *q* compared with hindsight value.

Sources: Wright, Fed Z1 (table B.102) and Shiller.

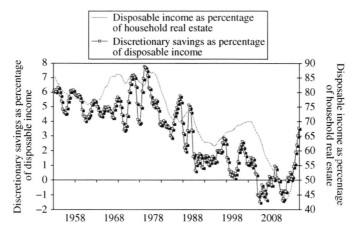

Figure 6.5. Household 'discretionary' savings and value of real estate in the US. Correlation coefficient 0.86.

Sources: NIPA (table 2.1), Z1 (tables B.100 and F.100).

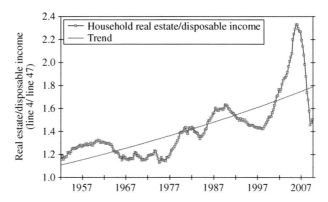

Figure 6.6. Housing affordability in the US.

Source: Z1 (table B.100).

from subsequent returns, fit with past values derived from q (similar though slightly less good results are shown if CAPE is used).[8]

6.6 HOUSE PRICES

There is a close parallel between the influence of house prices on the economy with that shown by equities. The impact of movements in house

---

[8]For a fuller account of these metrics of stock market value and the tests for their validity see Smithers (2009).

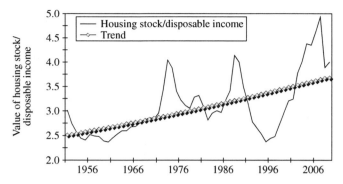

Figure 6.7. Housing affordability in the UK (the level and recent rise in house prices looks unsustainable).

Sources: housing stock from the Office of the Deputy Prime Minister to 1987 linked to ONS CGLK and updated for house prices for 2009 Q1. Disposable income ONS QWND.

prices on savings is very similar to the impact that movements in share prices have, as we illustrate in figure 6.5. House prices also appear to rotate around an equilibrium level and their over or undervaluation can be ascertained by reference to real incomes,[9] as illustrated in figures 6.6 and 6.7.

It also seems likely that short-term interest rates seem to have an ephemeral impact on house prices.[10]

6.7 FLUCTUATIONS IN RISK AVERSION BY HOLDERS OF DEBT ASSETS

The value of debt assets responds to three variables, which are the level of riskless interest rates of different durations, the default risk and the variable return that investors require from sacrificing liquidity. (The relative liquidity of an asset depends on the extent to which its price changes under the impact of transactions. The price of a highly liquid asset will change much less when, say, £1,000,000 is sold, than when a less liquid asset is sold.) It is possible to measure the 'compensation for illiquidity' by measuring differences in the return to debt assets of differing liquidity but otherwise similar characteristics, such as default risk and duration. One approach to this (Webber and Churm 2007) shows that the compensation for illiquidity has varied in a similar, but not identical,

---

[9]See Holly *et al.* (2010): 'This allows us to find a cointegrating relationship between real house prices and real per capita incomes.'

[10]This seems to have been accepted, albeit with some reluctance, by Bernanke in his AEA speech of 3 January 2010.

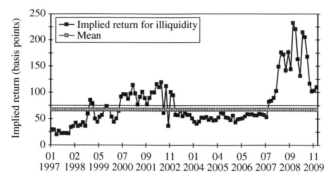

Figure 6.8. Risk aversion implied from investment grade bonds in the US. *Source*: Bank of England (updated).

way to concerns about default and often by as much as those concerns. I illustrate in figure 6.8 the compensation for illiquidity calculated by this approach for US investment grade bonds. Over the admittedly limited time for which we have the data, the figure shows that the compensation for illiquidity was well below average in 1997 and 1998 and again from 2004 to 2007.

A low return from the loss of liquidity is a clear sign that risk aversion is unusually low. In these circumstances banks are particularly vulnerable. When risk aversion rises, the value of debt of any given duration will fall and, as liquidity falls with duration, a rising level of risk aversion will cause both major types of assets held by banks, loans and securities, to fall in value.

When risk aversion falls to a low level, it is an obvious sign of danger, but the degree to which this poses a major risk to the economy depends not only on the level to which risk aversion has fallen, but the degree to which policy adjustments can readily counteract the damage. Policy moves to offset the negative impact on the economy of changes in risk aversion can be either fiscal or monetary. But monetary changes alone may not be sufficient and this will be particularly likely if asset prices fall, as will often be the case, and may be the trigger which sets off the sudden change in the perceived risks of default.

6.8 CONCLUSIONS

Economic policy aimed at maintaining low and stable inflation is a necessary but not sufficient condition for achieving economic stability. Low consumer price inflation is compatible with asset bubbles. These pose major risks to the economy and, together with other signs of excessive monetary ease, must be avoided. At present there is no adequate institutional structure for monitoring these risks and taking, or at least recommending, action to forestall them. It is essential to create such a structure if we are to try to prevent similar problems to those we have just experienced from recurring.

REFERENCES

Bernanke, B., and M. Gertler. 1999. Monetary policy and asset price volatility. In *Federal Reserve Bank of Kansas City Economic Review 4th Quarter*, pp. 17–51.

Holly, S., M. Hashem Pesaran and T. Yamagata. 2010. A spatio-temporal model of house prices in the US. *Journal of Econometrics*, in press.

Smithers, A., and S. Wright. 2002. Stock markets and central bankers—the economic consequences of Alan Greenspan. *World Economics* 3(1), 101–24.

Smithers, A. 2009. *Wall Street Revalued: Imperfect Markets and Inept Central Bankers.* John Wiley & Sons.

Webber, L., and R. Churm. 2007. Decomposing corporate bond spreads. *Bank of England Quarterly Bulletin* Q4, 533–41.

White, W. R. 2009. Should monetary policy 'lean or clean'? Federal Reserve Bank of Dallas Globalization and Monetary Policy Institute Working Paper 34 (August).

What Framework Is Best for Systemic (Macroprudential) Policy?

By Andrew Large

This chapter identifies a significant gap in today's policy framework and suggests for debate an approach to fill it. It addresses systemic financial failure which, as recent events have amply demonstrated, can give rise to significant fiscal and welfare costs.

Seeking to prevent such failures has encouraged a plethora of regulatory initiatives. This chapter suggests that, important though they may be, they will not on their own prevent crises. It proposes a policy framework for containing systemic dangers but recognizes that there are a number of significant and difficult issues on which at present there is no clear-cut conclusion. Important interfaces with other policy areas—such as monetary and regulatory—are considered. Encouragingly the policy debate and increasingly political intentions in both Europe and the US do now seem to be focusing on these issues and the new UK government has announced its plans to move in this direction.

EXECUTIVE SUMMARY

The policy framework needs to comprise a number of elements. It must provide for assessing the systemic conjuncture on a regular basis and for identifying emerging risks. Crucially, it must ensure that the diagnosis is translated into effective preemptive action, which in turn means ensuring that appropriate policy instruments are available and that the relevant bodies have full authority to use them. In addition, the framework must set out clear mechanisms for disclosure and accountability. Despite the difficulty of formal cost–benefit analysis, the chapter suggests that the welfare benefits of success would justify the deployment of significant resource and effort.

The need to monitor a range of indicators of financial stability (or instability) is emphasized, and it is suggested that leverage and overall indebtedness are especially important. The question of targets is addressed and

I am extremely grateful to Alastair Clark for his substantial input.

it is noted that, in contrast to monetary policy/inflation, the choice is more open and quantification is more difficult.

The questions of policy instruments and of governance arrangements associated with their use are raised. The former remains a subject of debate although the chapter suggests that overall capital ratios should be a candidate. However, there remain uncertainties about just how effective they would prove to be and about the interaction with microprudential policy (whose principal goal is the avoidance of individual firm failure). Questions are also raised about calibration and about automaticity versus discretion in deployment. On policy governance, it is suggested that the systemic authority should take decisions about the deployment of its 'own' instrument. However, it should also be mandated to make observations or recommendations to other policymakers whose areas of activity have a systemic stability dimension. This includes monetary policy, regulatory policy, competition issues and fiscal policy.

The relationship with monetary policy is specifically recognized but it is argued that, for reasons of accountability and effectiveness, it would be preferable to keep the policy areas apart.

The complex institutional issues for the successful delivery of policy are examined next. These include clarity of objectives, independence from the political process and requisite skills and experience. The importance of transparency of process is noted.

The institutional structure is likely to vary from jurisdiction to jurisdiction, but might focus on a 'Systemic Policy Committee' receiving inputs from diverse areas which may be located in different existing authorities. However, the case is made for housing the committee itself within (or attached to) the central bank. Questions of the implied concentration of power are noted.

Although policy delivery should ideally be on an international basis, the lack of global government makes this impractical to achieve. This chapter leaves to others the debate on how best this vital dimension should be developed. Accordingly, and ideally with clear guidance from and coordination by international authorities, the chapter suggests that individual jurisdictions will need to implement their own policy frameworks. It emphasizes that such frameworks need to be pragmatic and operationally practical as well as addressing the difficult areas of analysis.

Finally, to provide a concrete example, an outline of how such a framework might be constructed in practice is put forward, taking the case of the UK.

INTRODUCTION

The previous chapter, 'Can We Identify Bubbles and Stabilize the System?' by Andrew Smithers, discussed various indicators of systemic risk, notably 'overexuberant' asset prices and credit bubbles, and pointed out that we did not have an adequate institutional structure for monitoring these risks and taking, or even recommending, action to forestall them.

Although the current environment, with its continuing economic and financial strains, may complicate implementation and introduction of any new policy approach, the experience of the past three years demonstrates very clearly the need to reinforce policy in this area. That experience has also called into serious question several of the principles which, explicitly or implicitly, underpinned the approach to financial regulation (and indeed other aspects of financial and economic policy), notably the 'efficient markets hypothesis' and 'rational expectations'. It has in addition raised the issue of whether the range of 'conventional' policy instruments—short-term interest rates, the fiscal stance, regulatory capital requirements and so on—are adequate to deliver not only low inflation and sustained growth but also continuing financial stability. And if the conclusion is that they are not, the corollary is a need to establish a policy framework and identify instruments which will 'plug the gap'.

This chapter responds to that challenge and considers a possible framework for delivering such policies. It identifies a number of significant and difficult issues on which at present there is no clear-cut conclusion, but suggests some possible approaches for debate. The challenge is all the greater because of the need on the one hand to address the complex analytical issues while on the other to find a practical operational structure to ensure that policy is both developed and then actually delivered.

Encouragingly, the intellectual debate and increasingly political intentions do now seem to be focusing on creating such policy frameworks. Examples of this are emerging with the intended European Systemic Risk Board, which the ECB will chair; in the US as outlined in the recent Dodd–Frank Wall Street Reform and Consumer Protection Act; and in the UK.

Questions which arise include the following.

- Is it feasible/legitimate to try to turn financial stability into an executive responsibility along the lines of monetary stability, certainly at this stage of the debate? (It took a very long time to get there with monetary policy.)
- What should the mandate for this policy area actually be?

- What instruments would help in delivering the mandate, and who has or should have the ownership and power to deploy them?
- How will the interaction of supervisory/microprudential policy and systemic/macroprudential policy be handled without confusing and/or excessively complicating governance and accountability arrangements?
- Would capital requirements actually be effective as an instrument for controlling credit/gearing? If not, are there better candidates?
- How will/should systemic/macroprudential and monetary policy interact? To what extent should they be separated or handled together?

It may be helpful to make a few introductory points.

1. Global issues. In what is essentially a global financial marketplace, a global approach would be the ideal. But as in so many other areas, this runs up against the tension between global commercial models and national legislative and legal frameworks. This tension is all the more acute in the context of financial stability because at present only national governments have the discretion to apply fiscal resources to the resolution of crises, and in taking such action they are accountable to national electorates.

This of course raises the question of whether supra-national bodies— most plausibly perhaps the IMF in conjunction with the Financial Stability Board (FSB) and Basel Committees—should have a bigger role to play, going beyond any current contribution as standard setter, source of experience and provider of assessment capability. Whilst acknowledging the importance of the global issue, it is not the subject of this chapter.

In the absence, however, of such a global—or even regional—authority (other than that which is perhaps emerging in the EU), the delivery of policy will fall mainly to individual countries, who will need to implement measures in a way which commands legitimacy with all relevant stakeholders.

It would nevertheless be helpful if each jurisdiction adopted a similar conceptual framework and addressed the basic issues in a consistent way. This should ensure broad similarity of approach while accommodating the particular features of each jurisdiction. In addition, we have to start somewhere! If one or several jurisdictions put their toes in the water, others are likely to follow, encouraged by a mixture of pressure from the global authorities and from their peer group.

2. Microprudential/regulatory initiatives. There may be some who feel that, with the multitude of micro measures in place or in prospect, we should rest there for a moment and not attempt to develop a new area of policy involving difficult judgements and complex political issues. The counterargument is that, whatever the merits of these micro-measures, there are serious doubts about their collective capacity to deal with emerging systemic pressures.

Many would argue that, historically, systemic oversight and policy were the preserve of central banks and that this area of policy is not therefore new. What is new, however, apart from having to deal with vastly more complex markets and global interactions, is the need for such policies to respect modern approaches to law and accountability. Monetary policy has in many countries now been given the statutory backing needed to confer 'legitimacy'. Financial stability objectives, on the other hand, have been imprecisely specified or left in the too difficult box. Financial authorities were left with the alternatives of acting presumptively, i.e. as though they did have the requisite powers, or of deciding that they could not take the risks of so doing.

3. Nomenclature. A key underpinning for today's typical monetary policy frameworks is that people accept the benefits of price stability. In present circumstances, it seems plausible that they might also increasingly see the need for financial or systemic stability. The term 'macroprudential' policy, which is often used in much the same sense, whilst clear to policymakers, may appear to many rather technical and discourage a wider audience from engaging in the debate. So this chapter uses the term 'systemic policy' which describes the oversight, assessment and delivery of policy and can be seen as a complement to 'monetary policy'.

4. Timing. The timing of any move to put systemic policy frameworks into effect is complicated by the fact that we are far from the steady state which the framework is designed to maintain. On the other hand, the backdrop and aftermath of the crisis may provide a favourable time to think hard about how to implement a policy framework to reduce the probability of crises of this magnitude happening again.

5. Cost. Clearly there would be no point in trying to reinforce the systemic policy framework unless the welfare costs of doing so were demonstrably lower than those which might arise from failing to do so.

Recent evidence suggests that the fiscal costs of financial bailouts, and even more the overall welfare costs of dealing with the results of acute financial instability, are extremely high. It would therefore seem that, despite the absence of a formal cost–benefit analysis, there should be a large constituency for policies to mitigate the risks and costs of future financial crises.

This nevertheless leaves open the question of whether such policies might themselves impose a cost in terms of long-term growth. Growth in the mature economies may well have been slower in the decade up to 2007 if policy had leaned against the build-up of indebtedness. But there is no clear evidence that, over the longer term, average growth rates consistent with a sustainable level of leverage would be lower than those in the 'leverage unconstrained' world (when higher growth in upswing has to be combined with reduced or negative growth in busts). They may even be higher. Moreover, lower volatility in the growth rate might provide additional welfare benefit.

7.1 MANDATE

7.1.1 Proposal

The proposal for debate is that an overarching mandate be given to policy-makers in some public body (hereafter referred to as the Systemic Policy Committee (SPC): see section 7.5 below) along the following lines.

> To review and assess the systemic conjuncture, to identify actual or incipient threats to financial stability, to apply the policy instruments available to it directly and, where necessary, to recommend policy actions to be taken by other relevant policymakers, so as to secure and maintain financial stability.

Financial instability and the crises to which it can give rise occur when there is a sudden and general collapse in confidence in the soundness of the financial system. This is likely to be associated with doubts about the ability of one or more participants in that system to meet their obligations, in turn precipitating the familiar pattern of herd behaviour, a drying up of liquidity and the firesale of assets by banks or others. The question is, what are the circumstances which can create such doubts? Assessing the probability of a crisis occurring requires complex judgements in relation to a number of interrelated factors. So do decisions about when and how to signal concerns and/or to use the available policy instruments. (Excellent analyses are provided *inter alia* in recent publications by the de Larosière group on financial supervision in the EU (February 2009), the G30 on financial reform (2009), the Bank of England on macroprudential policy (November 2009) as well as by significant literature from the IMF, FSB and Basel institutions.)

7.1.2 Leverage and the Systemic Conjuncture

Previous financial crises demonstrate that confidence is likely to be more fragile the greater the degree of leverage in the system. The term 'leverage' is used here in a broad sense to cover 'balance-sheet-relevant' items (i.e. including special purpose vehicles, structured investment vehicles, etc.) as well as the embedded leverage in derivatives and other related products and is not confined to the banking system. The term 'systemic conjuncture' covers the level of leverage in the economy, the robustness of both the system as a whole and individual institutions to shocks, the fiscal and monetary environment and the state of confidence in the system's ability to repay debt in full and on time.

7.1.3 Executing the Mandate and Its Evolution

Assessing the systemic conjuncture as outlined above will mean reviewing a range of indicators. There is no single indicator of either leverage or confidence. Instead, the SPC will need to consider the relevance of a number of indicators—both in terms of levels and, where relevant, rates of change over time—including

- national and international imbalances;
- the overall level of leverage within the system;
- the level/rates of change of indebtedness of different sectors and of the economy as a whole (i.e. external indebtedness);
- the asset exposures and potential dynamic and behaviour of non-leveraged (long only) as well as leveraged asset managers;
- the level of asset prices (equity prices, house and commercial property prices, etc.) relative to their long-term trend or their relationship with other economic variables;
- market measures of uncertainty and risk (asset price volatility, credit spreads on bonds of various types, credit default swap prices, etc.);
- new products and securitization techniques which may be manifestations of arbitrage to avoid measures taken to mitigate systemic dangers;
- the outcome of stress testing of financial institutions and the system as a whole;
- trends in external measures of confidence and risk appetite.

Such reviews will need to be set against judgements about the resilience of the system and about the potential effectiveness of policy measures and sanctions available to the authorities, including the techniques for the resolution of problems affecting individual financial firms.

Depending on the conclusions, decisions will then need to be taken both about deployment of the instruments available directly to the SPC and on what advice, recommendations or 'encouragement' the SPC should give to other policymakers on issues deemed relevant to financial stability.

7.1.4 Targets

It is not proposed that the SPC should be given any single target variable, bearing in mind the untested nature of policy in this area, nor at this stage does it seem sensible to determine whether targets should be hard or soft. As part of its remit, however, the systemic/macroprudential authority should be asked to consider, in the light of experience, whether any particular target or set of targets should in due course be formalized. It is widely recognized that identification of such a target or targets is likely to be materially more difficult than for monetary policy, where the main focus has been on the delivery of low and stable inflation.

7.1.5 Issues Arising

Given the difficulty of defining a precise objective, there is a legitimate question about the feasibility of constructing any satisfactory policy framework. Is it achievable in practice and can it be effective? It is worth noting, however, that other areas of public policy, notably monetary policy, have faced similar issues at early stages in their development which have in many cases now been overcome. The view expressed by some that it is all too complicated to justify the attempt seems excessively negative, particularly given the substantial real cost of the recent crisis and the widely held view that, in the absence of additional measures to address this gap in policy, a similar or even more severe crisis might well occur within a generation. Furthermore, it seems doubtful whether, on their own, the multitude of microprudential and resolution measures introduced recently with the goal of mitigating systemic risks will actually achieve the desired result.

7.2 POLICY INSTRUMENTS

7.2.1 *Proposal*

The SPC would be mandated to act in two ways.

Firstly, it would have the authority to deploy its 'own' policy instrument. This is discussed below with the proposition that the instrument should be based on capital ratios. Secondly, it should assess the impact of other policy areas on systemic stability, and be mandated to make recommendations to the authorities responsible for these policies, to which the authorities would be expected to respond, perhaps on a comply-or-explain basis.

7.2.2 *The SPC's 'Own' Policy Instrument*

This should be capable of deployment on a regular and continuing basis and will need to satisfy a number of criteria, including the following.

- It should address the root causes rather than merely the symptoms of instability.
- It should ideally be independent of the instruments used in other areas of public policy. Without this independence, there is a risk of confusion and unclear accountability.

Accordingly, so long as they continue to be assigned to delivering an inflation target, short-term interest rates would seem to be disqualified from being the 'own' instrument, even though they are certainly likely to have a bearing on financial stability conditions and in some circumstances may indeed be the subject of recommendation by the SPC.

The candidate proposed for discussion would be a capital or gearing ratio (perhaps in conjunction with reserve requirements). This would have its principal impact on banks, which are the main agents for extending credit. Furthermore, given the effect on the cost of providing this credit, the impact would extend indirectly to credit users such as investment banks and hedge funds.

This of course could also fall foul of the problem of 'single-instrument two-policy objectives' (because capital ratios are at present assigned to microprudential supervisors, with the prime objective of achieving an acceptably low probability of individual-firm failure). However, capital ratios would meet the first criterion above in that they would bear directly on the cost both of creating credit and of increasing leverage, i.e. the cost of intermediation.

In relation to the second criterion it might be argued that the two objectives are in fact not genuinely distinct—that systemic and individual firm stability are *de facto* highly correlated. Although there must be some merit in this point it is hardly borne out by recent experience.

So, assuming that capital ratios were indeed the chosen instrument, it would be necessary to define a hierarchy, or at least some clear relationship, between the two policy areas. This could be to assign to the systemic/macroprudential policymaker 'ownership' of the overall level of the risk asset ratio (RAR) (the Basel 8%). This would give the SPC a way to influence the cost of creating, and thence the overall growth of, credit.

Meanwhile the microprudential supervisor—focused on the strength of individual firms—would be able to assign relative weights to different classes of assets in the RAR computation, also taking into account judgments on a firm's individual risk characteristics.

7.2.3 Policy Areas with Systemic Relevance

The SPC might also separately be mandated to make recommendations to other policymakers, including the microprudential supervisor, in relation to policy instruments that fall under their control, such as liquidity policies etc. The latter would be expected to respond, perhaps on a comply-or-explain basis.

7.2.4 Breadth of Mandate

Other policy areas relevant to systemic policy include monetary policy, fiscal policy, competition policy and microprudential policy—the last of which includes, for example, capital and liquidity standards and also incentives and remuneration policies. This raises the question of exactly what powers and responsibilities the SPC should have in relation to these other areas. For which should it have a remit/duty to make recommendations and for which should it merely take the relevant policy stance into account in making its own decisions? Microprudential and monetary policy might fall into the former category whilst fiscal policy might fall into the latter.

7.2.5 Other Instruments

It would be necessary to consider also what might be equivalent instruments to contain systemic pressures arising independently from and outside the banking sector. Instruments such as the solvency ratio, in relation to the insurance sector, might be considered here. As is the case more generally, it would be important to avoid measures which made sense at the individual firm level but which could prove destabilizing for the system as a whole.

7.2.6   Role of Interest Rates

Finally, putting to one side the issue of multiple targets for a single instrument, there is debate as to whether interest rates would be more effective than capital ratios in containing leverage growth. The balance is hard to predict; general interest rates levels impact banks' cost of funds whereas capital ratios influence the cost of intermediation and therefore affect the willingness of intermediaries to supply credit.

7.2.7   Granularity Issues

Our proposal is that it would be preferable for the SPC to 'own', and direct the use of, a single policy instrument, following the model of monetary policy. It would be possible in principle for the SPC to adopt a more granular approach to influencing the growth of credit, for example by setting different and/or variable capital ratios for different classes of assets (say mortgages or commercial real estate loans or loans to small and medium-sized enterprises).

Although in some circumstances such measures might seem attractive, they involve a number of serious downsides.

- First, it would complicate the conduct of systemic policy and potentially make it more difficult to reach clear conclusions or establish behavioural expectations and reaction functions as regards the SPC (see the section on calibration below).

- Second, it could potentially confuse or undermine the legitimacy and governance structure of the other authorities already charged with particular areas of policy.

- Third, use of micro instruments could lay the SPC process open to a greater degree of political pressure given the differential impact on different segments of the economy. (Note, however, that it may sometimes be easier politically to justify raising capital requirements for lending to a particular sector or sectors where credit growth has been 'excessive' and that in some circumstances a more granular approach could also alleviate tension with monetary policy goals.)

- Fourth, however, and perhaps most important, it is not clear that a granular approach could be made to work satisfactorily in practice. If the objective is to contain overall leverage and credit growth, applying constraints only to particular sectors is likely to generate a 'squeezed balloon' effect.
- And finally, micro-intervention seems inconsistent in principle with what is intended to be an overarching macro dimension to financial policy. This might be regarded as philosophically unacceptable in some jurisdictions.

7.2.8 *Calibration*

There is at present no reliable estimate of what effect a given adjustment of overall capital ratios would have on credit growth. Again, however, this is not a new challenge for policy: in the context of monetary policy, the impact of alterations in interest rates on inflation is also hard to judge.

Two factors are relevant in considering this problem.

- First, a regular and reasonably frequent process of assessment would allow 'course corrections' to be made if credit growth seemed not to be adequately restrained. Such assessments, as in monetary policy, would clearly need to take account of significant lags in the response to capital ratio changes.
- Second, as the policymakers' reaction function becomes more stable and better understood, so preemptive behaviour is likely to become more common and the degree of adjustment of the policy instrument needed to achieve a given impact is likely to be less. (Facilitating understanding of this reaction function is a further reason for keeping the instrument environment simple and avoiding multiple instruments.)

7.2.9 *Discretionary or Automatic*

An obvious further question is whether the instrument should be deployed on an automatic or a discretionary basis.

Automatic countercyclical adjustment of capital requirements is under discussion as part of the FSB and Basel Committee processes. It is perceived to be of value both in reducing credit cyclicality and in countering the danger of regulatory or supervisory forbearance or political interference. It seems probable, however, that discretionary use of the instrument will also be needed—and in any case it is wise to make provision for such use—given the many factors which influence credit conditions and the overall systemic conjuncture. In effect, the deployment of such adjustment by national systemic policymakers would be constrained by such globally set, and transparent, adjustments, but not overruled by them.

7.3 RELATIONSHIP WITH MONETARY POLICY

7.3.1 *Interplay of Policy Areas*

As proposed above, interest rates and capital ratios would be designated as the prime instruments to impact the root causes of inflation and credit/leverage, respectively. But the two instruments interact: movements in interest rates will affect the evolution of credit and leverage and capital ratios will affect the monetary transmission mechanism. And both may have an impact on growth. The question is whether this matters and, if so, what can be done about it.

At a minimum, it seems clear that policy assessment in each area should take into account policy actions in the other. This follows precedent in a number of jurisdictions where monetary policy takes fiscal policy into account. In a similar way, monetary policymakers might be formally enjoined to have regard to systemic stability issues and vice versa for the SPC, although there is clearly a critical question about what 'taking into account' would mean in practice. Over time, the two sets of policymakers may well develop expectations about each other's likely policy actions.

This raises the question of whether an 'equilibrium' delivering both price stability and financial stability objectives could be reached, or whether the set of actions and counteractions would be recursively self-defeating and potentially destabilizing. In practice, this seems unlikely to be the result any more than it is in relation to fiscal policy, although the outcome would depend on precisely how the systemic/macroprudential target came to be specified.

The additional credit/leverage constraint could of course have an impact on growth. But a possible criticism of the current policy framework is precisely that the growth rate compatible with the inflation target alone has in recent years been higher than was compatible with the maintenance of financial stability.

So arguably the following equilibrium might emerge. Higher capital ratios and slower credit expansion would allow price stability to be delivered with slightly lower interest rates. And while growth in the short-to-medium term might be slightly slower, the threat of financial instability as a result of rising leverage would be reduced and long-term growth might actually be enhanced.

7.3.2 *Combine Monetary Policy and Systemic Stability?*

Alternatively, it is argued by some that, if there is indeed a case for a policy initiative in relation to systemic stability, it might be better to extend the remit of the relevant monetary policymaker. Although there are significant and possibly decisive contrary arguments, this is an important point to address.

- Experience suggests that introducing more policy goals increases the risk of *suboptimal implementation*. For example, monetary policy in the UK already has price stability as its goal, albeit with a subordinate objective of supporting the government's wider economic objectives. Jurisdictions which attempt to deliver several goals (e.g. price stability and growth) with the single instrument of short-term interest rates face *inter alia* greater difficulties in explaining policy decisions, in creating a reaction function and in managing inflationary expectations. This arises for the obvious reason that there are often tensions between the actions indicated by the different objectives.
- The *experience and capabilities* required of those involved in formulating and executing monetary and financial stability policies differ in important respects. Experience of supervision and financial market dynamics are essential in the context of financial stability, just as an understanding of macroeconomic and monetary theory and practice are needed for monetary policy. It would be preferable to ensure that each area is fit for purpose rather than trying to embrace all the needs of both policy areas in a single committee.
- *Accountability*, on both the monetary and financial stability sides, is likely to be more effective if each is accountable for a single rather than multiple area of policy. Moreover, from the point of view of individuals it could be uncomfortable to be accountable for quasi-political judgements about the relative weight to be accorded to different policy objectives, especially since political perceptions of relative importance are likely to change over time.
- The nature of the *assessment process* is different. Monetary policy assessment is about stability within a band or around a target over time. And there is regular and reasonably clear-cut evidence on whether that is being achieved. In the case of financial stability

policy, while instability is also obvious, by the time that point is reached, policy has failed. Instead policy has to be based on unobservable probabilities that a state of instability might arise. Trying to combine both approaches in a single process could risk compromising the integrity of both.

- Finally, policy in the two areas is at *different stages of development.* There is still a great deal to learn in the area of financial stability policy. It needs to find its own place in the thinking and expectations of not just the authorities but also of the public and industry. It is vital that the public sees systemic policy issues as part of everyday life and not just during a crisis!

There are no doubt countries, particularly where the liberalization of the financial sector is not complete or the capital account remains partially controlled, where the two areas of policy are satisfactorily carried out together. Such countries may feel the absence of an explicit financial stability regime less strongly. In practice, they accommodate systemic issues within their monetary policy regime. India has been one such example. In the case of mature and fully open economies with existing monetary policy frameworks, however, the issues set out above become more important.

Finally, it is certainly the case that someone must in the end make the overall assessment of the combined impact of systemic and monetary policy measures. This will require careful thought. It would probably be assisted by housing the two areas of policy at or close to a single institution (the central bank), but that may in turn raise issues about concentration of power (see section 7.5).

7.4   INSTITUTIONAL FEATURES: QUALITIES NECESSARY FOR THE SUCCESS OF SYSTEMIC POLICY

More than for monetary policy, which is better understood, systemic policy decisions could at this stage be unpopular. The impact, for example, of constraining credit growth/leverage would be felt by many different groups—politicians, bankers, industrialists and consumers. So, however ill-advised, resistance to constraining the 'fuel' of credit growth can be expected from politicians whose 'growth story' may be compromised, from bankers (and bank shareholders) whose remuneration and profits are likely to be impacted, and from the public and other users of credit because 'live now, pay later' has an enduring appeal.

For these reasons the following qualities will be necessary for the success of systemic policy.

(i) *The objectives and mandate should be set by the political process.*

(ii) The conduct of policy within the framework should be *independent of political process but accountable to it.*

(iii) *The arrangements should incorporate features which have proved themselves in other policy areas, notably monetary policy.* This includes regularity of assessment, even if perhaps less frequent than for monetary policy.

(iv) *Particular qualities/experience and skills will be needed.* Irrespective of the precise institutional arrangements, an SPC would need individuals with experience and skills at the highest level covering

- central banking,

- supervision of financial markets and financial innovation,

- practical experience of systemic events,

- academic understanding of the issues and

- the handling of relationships with ministries of finance/treasuries.

(v) To command respect there needs to be adequate *accountability of policymakers* to legislatures and the public: the arrangements should have 'legitimacy' in the eyes of directly interested parties and the population at large.

(vi) To support this, *the process by which policy decisions are made should be transparent.* Where appropriate, the supporting analysis and assessment of early warnings should be disclosed, recognizing that in some cases immediate disclosure may be undesirable and risk generating a destabilizing erosion of confidence. This might apply, for example, to situations involving individual financial firms. A process for deciding what falls into that category would be needed and for judging cases involving potential breaches of commercial confidentiality. Financial Stability Reviews (FSRs) go some way towards achieving this but they typically stop short of reviewing the background to policy decisions as such. The transparency process proposed in this chapter could be seen as an extension of the thinking behind FSRs, beyond being a channel for early warnings and instead representing a more formalized and effective framework for policy accountability. It is in any event important to enhance public understanding of financial stability issues, which should in turn facilitate acceptance of 'unpopular' decisions if these are seen to be directed at avoiding the high social costs of financial crises.

(vii) There needs to be confidence that effective means and *authority* exist to implement policy decisions, whether the instruments are under the direct control of the SPC or lie with other bodies.

(viii) *Dedicated resources* will be needed to assist the SPC in carrying out proper assessment and providing support.

7.5 THE 'VEHICLE' FOR SYSTEMIC POLICY DELIVERY: INSTITUTIONAL ARRANGEMENTS

7.5.1 *A Committee*

The choice of institutional arrangements will be a function of the legal, cultural and political environment in each jurisdiction. The options include a new self-standing institution, a department of an existing institution or a semi-autonomous committee either within or anchored to an existing institution. Different approaches are already emerging (European Systemic Risk Committee at the ECB; separate committee as per the Dodd–Frank Wall Street Reform and Consumer Protection Act in the US).

For the sake of illustration as mentioned above we have assumed the creation of an SPC.

7.5.2 *Should the SPC Be Freestanding or Anchored to an Existing Institution?*

The proposition in this chapter is that a model with the SPC anchored or close to the central bank has merit. There are valuable precedents in terms of monetary policy in many jurisdictions.

This would build on and put onto a more formalized footing central banks' 'traditional' role in the area of financial stability. The following attributes of central banks are relevant.

- Despite recent setbacks central banks command respect because of their expertise on systemic issues, their independence (in many cases) from political manipulation, their unique role as creators of central bank money and implementers of monetary policy, and their position at the 'nerve-centre' of both national and international financial systems. Furthermore, they typically have wide experience

of macroeconomic policymaking through their historic relationships with finance ministries.

- Against this background, many people assume or expect central
banks to be responsible for handling systemic issues. In that sense
systemic policy is not 'new'. But in former times central banks
tended to act 'presumptively' without a formal or statutory mandate to do so.

- A difficulty arose when formalized mandates for monetary policy were given to central banks, complete with accountability provisions. This made it less comfortable—and indeed potentially
dangerous—to act presumptively in relation to systemic policy. And
governments/legislators shied away from trying to create such formalized processes for systemic stability because of the difficulties
in defining objectives and scope. The UK in 1997 is a case in point,
when responsibility for monetary policy was awarded to the Bank of
England but its role in relation to systemic stability was left unclear.
This effectively encouraged an emphasis on monetary policy which
tended to 'crowd out' systemic issues. It is that deficit which we are
now trying to address.

7.5.3   *Issues Arising in Relation to Location*

Power

If the central bank, an unelected body, is given responsibility for systemic
policy, in addition to monetary policy and its normal central banking
functions, would this mean that it became too powerful? Might it suffer
from political challenge and reputational risk causing its effectiveness to
be compromised?

The question as to the degree of power that different jurisdictions feel
comfortable placing in the hands of the central bank is an important
one to which there are no easy or general answers. The matter is further
complicated by the move in some jurisdictions to place responsibility
for microprudential supervision with the central bank as well. If housing
both systemic policy and micro-supervision, as well as monetary policy,
within the central bank were indeed thought to mean too great a concentration of power, there seems a strong case for assigning systemic policy
to the central bank and micro-supervision to a third party—either a uni-
tary supervisory authority like the Financial Services Authorities in Japan
and (presently) the UK or a stand-alone prudential supervisor like the

Australian Prudential Regulation Authority in Australia. But it is beyond the scope of this chapter to examine this issue further.

Interface with the Political Process

This interface clearly needs to be handled effectively. The mechanism suggested is that, following models in a number of jurisdictions, the mandate and objectives of systemic policy should be set by the political process, and that the execution of the mandate should be handled independently from, but be accountable to, it.

How Will the Interface with Fiscal and Competition Policy Be Handled?

Again paralleling the conduct of monetary policy, from the point of view of the SPC these would be taken as 'givens'. There would be debate, however, as to the extent to which it should be expected to make recommendations, and with what degree of authority, in relation to these other established policy areas (see section 7.1).

Handling Crises

The framework in this chapter is designed to handle mitigation of systemic risks in 'peacetime'. More debate is needed on how the arrangements would need to evolve in the event of an incipient or actual crisis, in particular how the key role of the ministry of finance/treasury in such conditions would be accommodated; on the 'trigger' mechanism for moving from 'peacetime' to 'crisis' mode; and on the role of the SPC itself at a time of crisis. Appropriate resolution machinery is separately widely under discussion.

APPENDIX. A FRAMEWORK FOR THE UK: AN ILLUSTRATION

This chapter concludes with an illustration of how such a process might be constructed in the UK taking account of the considerations mentioned in the chapter.

A new systemic policy framework could usefully borrow from the Monetary Policy Committee (MPC) experience. This might suggest the following.

(i) A committee, the 'Systemic Policy Committee' (SPC), should be established whose broad remit, following the issues outlined in section 7.1, would be determined in legislation and whose specific objectives would be specified from time to time by the government.

The SPC would be anchored at the Bank of England and would have independence in making its policy decisions. Its association with the central bank should help to reinforce its independence.

(ii) Membership would include

- governors of the bank,

- senior officials of the supervisory authority,

- those with practitioner experience of the financial sector (possibly non-conflicted and/or recently retired members of the financial services industry, including infrastructure providers)—this could include members of the bank's board (court),

- academics with a particular expertise in financial markets and institutions,

- an observer from HM Treasury.

(iii) Size of committee might be 8–10.

(iv) Members could be appointed through the political process, as per the MPC, and be fully accountable individually for decisions made, both before parliament and more generally.

(v) Consideration would be needed as to how to ensure the availability of reliable and timely data from a variety of sources. Any barriers to automatic exchange of data would need to be overcome and perhaps facilitated by including representatives of the suppliers on the committee.

(vi) Consideration would be needed as to how to establish a method for achieving consensus with a possible 'voting' framework, as well as the ability to explain directly to the political authorities how the SPC would behave if it feared that its policy objectives might not be met (the 'letter writing to the chancellor' process).

(vii) The SPC might normally meet quarterly, say, rather than monthly, given the frequency with which major items of data become available and the relative infrequency of periods of serious stress. As for the MPC, there could be provision for exceptional meetings to be held if it was felt necessary.

(viii) Minutes of SPC meetings would be published. Today's FSR assesses the systemic conjuncture, but the minutes would also explain the reason for the policy response.

(ix) Accountability for the effective functioning and resourcing for the committee could lie with the bank's board (Court).

Should We Have 'Narrow Banking'?

By John Kay

The credit crunch of 2007-8 was the direct and indirect result of losses incurred by major financial services companies in speculative trading in wholesale financial markets. The largest source of systemic risk was within individual financial institutions themselves. The capital requirements regime imposed by the Basel agreements both contributed to the problem and magnified the damage inflicted on the real economy after the problem emerged. This chapter argues that regulatory reform should emphasize systemic resilience and robustness, not more detailed behavioural prescriptions. It favours functional separation of financial services architecture, with particular emphasis on narrow banking—tight restriction of the scope and activities of deposit-taking institutions.

8.1 HOW WE GOT HERE

The traditional role of banks was to take deposits, largely from individuals, and to make loans, mostly to businesses. Deposits were repayable on short notice but loans could not in practice be called in immediately. Even a well-run bank was therefore potentially vulnerable if many depositors demanded their money back simultaneously. Banks maintained extensive liquid assets and the Bank of England, in common with other central banks, offered 'lender of last resort' facilities. The assumed willingness of the central bank to provide funds against good quality assets meant that a solvent bank need not fear failure.

In the modern era, financial innovation allowed banks to trade both credit risk and interest rate risk. These developments were at first called 'disintermediation' and subsequently 'securitization'. The credit and interest rate exposures which traditionally had been contained within banks, and made banks inherently risky, could now be reduced or eliminated through markets.

There was early recognition that such disintermediation also undermined the traditional conception, and role, of a bank. Some thoughtful commentators believed that the financial institutions of the future would be narrow specialists. An important book published in 1988 by a young McKinsey partner, Lowell Bryan (now director of the company's global financial services practice), defined that firm's view at the time. The title was *Breaking Up the Bank* (see Bryan (1988); Litan (1988) expounded similar arguments).

Bryan was half right, half wrong. All of the individual functions of established banks (with the possible exception of small and medium-sized enterprise (SME) lending) are now also performed by specialist institutions. In many cases these functions are best performed by specialist institutions. Dedicated mortgage banks, based on wholesale funding, have offered market-leading products. Supermarkets have diversified into simple financial services, such as deposit accounts and consumer loans. Private equity houses (venture capital firms) have transformed the provision of finance for start-up businesses. Successful proprietary traders set up their own businesses, attracting institutional money to hedge funds.

But, seemingly paradoxically, the trend to specialization was accompanied by a trend to diversification. Traditional banks became financial conglomerates. They not only sold a wider range of retail products but also expanded their wholesale market and investment banking activities. The bizarre consequence was that while the deposit-taking and lending operations of banks could—and did—use new markets to limit their risks, speculative trading in the same markets by other divisions of the same banks increased the overall risk exposure of the bank by far more.

In 2007–8, the process by which retail banks became financial conglomerates ended in tears. Almost all the businesses concerned experienced share price collapses, raised emergency capital and became reliant on explicit or implicit government support to continue operations. But these financial conglomerates not only failed their shareholders: their customers had been victims of endemic conflicts of interest for years. At the very moment in 1999 that the 1933 Glass Steagall Act that separated commercial and investment banking was repealed, the New Economy bubble was illustrating once again the abuse which had led to the Act's passage in the first place—the stuffing of retail customers with new issues from worthless companies which were corporate clients.

Within every diversified retail bank, there is evidence of the fundamental tension between the cultures of trading and deal-making—buccaneering, entrepreneurial, grasping—and the conservative bureaucratic approach appropriate for retail banking. It is a conflict in which the investment bankers and traders generally came out on top. These institutional conflicts are, perhaps, the heart of the matter. The attractions of financial conglomerates are more evident to the people who run them than to their customers, employees, shareholders—or the taxpayers who have been faced with bills of startling magnitude by their failure.

8.2 LESSONS FROM THE HISTORY OF REGULATION

History shows that regulation works most effectively when it is targeted on a small number of clearly identified public policy problems. Most other industries are regulated, not supervised, and neither regulators nor the businesses concerned normally use the term supervision. Regulation monitors observance of a limited number of specific rules, and emphasizes structure rather than behaviour.

The remit of supervision is general rather than specific. Supervision seeks to impose a particular conception of good business practice across the industry. In financial services, the terms regulation and supervision are used almost interchangeably. Yet they are not interchangeable. Supervision is, by its nature, wide ranging; regulation is focused.

Attempts to standardize financial services regulation intentionally did lead after 1987 to attempts to agree a common set of minimal rules. Yet the Basel accords based on capital requirements proved worse than useless in the years before the crisis of 2007–8. The rules stimulated regulatory arbitrage and the use of off-balance-sheet vehicles, which made the nature of the activities that banks were conducting opaque even to the management of these institutions themselves. Even more seriously, they relieved executives of management responsibility for determining appropriate capital requirements. Capital adequacy requirements failed to restrain imprudent behaviour in the years up to the credit crunch and aggravated the recession by enforcing contraction of lending when the credit crunch hit. The belief that more complex versions of the Basel rules would be more effective in future represents the triumph of hope over experience.

That experience, from other industries as well as from financial services, shows that such attempts at regulation become steadily more extensive in scope, without being more successful in their practical results. Supervision is subject to creep—a tendency for its scope to grow. Supervision involves a form of shadow management, but it is almost inevitable—and wholly inevitable in the financial services industry—that shadow management will be at a disadvantage to the real management in terms of the competence of its staff and the quality of information available to it.

Supervision is subject to regulatory capture, an inclination to see the operation of the industry through the eyes of the industry and especially through the eyes of established firms in the industry. Because the supervisor's conception of good practice is necessarily drawn from current practice, supervision is supportive of existing business models and resistant to new entry. Extensive and intrusive, yet ineffective and protective of the existing structure of the industry and the interests of its major players. That describes financial services regulation in Britain (and in other countries) today.

There is also a public interest in the promotion of a profitable and internationally competitive financial services industry. This activity, usually called sponsorship, should be distinguished from regulation and kept separate from it, as it is in most other industries. Examples of the dangers of blending sponsorship and regulation abound. In the BSE crisis over infected beef, a government department responsible for both consumer protection and industry sponsorship voiced misleadingly reassuring statements until the problem because too serious to ignore. In the long run, the results were damaging to both the interests of the industry and the interests of the public. Much the same has been true in financial services.

Textbooks of regulatory history point to the lessons of the US airline industry (Kahn 1988). The need for regulation to secure passenger and public safety has been evident from the earliest days of civil aviation. It seems plausible—indeed it is true—that planes will be better maintained by strongly capitalized companies with sound business models. It is only a short further step to perceive a need to review pricing policies, the qualifications of prospective new entrants, and the need for their services. And so on. Airline regulation spread to cover almost all aspects of the operation of the industry. Industry leaders met to discuss issues such as seat pitches and the composition of meals.

In the US in the 1970s, this structure was swept away by a broad-based congressional coalition. The right believed that market forces would serve customers and promote innovation better than regulatory solutions. The left believed that regulation had become a cartel: a racket operated on behalf of large, inefficient, long-established companies. Both these beliefs were justified, as subsequent experience showed. The deregulated market, initially unstable, grew rapidly. There were many new entrants: some incumbents failed, others thrived. Consumer choice expanded, and prices fell. Passenger needs are today generally better served, while aircraft are safer than ever.

The financial services industry should follow this example. Regulation should seek to work with market forces, not to replace them. Not because

211

free markets lead to the best of all possible worlds—in financial services, as in many other activities, they plainly do not. But it is much easier to channel a flow of water into appropriate downhill channels than to push it uphill. That is why structural regulation, which emphasizes the incentives given by regulatory measures, is often preferable to regulation which seeks to control behaviour. Competition where possible, regulation where necessary, and supervision not at all, should be the underlying principle.

There are many lessons to be learnt for financial services from both the management and regulation of other industries. We need to stop thinking of financial services as a unique business whose problems are *sui generis*, and whose economic role is one of special privilege. The historic deal, which limited competition in banking in return for an expectation of prudent behaviour, has been abrogated by the actions of banks and bankers. Today, both consumer protection and macroeconomic stability will be best served by the policies to promote competition which are rightly favoured in other sectors of the economy.

8.3   REGULATORY STRUCTURE

The appropriate regulatory strategy in financial services is one which has been followed in other industries, notably utilities. Define, as narrowly as possible, the areas in which uninterrupted supply is essential, or in which natural monopoly is inevitable and for which close regulation is therefore required. Sponsor competitive markets, more lightly regulated, in areas to which these conditions do not apply. Impose structural separation to reduce conflicts of interest and to establish a system that is resilient and robust, in which failures can be contained.

There are many interconnected networks in the economy, and failures within them cannot be prevented. The appropriate objectives in the control and regulation of all such complex processes are to establish modularity, redundancy and alternative provision throughout the system: to create firewalls which prevent problems from spreading. These measures entail costs, of course—perhaps substantial costs—but these costs are dwarfed by the collateral damage imposed by wide-ranging failures in the electricity grid, or the telecommunications network, or by the financial crisis of 2007–8.

The appropriate regulatory strategy, therefore, is one that focuses on structure rather than behaviour: that distinguishes between the parts of the financial system where light regulation is essential and those in which the public interest is best served by competition and diversity. The overriding aim is not to prevent failure, but to limit its impact.

The present debate simply fails to address the issue posed by the emergence of managerially and financially weak conglomerate institutions, mostly based on retail banks. Even if the assertion that supervision will prevent future failure were credible—and it is not—the outcome would not deal with either the political problem or the economic problem that 'too big to fail' raises. 'Too big to fail' is not compatible with either democracy or a free market. An organization that is 'too big to fail' can show disdain for its investors, its customers and for elected officials—and the rows over bonuses are a clear, if trivial, illustration that such behaviour is a reality. On the other hand, supervision that succeeded in ruling out even the possibility of organizational failure would kill all enterprise.

The development of such mechanisms to combine competitive markets with resilient systems is not only the route ahead, but the only possible route ahead. Government underwriting for all or most financial sector counterparty risk in wholesale financial markets is not acceptable. Not just because this is not an appropriate government expenditure, but because the existence of such support undermines the imposition of risk disciplines within financial institutions and the evolution of market mechanisms to deal with counterparty risk. The problem is not simply, or even primarily, that the belief that the government will rescue failing institutions encourages these institutions to take more risk. The belief that the authorities will intervene in this way substitutes ineffectual regulatory supervision of risk-taking behaviour for the far more effectual monitoring of risk exposures by private-sector counterparties. The notion that supervision will in future prevent failures such as those of Long Term Capital Management or Lehman and that these problems of moral hazard will therefore not arise is an engaging fantasy.

There should be a clear distinction in public policy between the requirement for the continued provision of essential activities and the continued existence of particular corporate entities engaged in their provision. In today's complex environment, there are many services we cannot do without. The electricity grid and the water supply, the transport system and the telecommunications network are all essential: even a temporary disruption causes immense economic dislocation and damage. These activities are every bit as necessary to our personal and business lives as the banking sector, and at least as interconnected.

But the need to maintain the water supply does not, and must not, establish a need to keep the water company in business. Enron failed, but the water and electricity that its subsidiaries provided continued to flow. Railtrack failed, and the trains kept running. The same continuity of operations in the face of commercial failure must be assured for payments and retail banking.

Financial services companies should therefore be structured so that in the event of an overall failure of the organization the utility can be readily separated from the casino. That means the establishment of distinct narrow banks. These might operate as stand-alone entities or as separately capitalized and ring-fenced subsidiaries of financial holding companies. The claim that innovation in modern financial markets makes it essential to have large conglomerate banks is precisely the opposite of the truth—these innovations make it possible *not* to have large conglomerate banks. The activities of managing maturity mismatch, and spreading and pooling risks, which once needed to be conducted within financial institutions, now can, and should, be conducted through markets.

A special resolution regime should enable the activities of the narrow bank to be continued under public supervision or administration—supervision is obviously appropriate at this point—while the remaining activities of the company are liquidated. In some cases, the operation of the utility activity may require injection of public funds. In no circumstances should there be public support, or government underwriting, of non-utility activities.

There should be no 'too big to fail' doctrine, and no government insurance of counterparty risk in wholesale financial markets. The normal principle should be that financial institutions that cannot function without government support or subsidy, including so-called lender of last resort facilities,[1] should be put into resolution. If such institutions are unable to rectify their problems without public assistance, the corporate entities concerned should be wound up and their senior management removed. In order to secure proper monitoring of the behaviour of financial institutions, it is important that creditors as well as shareholders expect to lose money in such an event. The market mechanism for securing competent management is the prospect of failure. Government supervision of risk management in complex financial institutions is neither possible nor desirable, and regulation will never be an adequate substitute.

---

[1] The traditional lender of last resort function, as described by Bagehot in 1873 after the collapse of Overend Gurney, has been made redundant by deposit protection and disintermediation. The term is now used in a general way to describe central bank support of failing financial institutions.

8.4 REGULATING THE UTILITY

The utility element of the financial services system is the payments system. Like the electricity grid or the telecommunications network, failure even for a few hours imposes economic damage. The payments system is inherently a natural monopoly, like the electricity grid or the telecommunications network. There are alternative, and to some degrees competing, payments systems but—as with telecommunications networks—all are ultimately dependent on the core clearing and settlement systems.

In order to use the payments system, individuals and businesses must make deposits, or have access to associated lines of credit. Provision of these facilities can be, and should be, a competitive industry. Ownership and control of the network should be separated from ownership and control of these deposits. If there is vertical integration from deposit-taking into transmission, deposit takers will use the economic power that such vertical integration gives them to distort competition in their favour—to advantage a single firm which is owner of the network, or to benefit established firms at the expense of entrants if ownership is collective. That distortion of competition is what currently happens.

Narrow banks are institutions that have access to the payments system and take the deposits necessary for that access. There is a strong case and a political necessity for government guarantee of the deposits of narrow banks. The scope of such guarantees is open to discussion, but it should cover normal transactions balances and the modest savings of individuals. Theoretically, the guarantee of deposits in the UK and some other countries is provided by the financial services industry, but both the perception and the reality is that the UK government is the guarantor, and this should be made explicit. The fiasco of the collapse of the Icelandic banks exposed this fiction, in both Iceland and the UK: in Iceland the compensation scheme collapsed, and the UK (and other European) governments met the shortfall and are demanding reimbursement from the Icelandic government. The costs of the failures of British banks (including the British subsidiaries of Icelandic banks) to the UK Financial Services Compensation Scheme were met through a 'loan' from the Bank of England. There are no current proposals for the repayment of this 'loan'. If financial services activities are to be subject to a special tax, this can and should be done in other ways.

Only narrow banks could describe themselves as banks, take deposits, or access the payment system. Narrow banks would state that their deposits were guaranteed by the UK government (to the extent that they were) and all other financial institutions would be required to indicate on all statements and promotional material that funds entrusted to them were not underwritten by the UK government. The simplest rule is that all deposits with narrow banks are guaranteed and only deposits with narrow banks are guaranteed. Narrow banks would be required to restrict the investment of such deposits to safe assets. The definition of safe assets would be in the hands of regulators, not rating agencies: the privatization of this activity manifestly failed.

In the light of recent experience, there is a good case for restricting the category of 'safe assets' to UK government securities, or (possibly) securities of major OECD member governments. Such a regime would allow some exposure within the bank to maturity, or perhaps currency, mismatch, but not credit risk, and relatively modest capital requirements should be sufficient to cover these. Such elimination of credit risk is the only means of minimizing the cost to taxpayers, and of minimizing the competition-distorting advantage to banks which are covered by deposit protection or the current government implied guarantee of bank liabilities.

These provisions would be significantly more restrictive than a simple restoration of the situation that existed before the aggressive diversification of UK retail banks and building societies from the 1970s. These limitations are necessary because during that period the treasury activities of retail savings institutions metamorphosed from the purpose of meeting the routine financing needs of everyday banking into functions that were treated as profit centres in their own right.

The direction of change proposed by the so-called Volcker rule—the separation of proprietary trading from banking—gets to the heart of these issues, but the difficulty of defining 'proprietary trading' becomes evident if speculative trading on the bank's own account is intertwined with the ordinary practices of cash management. Such linkage has enabled institutions such as the (former) investment banks to claim that proprietary trading is a small part of their activities even though trading in general is a major part of their activities and a large part of their declared profits: these banks define proprietary trading essentially as what takes place within a department labelled 'proprietary trading'. Only a stringent view of what constitutes the ordinary activities of a bank can solve the problem of effectively distinguishing the utility from the casino. The implications of such restriction for the financing of conventional narrow banking activities—such as mortgages and SME financing—is discussed further below.

8.5 THE ROLE OF GOVERNMENT

For the purpose of considering the role of government in ensuring the provision of vital supplies, three categories of goods and services may be distinguished.

Utility: even very brief disruption causes systemic disarray and extended economic loss (e.g. the electricity grid, the telecommunications network).

Essential goods and services: continued supply is necessary but partial or temporary disruption can be accommodated (e.g. food, fuel).

Nice to have: free markets can and should generally be allowed to define market price and availability. If the market does not provide, too bad (most goods and services).

Public intervention in utility markets, which are generally natural monopolies, has as its primary goals regulation of prices and of access and the assurance of continued supply. The mechanism for achieving the latter objective is normally a combination of a special resolution procedure (which has continued service to the public as its primary purpose) and firewalls which enable the utility assets to be readily separated from any other assets of the business in the event of the failure of the overall corporate vehicle. Such procedures were involved in cases such as the failures of Railtrack, Metronet and Enron (owner of Wessex Water and some UK electricity companies). The absence of any specific resolution regime for financial services companies substantially aggravated the problems created by the failures and near failures of UK retail banks in 2007–8.

The supply of credit to SMEs, and for consumer lending and mortgages, fall into the second category. Although they are essential services, hiatuses in supply can be handled so long as they are of brief duration. The characteristic, and appropriate, strategy for government involvement in securing supplies is very different here. That strategy is to stimulate a competitive market with diversity of providers. The proper role of government is to promote competition and to seek to minimize dependence on any single source of supply. More detailed regulation (other than for reasons of consumer protection and safety) is not normally required. There should be—as there is for commodities such as food and fuel— the capacity to declare emergency in the face of fundamental disruption to the supply of credit. A public agency would assume responsibility for the direction of supply, normally with the cooperation of management but without it if necessary in these extreme circumstances. The objective is to withdraw and restore market forces as soon as possible.

Such emergency powers to direct the supply of credit were lacking in 2007, and are all too evidently lacking still. UK government influence on lending policies, even of banks which the government substantially owns, or whose credit the government has substantially underwritten, has amounted to pushing on a string. Supplies of credit for many ordinary business purposes have remained severely constrained well after the immediate crisis has passed. Regulatory interventions have emphasized the financial health of providers rather than the supply of services to customers. It is as though, when consumers were faced with fuel shortages, the government had released stockpiles to oil companies, which promptly used the supplies to rebuild their own stocks and then sold the remainder at a profit on international markets.

Most other financial services fall into the third, 'nice-to-have', category. Their provision, or otherwise, should be left to market forces. I doubt whether much securitization would take place in the absence of gains from regulatory arbitrage and the extensive risk mispricing which occurred in 2003–7. It is commonly argued that since much (for example) mortgage debt was funded through securitization, mortgages would not be provided on any scale in the absence of securitization (Crosby 2008). But this claim rests on an elementary confusion between the channels of intermediation through which capital is provided and the availability of capital itself. Although Tesco accounts for a significant share of sales of cornflakes, cornflakes would continue to be supplied even if Tesco did not sell them. The mortgage market existed in Britain for many years before the wide use of either securitization or swaps, and that period covered the largest extension of home ownership in British history. Securitization should neither be supported by government nor actively discouraged, and the same is true of most other wholesale financial market activities.

8.6 RESTRUCTURING THE FINANCIAL SERVICES INDUSTRY

Many people think that narrow banks would be boring. They would be boring for people whose aspirations are to welcome chief executives to panelled meeting rooms to plot global acquisitions, or for those who enjoy securities trading or the profits derived from them.

Retail banking is, however, a retail activity, as its name suggests, and the consequence of disintermediation is that the skills needed to run a retail bank are increasingly those of the retailer, not the traditional skills of the banker. Bank managers have long ceased to be the knowledgeable and influential figures in local communities they once were, and the function of credit assessment has largely been taken out of branches and replaced, perhaps excessively, by centralized and mechanical credit scoring systems. Narrow banks would compete, as retailers do, on product design, cost efficiency and customer service, which is what most people who occupy management positions in retail banks want to do. At present, however, traders and investment bankers dominate the power structure of most conglomerate banks and are the dominant influence on the culture of the organization.

High street retailers are focused on establishing the needs of their customers and aggressively demand that suppliers meet these needs with good products at low prices. High street financial institutions mostly promote the services the wholesale divisions of the same institution want to sell. Customers currently rate their banks unfavourably relative to other retailers on the trust they place in them and on their quality of service, and with good reason. One of the probable effects of narrow banking would be to change these perceptions by facilitating new competition and encouraging innovation in the segment of the financial service industry where such innovation generates real benefit to customers. Strikingly, and erroneously, the industry currently appears to see this loss of trust as a problem of public relations rather than the product of its own behaviour.

Would narrow banking imply lower interest rates or higher charges for those who hold accounts with narrow banks? In the first instance, the answer to that question is certainly yes, because narrow banking effectively withdraws the subsidy currently provided to banks through the free deposit insurance. (Deposit insurance is not entirely free, because some part of compensation costs is recouped from the industry, but experience in the UK with deposit protection and in other countries with explicit insurance schemes is that this fraction is small. To the extent that deposit insurance is currently paid for, the impact on customers of the withdrawal of the subsidy would be reduced.)

We do not know the extent to which the benefit of deposit insurance is currently split between higher interest rates to lenders, lower interest rates to borrowers, or absorbed in bank profits or inefficiencies. In normal circumstances, however, the size of the subsidy—essentially the difference between inter-bank and central bank interest rates—is not large, although it has reached substantial levels in the last two years and is likely to remain at levels significantly above the historic norm.

Companies, and individuals with substantial balances, might wish to give up the government guarantee in return for somewhat higher interest rates and associated risks. Charles Goodhart, in particular, has emphasized 'the boundary problem': the line between guaranteed and non-guaranteed deposits. Such a boundary problem exists unless all bank liabilities are guaranteed or no bank liabilities are guaranteed, neither of which are acceptable solutions. The worst of all worlds is one in which there is continuing uncertainty about the actual scope of the government guarantee—the present situation. US experience with Fannie Mae and Freddie Mac has demonstrated just how costly such ambiguity can be.

It is important, therefore, that there be an unequivocal distinction between balances that are underwritten by government and those that are not. Some measures that might help sustain that distinction follow.

- Only narrow banks could call themselves banks, or call their activity deposit taking.
- Non-guaranteed cash balances would be invested only in money market funds, registered as open ended investment companies, or under a similar regime, and would be subject to corresponding requirements for disclosure and spread of investments.
- Both guaranteed deposits and non-guaranteed money market funds would clearly describe their status on all promotional material and on statements of account.
- Funds could be offered only on an accumulation basis and no explicit promise or implied assurance that they could not fall in value would be given.
- Funds would be required to state prominently that redemptions might in emergency be suspended for up to (say) three months.
- Funds would not be marketed through branches of narrow banks, but only online or by post or telephone.
- Funds should have a substantial minimum investment (e.g. £10,000 or perhaps higher).
- Funds would not be permitted to invest in liabilities of the fund manager or in associated companies.

Such money market funds would be expected to make a substantial contribution to the finance of mortgages and SME lending, either via securitization or direct funding of specialist mortgage or SME lenders. The emergence of such specialists should be a deliberate policy objective: some lenders would be subsidiaries of financial holding companies with narrow banking subsidiaries, others might be stand-alone institutions. Obviously, however, there could be no express or implied guarantee of the obligations of such institutions by narrow banks in the same group.

Goodhart has expressed views that the boundary might provoke instability—funds might shift en masse from one side of the boundary to the other, depending on the state of the cycle and investor psychology. Market variations in the premium between insured and uninsured deposits should, however, take care of the issue. A range of different funds would offer different risk profiles, with corresponding implications for the quoted yields. In optimistic phases of the cycle, these spreads would compress; in pessimistic ones, they would widen.

The splitting of utility and casino banking is not the last word on functional separation of financial services activities. Investment banks, whether stand-alone institutions or divisions of financial conglomerates, are themselves conglomerates. They are market-makers, traders on their own account, issuers of securities, asset managers and providers of advisory services to large corporations. Each of these functions potentially conflicts with the others. The conflict is a reality, and is not adequately addressed by claims for the effectiveness of Chinese walls. Deregulation in Britain and the US from the 1970s to the end of the century allowed the creation of financial conglomerates (and encouraged many continental European universal banks to transform themselves into similar institutions). Such deregulation and restructuring has proved to be a mistake and one which has imposed large costs on the global economy by reducing the overall resilience of the financial system. It is time for that deregulation to be reversed.

8.7 Issues and Problems

Could narrow banking be implemented unilaterally by the UK? In my pamphlet *Narrow Banking* (Kay 2009) I discuss this issue and suggest that measures towards narrow banking would be necessary to protect UK taxpayers in the absence of action elsewhere, i.e. that the failure to take similar steps in other countries adds to, rather than detracts from, the urgency of such action in the UK. The FSA's *Turner Review* reaches a similar conclusion (FSA 2009). With nothing to add to that discussion, I refer the reader to it.

Other questions raised about the implementation of narrow banking fall into three main groups.

- The proposal is unnecessarily radical, since other measures, including but not necessarily confined to, more demanding capital requirements, more intrusive supervision, extension of the scope of regulation, better international coordination, and the implementation of better resolution procedures will be sufficient to secure the future stability of the financial system.

- Narrow banking could not have solved the problems that emerged in 2007–8; in particular, Northern Rock failed although it was a narrow bank, while the failure of Lehman caused a major international crisis even though Lehman was not involved in retail activities.
- The proposal is impractical, in the sense that the financial services industry could not feasibly be organized in a manner so substantially different from the current structure, or could not be so organized without imposing very large transitional and ongoing costs.

Each of these objections derives from a common implicit, but false, premise: that the existing structure of the industry and its products is basically appropriate and that the primary requirement is to put in place a set of measures which, if it had been implemented in 2003, would have prevented the developments which occurred between 2003 and 2007 and which led to the subsequent crisis. It is common for regulators to be concerned to shut the particular stable door through which the horse has recently bolted, but this argument represents a particularly egregious form of that error.

The events of 2003–7 were not a unique aberration, but a manifestation of an underlying problem. Financial services have become the main source of instability in the global economy. Although there is a long history of financially induced crises, advanced societies have become much more resilient to the consequences of natural disasters and geopolitical crises, which were historically the major causes of economic disruption. The increase in the ability of wealthy democratic states to resist natural and political events appears to have been accompanied by increased vulnerability to financial disaster.

The global economy has experienced three major shocks in the last fifteen years—the Asian and emerging-market debt crisis, the New Economy bubble and its aftermath, and the credit expansion and crunch. The same underlying factors have been at work in each case, even if the proximate manifestation has been different. The process is characterized by competitive herd behaviour which has produced widespread and gross asset mispricing which has been eventually and dramatically corrected. In each of these crises, the activities which gave rise to them has enriched many individuals involved, while the aftermath imposed substantial and widely dispersed costs on people outside the industry. These economic losses are partly direct loss of savings or pension expectations, or higher taxes to finance public subsidies for the liabilities of failed institutions.

But the indirect losses resulting from downturns in economic activity precipitated by the effects on business confidence and the disruption in the supply of financial services to the non-financial economy have in each case been far larger.

These recurrent events frame the argument for imposing functional separation, seeking simplification and aiming to create smaller, more specialist institutions of more diverse character in the financial services industry. Thus the test of narrow banking and alternative reform proposals is not 'Would these measures have averted the credit crunch?' but 'Would they establish a structure more robust to the next shock, which will certainly arise from a quite different, and currently unpredictable, source?'

The packages under discussion undoubtedly include measures which are relevant to these questions: in particular, the extension of the scope of central clearing and the introduction of resolution procedures. 'Living wills' would, if sufficiently rigorously implemented, represent a big step towards creating a more robust system for dealing with failing conglomerates, but it is evident that the measures introduced fall far short of this. To be effective, living wills would require the same kind of functional separation involved in narrow banking. In fact, an effective living will would introduce narrow banking.

While some current proposals are helpful, other post-crisis measures aggravate potential problems. In particular, the doctrine of 'too big to fail' has unfortunately been made more explicit. That doctrine put government in the position of unpaid insurer of counterparty risk incurred by systemically important institutions in their dealings in wholesale financial markets: an indefensible situation which not only imposes direct and indirect costs on taxpayers, but aggravates the problem of moral hazard. The moral hazard created is not just the incitement to risky behaviour by 'too big to fail' institutions themselves: of more importance is the undermining of incentives for surveillance of 'too big to fail' institutions by their own counterparties. Perhaps most seriously, the 'too big to fail' doctrine gives substantial advantages to large incumbent firms over entrants and smaller competitors, regardless of their relative efficiency or capacity for innovation.

Narrow banking is neither necessary nor sufficient to prevent bank failures: Northern Rock was a narrow bank and failed, while regulation of narrow banks would not have affected behaviour. As a matter of fact, Northern Rock was not a narrow bank in the sense defined here, and would not have failed if it had been. But this is not the main point. That point is that the objective of reform is not to prevent bank failure—to do so would have many adverse consequences—but to allow banks to fail without unacceptable or unmanageable consequences by creating a more resilient financial system. The requirement is therefore to put in place measures which would have enabled effective resolution of a failure like Northern Rock—the regulator and/or administrator should, as with the utilities described above, have power to take over the ring-fenced assets and liabilities. Trading on wholesale financial markets was Lehman's principal activity. The notions that public agencies can and should regulate businesses like Lehman so that they cannot fail, and that taxpayers should underwrite the trading risks assumed by the counterparties of such a company, are both preposterous. The objective must be not to prevent such entities from going bust, but to limit the consequences for essential economic activities when they do.

The objective of reform is not to support the existing structure of the industry, but to change what people do, and the culture of the institutions in which they do it. Most people within the financial services industry, and many outside it, either find it hard to believe that the industry could be organized in a significantly different way or do not wish to contemplate that the industry could be organized in a significantly different way. But plainly it could, and historically it was. To repeat an earlier example, the UK mortgage market operated without securitization for decades and could do so again.

The counterargument must be that there would be substantial cost, both transitional and continuing, from any restructuring. It is not sufficient to suggest that there might be such costs: these costs have to be compared with the scale of costs imposed by the recent crisis, which amount to several percentage points of national income—costs sufficiently large, in fact, as to more than offset any plausible estimate of the benefits of recent financial innovation.

There is evidence of economies of scale in retail banking, but also evidence that they are effectively exhausted at size levels far below those of large retail banks (Ferguson 2007). The suggestion that there are gains to shareholders and the public when banks reduce risks through diversification is theoretically capable of being valid, but was refuted by recent experience: diversification led to the failure and near failure of several universal banks through contagion from activities that were poorly understood and controlled. The more relevant claim is that there are economies of scope in financial services, mainly in allowing individuals and businesses to obtain a range of financial services from a single provider.

Representatives of consumers and SMEs are inclined to emphasize the benefits of competition rather than the advantages of a 'one-stop shop'. Descriptions of the benefits of cross-selling by retail financial institutions tend to emphasize the gains to the institutions themselves rather than their customers. While there might be benefits to large corporations from the existence of a single point of contact for their financial services, in finance, as in most other specialist activities, large companies tend to employ that point of contact themselves and rely on him or her to find the most appropriate provider of particular services. There may be advantage, for example, in being able to buy a complex derivative instrument from a trader who participates in the market for all the elements that go into the construction of that derivative, but it is easy to envisage alternative arrangements that would produce that result. In general, market arrangements are likely to emerge to enable any different structure to meet the needs of customers—that capacity for adaption is one of the fundamental strengths of markets.

8.8 CONCLUSIONS

The case for narrow banking rests on the coincidence of three arguments. First, the existing structure of financial services regulation (supervision) has failed. Consumers are ill served, the collapse of major financial institutions has created the most serious economic crisis in a generation, and the sector has been stabilized only by the injection of very large amounts of public money and unprecedented guarantees of private-sector liabilities. It is time to learn lessons from the more successful regulation of other industries. Those lessons point clearly to the need to retreat from supervision and to regulate through the mechanism of relatively simple, focused structural rules.

Second, the most effective means of improving customer services and promoting innovation in retail financial services is market oriented. That approach is based on the ability of strong and dynamic retailers to source good value products from manufacturers and wholesalers and to promote consumer-oriented innovations. The growth of financial conglomerates, a consequence of earlier measures of deregulation, has not been in the interests of the public or, in the long run, of the institutions themselves.

Third, a specific, but serious, problem arises from the ability of conglomerate financial institutions to use retail deposits which are implicitly or explicitly guaranteed by government as collateral for their other activities and particularly for proprietary trading. The use of the deposit base in this way encourages irresponsible risk-taking, creates major distortions of competition and imposes unacceptable burdens on taxpayers. Such activity can only be blocked by establishing a firewall between retail deposits and other liabilities of banks.

This is a game of high stakes. The financial services industry is now the most powerful political force in Britain and the US.[2] If anyone doubted that, the last two years have demonstrated it. The industry has extracted subsidies and guarantees of extraordinary magnitude from the taxpayer without substantial conditions or significant reform. But the central problems that give rise to the crisis have not been addressed, far less resolved. It is therefore inevitable that crisis will recur. Not, obviously, in the particular form seen in the New Economy boom and bust, or the credit explosion and credit crunch, but in some other, not yet identified, area of the financial services sector.

The public reaction to the present crisis has been one of unfocused anger. The greatest danger is that in the next crisis populist politicians will give a focus to that anger. In the recent European elections, these parties of dissent gained almost a quarter of the British vote, and made similar inroads in several other European countries. The triumph of the market economy was one of the defining events of our lifetimes. We should be careful not to throw it away. It is time to turn masters of the universe into servants of the public.

References

Bryan, L. 1988. *Breaking Up the Bank.* McGraw-Hill.

Conservative Party. 2009. White paper on financial regulation (20 July).

Crosby, J. 2008. Mortgage finance: a report to the chancellor of the exchequer. HM Treasury (24 November).

Ferguson, R. W., P. Hartmann, F. Panetta and R. Portes. 2007. *International Financial Stability.* London: CEPR.

Friedman, J. 2009. Causes of the financial crisis. *Critical Review* (July).

FSA. 2009. *The Turner Review* (18 March).

Johnson, S. 2009. The quiet coup. *Atlantic Monthly* (May).

Kahn, A. E. 1988. *The Economics of Regulation,* 2nd revised edn. Cambridge, MA: MIT Press.

Kay, J. 2009. *Narrow Banking: The Reform of Banking Regulation.* London: CSFI.

Litan, R. 1988, *What Should Banks Do?* Washington, DC: Brookings Institution.

Milne, A. 2009, *The Fall of the House of Credit.* Cambridge University Press.

---

[2] A powerful exposition is provided by Johnson (2009).

Why and How Should We Regulate Pay in the Financial Sector?

By Martin Wolf

This chapter investigates whether there is a case for regulation of financial sector pay and, if so, how it should be done. It concludes that regulators should not be concerned with the level of pay. That should be left to tax policy, though there is also a strong case for investigating the degree of competition in the sector and exploring remedies if significant monopolies are discovered. But regulators do have a vital interest in the structure of pay, since shareholders and managers can benefit from 'gaming' the state's role as insurer of last resort of these highly leveraged and therefore inherently risky businesses. Structural reforms, including much higher capital requirements, would help. But, so long as anything like the present situation prevails, in terms of the structure of the financial industry, it is vital to prevent management of systemically significant institutions from benefiting directly from decisions that make failure likely. The answer is to make decision makers bear substantial personal liability in the event of such failures.

> *Simply stated, the bright new financial system—for all its talented participants, for all its rich rewards—failed the test of the market place.*
>
> Paul Volcker[1]

What, if anything, should be done to regulate the level or structure of remuneration in the financial services industry? This is one of the most contentious questions to have arisen out of the global financial crisis. To answer it, we need to address two further questions. First, what, precisely, is the problem? Second, what might be the solution?

9.1 PROBLEMS WITH FINANCIAL SECTOR REMUNERATION

We live in an era of widening pay inequality in western economies (see, for example, Dew-Becker and Gordon 2005; Piketty and Saez 2006). The extraordinary rewards secured by those in the financial sector have played a substantial part in this growing inequality. Many would argue that such inequality is itself socially damaging, whatever the explanation

---

[1] Address to the Economic Club of New York (8 April 2008).

for it: it undermines the sense of social cohesion, worsens social tensions and undermines equality of opportunity.

Yet such objections are multiplied in force when, as is the case for the financial sector today, these exceptional incomes appear to be the reward not of either merit or skill, but of rent extraction or 'heads-I-win-tails-you-lose' gambling.[2] The fact that states had to rescue the financial sector in 2008, through a combination of aggressive monetary policy and direct fiscal support, and then nursed it back to health, via regulatory forbearance and transfusions of cheap money, makes this sense of injustice stronger still. Contrary to the already notorious statement by Lloyd Blankfein, chairman and chief executive of Goldman Sachs, that his company does 'God's work', it is now widely felt that they are instruments of the devil, making their practitioners wealthy beyond the dreams of avarice, while they lay waste economies, only to benefit from state-led rescues when threatened with destruction themselves (see Arlidge 2009).

Beyond these broader objections to the growth of inequality, in general, and of unjust rewards, in particular, concern is expressed over more specific defects to do with incentives in the financial sector.

The argument here has several steps.

First, financial sector booms and busts create gigantic losses for society, not only via the direct costs of 'bailouts', but still more via the indirect costs of economic instability on the economy.

Second, to the extent that institutions take synchronized risks, they increase the likelihood and severity of such crises by creating the conditions in which ultimately ruinous bets are rewarded, at least for a while.

Third, asymmetric information is pervasive. Thus, strategies with zero expected excess returns in the long run may look successful in the short run, either as a matter of luck or because of the nature of the strategy—high probability of small gains with a low probability of huge losses, for example. Such strategies are extremely common: the 'carry trade' is such a

---

[2]On rent extraction, Adair Turner (see FSA 2009, p. 49), chairman of the UK's Financial Services Authority, notes:

> It seems likely that some and perhaps much of the structuring and trading activity involved in the complex version of securitized credit, was not required to deliver credit intermediation efficiently. Instead, it achieved an economic rent extraction made possible by the opacity of margins, the asymmetry of information and knowledge between end users of financial services and producers, and the structure of principal–agent relationships between investors and companies and between companies and individual employees.

strategy; so was the strategy of buying AAA-rated collateralized debt obligations in place of the liabilities of AAA-rated governments. As Raghuram Rajan of Chicago University's Booth School of Business has rightly noted (Rajan 2008):

> True alpha can be measured only in the long run and with the benefit of hindsight... Compensation structures that reward managers annually for profits, but do not claw these rewards bank when losses materialize, encourage the creation of fake alpha.

Fourth, shareholders lack the capacity to monitor risks in complex institutions. Worse, in highly leveraged limited-liability companies, they also lack the interest to monitor such risks properly, since—as Lucian Bebchuk and Holger Spamann of the Harvard Law School point out, convincingly—they enjoy the upside, while their downside is capped at zero (see Bebchuk and Spamann 2009; see also Wolf 2010). Thus, 'leveraged bank shareholders have an incentive to increase the volatility of bank assets', which enhances their potential gains.

Fifth, not only shareholders, but also creditors, lack the interest to price properly the risks being assumed, since they enjoy a high probability of rescue in the event of failure: this is the operational core of the idea of 'too big to fail'.

Sixth, managers also have an incentive to bet the bank to the extent that their interests are aligned with those of the shareholders. Since share options are a leveraged play on the gains to shareholders, they make management even more prone to bet the bank than shareholders. Moreover, the fact that managers sometimes lose does not show that they were wrong to take such bets. Yet the evidence suggests that even the management of failed institutions have been able to cash out substantial winnings before the collapse (see Bebchuk *et al.* 2009).

Finally, the combination of asymmetric information with the complexity of such institutions makes it effectively impossible for regulators to monitor the risks being taken.

The problem of remuneration is, therefore, an extreme version of the deep problem in this sector: the misalignment of incentives between the various decision makers inside the system and ultimate risk-bearers, particularly the taxpayers and the wider public. This is not to say that decision makers do not also make mistakes induced by over-optimism. But perverse incentives create what I have called 'rational carelessness', which makes decision makers underplay risks or even choose to ignore them altogether (Wolf 2010). Thus, it is impossible to distinguish between the impacts of perverse incentives and cognitive biases. For this reason, too, it is vital to start our analysis with the challenge of incentives.

9.2 Solutions to Financial Sector Remuneration

So what should, or can, be done about these problems with financial sector remuneration?

9.2.1 *Inequality, Rents and Competition*

As a general proposition, inequality should be dealt with by general taxation, not by interference in pay levels, least of all interference in pay levels in individual industries. It may be necessary, however, to limit political lobbying and election spending to ensure that this is possible. Experience has also found that direct government control of pay creates a host of perverse and unintended consequences. But monopoly rent can be attacked, either by competition policy or, where monopoly rent is an inherent feature of a market, by turning the industry into a regulated utility. This may well apply to the activity of market-making, for example.

It would make excellent sense to conduct a rigorous inquiry into the extent of obstacles to competition in the sector, ideally on a global basis. Where lack of competition is found, policymakers can then choose between actions that would enhance competition and moves towards a more regulated industry model. It appears plausible that reforms which increase competition—but also shrink the size of the sector, increase capital requirements, lower equity returns and reduce excessive risk-taking—should also lower the scale of the rewards available. Indeed, Thomas Philippon of New York University's Stern School of Business and Ariell Resheff of the University of Virginia have recently estimated that rents accounted for between 30% and 50% of the wage differential between the financial sector and other industries (Philippon and Resheff 2009). It would seem to follow that a successful attack on those rents would also lower these rewards.

9.2.2 *Fixing Incentives*

So far as possible, the problems identified above need to be fixed by changing incentives—radically so, if necessary. The alternative—effective supervision—is substantially less plausible and is, in any case, only a second line of defence against irresponsible risk-taking. So how might this be done?

Broadly speaking, there seem to exist two strategies. The first is to restructure the financial industry in such a way that the risk-taking parts—sometimes called the 'casino'—will never need public bailouts, in which case one could leave the monitoring of pay structures to share-holders, themselves monitored by creditors fully aware of the risks they are running. The second strategy is to assume that the public sector will always be the risk-taker-of-last-resort, and so intervene in the structure, but not the level, of pay, to ensure that the interests of the public are reflected in those incentives.

On the first of these two approaches, the relevant question is whether restructuring of this kind would be both feasible and effective. One possibility would be narrow banking, as recommended by John Kay (2009). But the rest of the system would then have to be credibly free from government insurance, in the sense that all participants would know that they would live and die by the market. The second, even more radical, alternative would be 'limited-purpose banking', which is recommended by Laurence Kotlikoff (2010) of Boston University, in which intermediaries would be prevented from taking risk on their own books, unless they had unlimited liability. Instead, any changes in the valuation of assets would be passed through at once to investors, as mutual funds or unit trust do today. Financial assets would then be marked-to-market at all times. Thus, under Kay's proposal, the credit system as we know it would be set free, though it would be separated from deposit-taking; under the proposal of Kotlikoff, it would effectively disappear.

I am sceptical about the effectiveness of these two structural alternatives. I believe it is impossible for governments to make a credible pledge to let the credit system as a whole implode in a crisis. But if this commitment were not credible, there would surely be excessive risk-taking, which would, in turn, make crises highly probable. Thereupon, governments would almost certainly prove the truth of the beliefs of those taking the risks. For this reason, narrow banking alone would be insufficient to make the system more stable.

Limited-purpose banking looks more hopeful, though it is extremely radical: the financial system as we know it would cease to exist: we would no longer have traditional term transformation. The big question, however, is whether the government would stand aside when asset prices collapsed. It is used to doing so when equity prices collapse. But the US authorities did not dare to stand aside when the money market funds were imperilled by massive withdrawals during the financial crisis of 2009. Instead the Federal Reserve intervened. True, it is possible that this would not happen if the vulnerability of the banking system to cascading asset prices were eliminated.

In any case, there is little likelihood of either of these radical structural alternatives being adopted. This then leaves us with the aim of changing incentives within a system that continues to enjoy a substantial degree of implicit and explicit insurance by the state. So how might one change the incentives affecting such institutions?

The first step would be to force financial institutions to become either full partnerships or, more plausibly, to increase their equity capital and possess large cushions of contingent capital (perhaps a combined total of as much as 20–30% of assets).[3] The advantage of greater equity capital (or near equivalents) is that it would greatly reduce the likelihood of any need for a government rescue, though it could not eliminate it. Moreover, with much greater equity, the asymmetry of shareholder incentives would also be reduced, since the owners of the firm would have far more to lose.

Nevertheless, so long as there were outside shareholders, the latter would still have only a limited ability to monitor the activities of management and employees. Moreover, if the social interest in containing risk-taking in financial institutions continued to exist, as it surely would, the regulator would have a legitimate interest in the structure of incentives even if shareholders could monitor their employees. This is, indeed, already widely accepted. So the question is not whether there should be intervention in the structures of remuneration, but rather what the principles of such reformed structures should be. Let us list the broad considerations that should apply, before turning to some details.

First, the regulator, representing the public interest, is interested in the soundness of the institutions under its supervision, not in maximizing expected returns to shareholders. At a minimum, therefore, it wants the interests of decision makers to be aligned with those financing the balance sheet as a whole, not just with those of the shareholders, who finance an extremely limited part of the balance sheet.

Second, the regulator wants to ensure that employees of the firms cannot benefit under any circumstances from risk-taking behaviour which risks the safety of the balance sheet as a whole—that is to say, makes bankruptcy a likely outcome.

Third, in carrying out this objective, the regulator must make it clear that it is the responsibility of management and senior staff (namely, those

---

[3]In practice, it would be impossible to raise the capital required by large financial institutions from a partnership. That was why the limited-liability company was invented in the first place. It seems particularly important for large financial institutions.

charged with oversight of risk-management in the firm) to protect its balance sheet, in the public interest.

Fourth, the regulator should also make clear that these decision makers exercise a public trust, for whose competent execution they will be held personally liable.

Finally, in ensuring such liability, sufficient time must pass between the making of decisions and the judgement on whether decision makers have fulfilled their trust appropriately.

Thus, the fundamental idea is that the decision makers in the firm exercise a public trust, which is to protect the balance sheet as a whole, for whose discharge they are to be held personally liable over a long enough period to make the judgement on their actions feasible.

How might these ideas be made effective, in practice?

The Squam Lake Report, authored by a distinguished group of American economists, makes the following recommendation (French *et al.* 2010, pp. 81–82):

> Systemically important financial institutions should withhold a significant share of each senior manager's total annual compensation for several years. The withheld compensation should not take the form of stock or stock options. Rather, each holdback should be for a fixed dollar amount and employees would forfeit their holdback if their firm goes bankrupt or receives extraordinary assistance.

Effectively, this would mean that management would bear substantial personal liability in the event of a failure. As the authors rightly note, pay in deferred stock or in stock options aligns the interests of the managers only with those of shareholders, not with those of the people who finance the balance sheet as a whole, including the state as insurer of last resort. As they also note (French *et al.* 2010, p. 82), under such payment schemes,

> Managers and stockholders both capture the upside when things go well, and transfer at least some of the losses to taxpayers when things go badly. Stock options give managers even more incentive to take risk. Thus, compensation that is deferred to satisfy this regulatory obligation should be for a fixed monetary amount.

Then, in the event of failure or government rescue (excluding access to lender-of-last-resort facilities at the central bank), the sums would be forfeit, unless some value were left over after all other creditors were made whole. It would be crucial that such obligations could not be expunged by leaving the firm, but would be in place for a significant and fixed period of time.

On similar lines, Neil Record (2010), writing in the *Financial Times,* argues that

> Bankers who wish to receive a bonus above a threshold (say £50,000, or twice average earnings) would become personally liable for the amount of the bonus for a period, perhaps ten years. They would sit between equity holders and other creditors of the bank—and so would be called upon should any bank find that its equity capital is wiped out by losses. In practice, this would mean their liability would be triggered by a government or other (private-sector) rescue. If there turned out to be no rescue, then they would be liable to the liquidator. If there were a rescue, the rescuer would pay over support monies, and then reclaim them from the limited-liability bankers. The bankers would be released from this liability over time, but of course with every new bonus payment they would incur a new liability. By this mechanism, all senior bankers would have a rolling portfolio of liabilities to the extent of the cash they had taken out of the bank in bonuses... I would also suggest that bankers' liability should not be an insurable risk; bankers would be prevented by law from insuring their exposure (just as one cannot insure against criminal penalties).

The details of such proposals are to be worked out. But the nature of the regulatory requirements seems quite clear.

First, regulators should establish the principle of personal liability of the decision makers in the firms.

Second, they should also establish principles on which the relevant key decision makers would be identified.

Third, regulators should publish the criteria for determining such personal liability.

Fourth, the liability should be for a substantial portion of total remuneration, whether paid as bonuses or salary, with the portion rising together with the seniority of the decision maker at the time he or she received the remuneration. For the chief executive, that portion should be close to 100% of a sum determined to be exempt from the levy—possibly the average salary of professionals in the firm.

Fifth, the liability would be a cash amount, indexed to inflation. The required sums would be held in an escrow account, to be paid out after the end of the required holding period.

Sixth, the period over which such liability would continue should be substantial—up to ten years after receipt of the remuneration. This would be long enough to establish the viability of many (if not all) strategies. Thus, there would be a rolling responsibility.

Seventh, stock awards would be permitted, but stock options would be precluded for such decision makers.

Eighth, the liability would be uninsurable. It would have to be borne by the decision maker.

Ninth, regulators would also have a say in the remuneration structures of the non-key decision makers in the firm. The principle of clawback of remuneration, in the event of failure, would be part of such discussion. In the event of failure and subsequent rescue, all stock options and stock awards should be cancelled for all employees.

Tenth, senior executives of failed financial firms would be barred from subsequent employment in the industry for a substantial period of time.

Evidently, such reforms would be far better implemented if they applied across borders. But, if necessary, countries should go their own way, since they have a vital national interest in ensuring the safety of the balance sheets of their own firms. Regulators would then have to agree the principle of remuneration for senior executives in all systemically significant national financial businesses.

9.3 CONCLUSION

The question of pay is unavoidably fraught. It concerns not just the financial sector but the wider economy and, indeed, its political and social stability. It is plausible, in fact, that the liberalization of the financial sector has had substantial direct and indirect impact on the widening inequality of private-sector pay in many countries over the past three decades. It is also plausible that remuneration is one factor, among others, that led financial firms to take a risk-seeking approach to the exploitation of their balance sheets, with ultimately disastrous results.

On both aspects, therefore, there is a case for policy action. So far as the economy, as a whole, is concerned, the obvious policy instrument is taxation, since direct controls on pay are likely to have unintended adverse consequences. But, in the case of finance, it also makes sense to undertake a rigorous assessment of competition. Should there be severe competition issues, policymakers should consider remedies: either competition should be enhanced or regulation be introduced, as in any other monopolistic industry. Market-making is an obvious area for such treatment.

Beyond this, the structure—rather than the level—of pay in the financial sector must be regarded as a matter of public interest, since taxpayers are the risk-takers of last resort. The fundamental problem is that, in the case of the financial industry, with its highly leveraged balance sheets, limited liability creates perverse incentives for both shareholders and management. These are not fully offset by the watchfulness of creditors, partly because the latter rightly believe that they enjoy the benefits of explicit and implicit taxpayer insurance. These perverse incentives encourage rational carelessness, with intermittently catastrophic results.

So what is to be done? The regulators have a duty to correct the perverse incentives at work. Higher capital requirements would help. But it would not be enough. Massive structural change in the financial system might also help. But it is unlikely to occur. Thus, it is also important to motivate management to protect the balance sheet as a whole and not just identify their interests with those of shareholders, since maximization of expected shareholder returns can leave huge tail risks with taxpayers.

For this reason, regulators should insist in a change in the structure of incentives, to discourage executives with responsibility for risk-management from 'gaming the state'. Since outside supervision is likely to fail, the best way to achieve this result is to make management liable in the event of bankruptcy or state rescue. This can be achieved by forcing a substantial part of remuneration to be held back for an extended period, up to ten years, and then be lost in the event of failure. In this case, the management of failed institutions would lose much of their accumulated wealth. In addition, stock options, with their perverse, one-sided incentives should be eliminated for all employees of systemically significant financial institutions and all variable pay within the firm should be subject to clawback in the light of subsequent performance.

Aligning the interests of those who work in the financial sector with those of creditors, including the creditor of last resort—the state—would surely not solve every problem in the industry. But it is the best way to realign incentives. The crucial step is to abandon the idea that shareholder interests alone count. They do not. In the case of financial institutions, there is a wider public interest in actions that minimize the chances of bankruptcy. Making decision makers substantially liable in the event of failure of the business under their control is also a vital part of the solution.

REFERENCES

Arlidge, J. 2009. I'm doing God's work. Meet Mr Goldman Sachs. *Times* (8 November).

Bebchuk, L., A. Cohen and H. Spamann. 2009. Bankers had cashed in before the music stopped. *Financial Times* (7 December).

Bebchuk, L., and H. Spamann. 2009. Regulating bankers' pay. Harvard Law and Economics Discussion Paper 641 (May).

Dew-Becker, I., and R. Gordon. 2005. Where did the productivity growth go? National Bureau of Economic Research Working Paper 11842 (December).

French, K. R. *et al.* 2010. *The Squam Lake Report: Fixing the Financial System.* Princeton University Press.

Kay, J. 2009. *Narrow Banking: The Reform of Banking Regulation.* London: CSFI.

Kotlikoff, L. J. 2010. *Jimmy Stewart Is Dead: Ending the World's Ongoing Financial Plague with Limited Purpose Banking.* John Wiley & Sons.

Piketty, T., and E. Saez. 2006. The evolution of top incomes. National Bureau of Economic Research Working Paper 11955 (January).

Philippon, T., and A. Resheff. 2009. Wages and human capital in the US financial industry: 1909–2000. National Bureau of Economic Research Working Paper 14644 (January).

Rajan, R. 2008. Bankers' pay is deeply flawed. *Financial Times* (9 January).

Record, N. 2010. How to make the bankers share the losses. *Financial Times* (7 January).

FSA. 2009. *The Turner Review: A Regulatory Response to the Global Banking Crisis* (March).

Wolf, M. 2010. Reform of regulation has to start by altering incentives. *Financial Times* (24 June).

Wolf, M. 2010. The challenge of halting the financial doomsday machine. *Financial Times* (21 April).

Will the Politics of Global Moral Hazard Sink Us Again?

By Peter Boone and Simon Johnson

During the last four decades governments in wealthy countries have built up large contingent liabilities due to the implicit guarantees they have provided to their financial sectors. Politicians are motivated to create near-term growth and are always reluctant to permit hardships that would otherwise arise from defaults and greater austerity. As a result, the industrialized world has experienced excessive and dangerous financial sector development. Including all promises, US and European taxpayers back over 250% of their GDP in implicit obligations, all of which contribute to the development of moral hazard in lending around the world. If this incentive system remains in place and these liabilities continue to grow unchecked, the eventual end of this 'doomsday cycle'—with repeated bailouts for distressed lenders—will be large sovereign defaults and economic collapse. The current round of regulatory reform is not sufficient to stop this trend.

10.1 INTRODUCTION

One of most widely held views within economics is that more financial development—as proxied, for example, by higher credit relative to GDP—is good for growth. Over the past four decades, a great deal of empirical evidence has been interpreted as pointing in this direction, and much supportive theory has also developed. At least since the Asian financial crisis of 1997-98, an increasing number of caveats have been attached to this view—particularly with regards to international capital flows—but the mainstream consensus remains that a larger financial sector relative to the overall economy is a sign of economic health: generally good for future growth and, at worst, not seriously harmful.

Events since September 2008 suggest that this view needs substantial revision. It is now self-evident that the financial system in Europe and the US has become dangerous—it is prone to catastrophic collapse in

Along with James Kwak the authors run a website on the global financial system at http://baselinescenario.com.

part because major private-sector firms (banks and non-bank financial institutions) have a distorted incentive structure that eventually encourages costly risk-taking. Unfortunately, the measures taken in various US and European bailout rounds during 2008-9 (and again in 2010 for the Eurozone) have only worsened, and extended to far more entities, these underlying 'moral hazard' incentive problems. The takeaway for systemic creditors everywhere, whether they be executives and traders at big banks or profligate politicians in Eurozone nations, is clear: they get bailed out with official finance and stimulus policies just after financial crises, so why fear a new cycle of excessive risk-taking and deficit spending?[1]

Not only have the remaining major financial institutions in North America and Western Europe, along with each one of the Eurozone nations, asserted and proved that they are 'too big to fail'—so they need to be saved at great taxpayer expense (both directly and through indirect off-budget measures), but they have also demonstrated that no one in leading governments is currently willing or able to take on their economic and political power. The financial reform process currently underway in the US and other industrialized countries will result in very little (if any) effective constraint on reckless risk-taking by 'too big to fail' financial institutions as the next credit cycle develops.

This cycle of boom followed by bailouts and bust amounts to a form of implicit taxpayer subsidy that encourages individual institutions to become larger—and the system as a whole to swell. Our willingness to bail out their creditors means that systemic institutions are able to raise finance cheaply in global markets. The implicit subsidy to creditors encourages greater debt, which makes the system ever more precarious.

There are now major fiscal threats posed by the size of the largest institutions (easy to measure), as well as by the nature of system risk (for which the measures remain much more rudimentary). The fiscal impact of the financial crisis of 2007-9 will end up increasing US net federal government debt by about 40 percentage points (i.e., from around 40% to around 80% of GDP). The IMF estimates that European debt will rise by a similar amount, albeit starting from higher levels.

However, this only captures a fraction of the total costs to taxpayers, savers and workers. Each time we have a new bust, our major central banks rush to relax monetary policy, thus lowering interest rates for

---

[1] Financial sector bonuses in the US were high in 2008, despite the financial crisis. Wall Street compensation as a whole was even higher in 2009. Some traders and executives lost their jobs (e.g. from the fall of Bear Stearns and Lehman Brothers), but most did very well.

savers while giving banks greater profits. These transfers from savers to financial institutions are effectively a tax on savings—if capital had been allocated better, savers could have earned higher returns. We also lose, as a society, due to the unemployment of labor and capital—and thus lost output—caused by these crises. If US and European unemployment rises by an additional 5% for five years, the total cost to society is 25% on annual workers' output.

We should be even more concerned about the contingent liabilities that arise from our failure to deal with this dangerous system. The potential liability arising from our collective failure to deal with 'too big to fail' financial institutions is of much larger magnitude since the liabilities of these entities are well above the size of GDP. In a bad crisis we could be liable for sums we simply cannot afford. In some Western European countries this contingent liability dwarfs US numbers—because European financial systems, such as those in the UK, Germany and Ireland, are much bigger relative to their economies. The concept of 'too big to fail' is now enshrined at the heart of the global financial system. The Eurozone countries have also, with their determination to prevent defaults inside the Eurozone, taken on their collective shoulders the current and future debts of all member nations.

Having chosen to take on these contingent liabilities, with the dangerous incentives in place for these to expand and grow, our only course of action to prevent calamity is to build a regulatory framework which keeps dangers in check. This has primarily been the task of our national regulatory institutions, who themselves are guided by legislative bodies and political leaders. We have also attempted to coordinate such regulation through international agreements such as successive Basel accords.

Unfortunately, these systems of regulation have proven to fail repeatedly at their main task of checking excessive expansion and risk. As we outline in case studies, these failures arise in many institutional contexts, but the root cause is an array of powerful incentives which cause our political leaders, legislative bodies and, of course, those being regulated to dismantle regulation after each bout of tightening.

Tough regulations are naturally opposed by financial institutions who fight them aggressively in order to increase profits. Politicians receive donations from the financial sector and they benefit from the booms that can be won with relaxed regulation. When one nation relaxes regulations, it harms others. Countries with tough regulators will see capital flow out to the less regulated economies as foreign banks bid up interest rates and take more risk. This in turn increases the call by local banks for relaxed regulation in order to maintain competitiveness. With such a global macroeconomic dynamic at play, there is invariably a race to the bottom across nations as regulatory standards are relaxed.

Despite attempts to reform the system now, politicians and regulators are once again making the same errors that they have made repeatedly during each cycle of boom and bust since the 1970s. The reform process that is currently underway does not resolve the deep incentive problems that have repeatedly caused our regulatory system, which we badly need to prevent excess, to spectacularly fail after each attempt to fix it.

We can already imagine how the next cycle of our financial system will evolve.

Emerging markets were star performers during the 2007–9 crisis; in fact, most global growth forecasts made at the end of 2008 exaggerated the slowdown in middle-income countries. To be sure, issues remain in places such as China, Brazil, India and Russia, but their economic policies and financial structures proved surprisingly resilient and their growth prospects are now perceived as good. In the near term, these economies will grow relatively quickly, while simultaneously generating significant savings in particular pockets (e.g. within the manufacturing export sector and/or in natural resource extraction). They will also demand capital for investments in the private sector and in quasi-state-backed activities. This global macroeconomic dynamic will push capital out of (some parts of) emerging markets and into perceived 'safe havens' around the world, while also pulling capital from those havens back into other parts of those same (or other) emerging markets. This is a circle of debt, not equity, financing, which will lead to a build-up of financial claims both in industrialized countries and in emerging markets.

There are striking parallels with the 'recycling of petrodollars' that occurred during the 1970s. In that episode, current-account surpluses from oil exporting countries were placed on deposit in money centre banks (mostly the US), which then lent the funds to emerging markets in Latin America and to communist Poland and Romania. When the global macro cycle turned, due to monetary policy tightening in the US, short-term interest rates increased and most of these debtors faced serious difficulties. Major banks in the US were technically insolvent, but regulatory forbearance allowed them to continue operating.

We now seem likely to repeat a version of this scenario, but the major changes in the nature of the financial sector over the intervening three decades means that more capital is likely to flow around the world (in

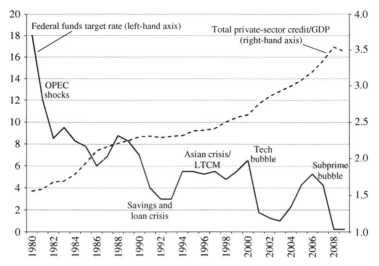

Figure 10.1. US private sector credit as fraction of GDP and federal funds rate. *Source*: Federal Reserve.

absolute terms and relative to the size of key economies) and more leverage may be piled on, including in the non-financial sector.

This is our next 'global doomsday cycle' or 'debt super-cycle', following repeated rounds of boom–bust–bailout over the past three decades, and it seems likely to end badly. [2]

Section 10.2 explains the structure of this global doomsday cycle. Section 10.3 reviews recent case studies illustrating how crises can emerge from multiple and different sources of failure around the world. Section 10.4 discusses incentive problems in the Eurozone in more detail. Section 10.5 argues that the latest round of regulatory reforms for the financial sector is unlikely to make much difference. Section 10.6 concludes with the implications for the global macroeconomy.

10.2 THE GLOBAL DOOMSDAY CYCLE

10.2.1 *Cycle Structure*

The size of the US financial system—as measured by total credit relative to GDP, for example—has more than doubled over the last three decades, and the changes in other industrialized countries are of the same order

---

[2]Haldane and Alessandri (2009) discuss an economic 'Doom Loop' where they focus on the time inconsistency of promises not to bail out banks, and the dangers to global financial stability that arise from this.

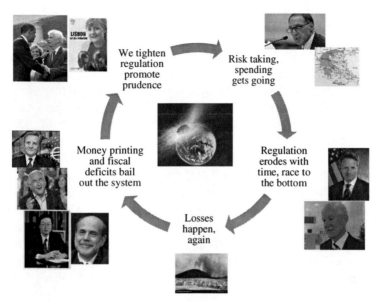

Figure 10.2. The global doomsday cycle.

Note: the photos in this figure are of US President Barrack Obama with Senator Christopher Dodd; Angela Merkel, Chancellor of Germany; Dick Fuld, former chairman and chief executive of Lehman Brothers; a map of Greece; US Treasury Secretary Timothy Geithner (former president of the New York Fed); Patrick Neary, former chief executive of the Irish Financial Regulator; the Icelandic volcano; Ben Bernanke, chairman of the Federal Reserve Board; Zhou Xiaochuan, the governor of the People's Bank of China; Dominique Strauss-Kahn, managing director of the IMF; and Jean Claude Trichet, president of the European Central Bank.

of magnitude (the dashed line in figure 10.1 shows credit relative to GDP since 1980). Each time our financial system runs into problems, the Federal Reserve quickly lowers interest rates to revive it (the solid line in figure 10.1 shows the federal funds target rate since 1980, including indications for the timing of particular cycles). These crises appear to be getting worse and worse: not only are interest rates now near zero around the globe, but a significant number of industrialized countries are on fiscal trajectories that require large changes in policy to avoid an eventual collapse of confidence in the government bond market. What happens when the next shock rears its head?

We may be nearing the stage where the answer will be, as it was during the Great Depression, a calamitous global collapse. The root problem is that we have let a 'doomsday cycle' become central to our economic system. This cycle, as illustrated in figure 10.2, has roughly five distinct stages.

At the start of the cycle (in the upper right part of figure 10.2), banks and other financial intermediaries begin to build dangerous levels of leverage. For example, banks take risks as creditors and depositors provide cheap funding to banks because they know that, if things go wrong, our central banks and fiscal authorities will bail them out. In the cycle that ran through September 2008, banks such as Lehman Brothers and Royal Bank of Scotland used such funds to buy risky portfolios of real estate assets and engineer massive mergers, with the aim of providing dividends and bonuses, or simply trophies, to shareholders and management. Through our direct (such as deposit insurance) and indirect (central bank and fiscal) subsidies and supports, we actually encourage our banking system to ignore large socially harmful 'tail risks', i.e. those risks where there is a small chance of calamitous collapse. As far as banks are concerned, they can walk away and let the state clean it up. Some bankers and policymakers even fare well during the collapse they helped create.

Regulators are supposed to prevent this dangerous risk-taking, but short-sighted governments often prefer to relax regulation, thereby promoting a credit boom, while banks wield large political and financial power and are hence able to outwit or overrule regulators. The system has become remarkably complex, so eventually regulators are compromised and lose their ability to rein in or even measure risk-taking—but hardly anybody cares enough to notice. The extent of regulatory failure ahead of this last crisis was mind boggling. Many banks, such as Northern Rock, convinced regulators they could hold just 2% core capital against large, risky asset portfolios. The whole banking system built up $70 trillion in interconnected derivatives exposures which meant that, when one large bank went down, it could have taken the rest of the system with it.

These resulting risks were not the result of errors. For example, it was easy to spot that derivatives had created massive systemic risk, and that lax rules on hybrid capital made those instruments ineffective.[3] Instead, our leading politicians and regulators took the easy route that so many

---

[3]Hybrid capital primarily differs from debt through its ability to absorb losses, i.e. providing a buffer like that provided by common equity. Banks like hybrid capital because tax laws permit the interest paid on it to be deducted. When the crisis came, most banks did their best to avoid cancelling coupons, or writing down hybrid debt, because they wanted to maintain reputations that they always paid—in order to keep financing cheaper in the future. The investor base in these instruments was also invested in the banks' debt and other securities, so maintaining good relations was important.

It was also soon revealed that some banks had issued supposedly hybrid capital instruments which could not legally be used to absorb losses. For example, the Belgian banking group KBC was ordered to not pay coupons on hybrid debt by the European Competition Commission after it received a government bailout, but it still made the payments—

have taken time and again in the past. They avoided confrontation with powerful banks, and financial sector lobbyists and donors, while paying lip-service to arguments that 'efficient markets' would sort this out. When the financial sector argued that tough regulation made them uncompetitive against neighbours, regulators invariably relaxed regulations even more.

Given the inability of our political and social systems to handle the hardship that follows financial collapse, when things finally do go wrong, we rely on our central banks to cut interest rates and direct credits to bail out the loss makers. While the faces tend to change, each central bank and government has operated similarly. This time it was Ben Bernanke (in his dual role as monetary steward and regulator as governor and now chairman of the Federal Reserve since 2001), Tim Geithner (first as regulator while president of the Federal Reserve Bank of New York, and now as chief architect of the administrations strategy to refine regulation as treasury secretary), Mervyn King (governor of the Bank of England since June 2003) and Jean-Claude Trichet (architect of the Eurozone and president of the ECB since November 2003), who all regulated and oversaw policy as the bubble was built and are now designing our rescue from the system that they helped create.

When the bailout is done, we start all over again. This has been the pattern since the mid 1970s in many developed countries—a period which coincided with large macroeconomic and regulatory change, including the end of the Bretton Woods fixed exchange rate systems, reduced capital controls in rich countries and the beginning of forty years of continuous regulatory easing (although during brief periods after each successive crisis some new rules are imposed only to find they get watered down soon after).

The real danger is that as this loop continues to operate, the scale of the problem becomes larger. If each cycle requires a greater and greater level of public intervention, we will surely eventually collapse.

---

because the language in their original prospectuses required this. Commerzbank issued hybrid debt instruments with legal requirements that they pay coupons as long as they paid coupons on any similar seniority debt. After acquiring Dresdner Bank, which had issued hybrid debt on which coupon payments were legally required, Commerzbank will probably be forced to pay coupons on all similar seniority debt instruments with this so-called 'pusher' language.

Other banks paid coupons despite their financial difficulties, even when these payments were not obligatory. This was accepted by the regulators due to the fact that pension funds and insurance companies are major owners of these securities and it would lead to systemic problems if holders of these securities were to face large losses. See Goodhart (2010) for more discussion of contingent capital instruments.

10.2.2 *Why Does Regulation Repeatedly Fail?*

There are really two broad ways to view the past regulatory failures which have brought us to today's dangerous point. One is to argue that mistakes were made that can be corrected through better rules. This is the path of virtually all the reforms currently underway, including the Basel Committee and the Financial Stability Board—backed by the G20—which are now designing supposedly comprehensive new rules that will close past loopholes that permitted banks to effectively lower core capital. Furthermore, they are adding new rules that will ensure greater liquidity at banks. Even Ben Bernanke, who heads a Federal Reserve that will soon be empowered with far greater powers under regulatory reform, has argued that the US simply needs 'smarter regulations' to save the system. Having worked for many years in formerly communist countries, this reminds us of the repeated attempts by central planners to rescue their systems with additional regulations until it became all too apparent that collapse was imminent.

The second view is that the long-standing and repeated failure of regulation to check financial collapses reflects deep political and operational difficulties in creating regulation for modern finance. The most important point is that our politicians naturally like looser regulation. When we loosen regulation we give our borrowers, who are implicitly backed by taxpayers, the opportunity to borrow more and profit more. This generates a credit boom, which may be financed by bad credits, but does well for sitting politicians. The great era of deregulation under Gordon Brown and Bill Clinton/George Bush undoubtedly supported those unsustainable boom years which commentators wrongly attributed to strong fundamentals.

When regulation is tight, banks naturally spend much money and time lobbying against it. The banks have the money, they have the best lawyers and they have the funds to finance the political system. Politicians rarely want strong regulators—even after a major collapse, they are more concerned about restarting growth than about limiting future dangers. So, politics rarely favours regulation.

The operational issues are also large: how should regulators decide the risk capital that should be allocated to new, arcane derivatives which banks claim should reduce risk? When faced with rooms full of papers describing new instruments, and their risk assessments, regulators will always be at a disadvantage compared with banks.

It is a great leap of faith to hope that this system will not be captured or corrupted again over time. So the fact that it has failed, in a spectacular manner, to successfully limit costly risk, should be no surprise. In our view the new regulations discussed in Basel III will fail, just as Basel I and Basel II already have. They sound 'smart', as Mr Bernanke would claim, because they are correcting past egregious errors, but new errors will surface over the next five to ten years, and these will be precisely where loopholes remain and where the system gradually becomes corrupted again.

10.2.3   *The Growing Sources of Moral Hazard in Our Doomsday Cycle*

In addition to 'too big to fail' banks in the US, Europe and many emerging markets, there are many other sources of moral hazard which contribute to rapid growth of credit and gross leverage. Whenever creditors think they may get bailed out, i.e. protected by a third party from loss when a borrower is on the verge of failure, they are willing to lend cheaply. If that third party can't adequately check the lending, we are all in danger of a debt cycle. Note that while the 'third party' in developed countries is often a government, the structures involved are often more complicated in emerging markets, broadly speaking.

The relationship between Abu Dhabi and Dubai World is a nice example. Despite its limited oil revenues and funds, creditors provided over $100 billion in loans and bonds to Dubai entities under the premise that Abu Dhabi was always likely to bail Dubai out. For many years, billions of dollars in global savings were allocated to highly questionable ventures selected by Dubai World.

The IMF is another potential source of moral hazard. It now has approaching $1 trillion available as loans. It is currently in the process of asking for far more funds in order to provide emergency bailouts to wealthy nations. Creditors can safely lend to nations that are likely to get IMF bailouts, thereby permitting such nations to build up larger debt burdens. It is entirely plausible that both Argentina and Russia's unsustainable credit-led booms in the 1990s were made possible by—and became larger as a result of—the implicit backing of the IMF, which creditors knew would forestall or prevent collapse.[4]

---

[4] The IMF's Independent Evaluation Office determined that the IMF stayed engaged with Argentina too long in the late 1990s/early 2000s. Presumably this engagement allowed Argentina to borrow more money from foreign creditors than it would otherwise have been able to do.

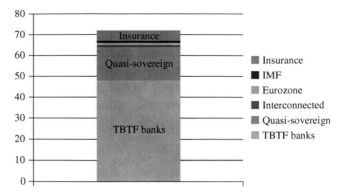

Figure 10.3. Estimates of total balance sheets that contribute to global moral hazard in Europe and the US ($ trillion).

Note: we have added together the liabilities of 'too big to fail banks', major quasi-sovereign companies, companies that have proven interconnections so are likely to be bailed out, the balance sheet we estimate the Eurozone is willing to put behind members, capital at the IMF, and the liabilities of major insurance companies. *Source*: authors' estimates.

In the US, agency debt has proven a major source of moral hazard, helping to fuel the housing boom and bust.[5] In Europe, the arrival of the ECB and the common currency created a lender of last resort which dramatically increased access to international loans for member nations and their 1,400+ banks, and which therefore financed large credit booms in nations such as Spain and Ireland, along with profligate spending in Greece and Portugal.

A rough list of governments, institutions and other entities involved in such moral hazard in industrialized countries is given in figure 10.3. This figure shows examples of entities, such as commercial banks, that are implicitly backed by governments. It also shows the backing of entities, such as the IMF, that is available to support sovereigns or other entities. The sum of these provides an indication of the balance sheets themselves, or the 'available credit line' that supports other balance sheets, with potential moral hazard issues if regulation fails.

These guarantees greatly expanded over the past twenty-four months as the Federal Reserve, ECB and Bank of England all provided effective bailouts to far more banks and other financial entities than ever before. By these crude but illustrative estimates, the grand total now stands at around $65 trillion, which is roughly 2.5 times total North American plus

---

[5]We do not subscribe to the theory that the financial crisis in 2007–8 was primarily due to Fannie Mae and Freddie Mac—in contrast, for example, to Calomiris and Wallison (2008).

European GDP.[6] The chart shows that the bulk of the risks stem from bank balance sheets, and so our prime focus should be on dealing with this issue. However, other areas are growing quickly. The IMF is now in the process of requesting much larger funding in order to provide emergency 'liquidity support' to nations under much easier terms than current programmes. This support is presumably aimed at bailing out wealthy European nations. The ECB and EU have repeatedly declared that no Eurozone member will be permitted to default or restructure debts, thereby effectively telling global creditors that the EU nations stand jointly behind the risks of each nation.

The guarantees and other support exemplified in this chart each serve a good purpose, but they also pose severe dangers. To limit the dangers, we would need to design regulatory systems that monitor the risk and prevent it from growing. This is where we invariably, eventually fail.[7] The larger the sums 'guaranteed' the greater the lobbying should be, and also the greater is the incentive for politicians to relax regulation in order to win a short-term credit boom. As the case studies below show, the problems are deep institutional issues with a critical global dimension. We need reform in areas that the official consensus is currently unprepared to even consider.

10.3 FISCAL DISASTER FROM FINANCIAL CRISIS: CASE STUDIES

10.3.1 *Iceland*

Iceland has long had a prudent sovereign with cautious fiscal policy and little debt. Ten years ago no one would have guessed this small island with a population of 317,000 could cause shock waves throughout the global financial system. Within the last decade, its banks started to expand—initially with financing from Europe, but more recently by taking positions in the collateralized debt obligation securitization market in the

---

[6]The gross liabilities protected are not the total potential losses of the guarantor as some of these are backed by good collateral. However, the large numbers show the importance for political incentives. A modest relaxation of regulation would conceivably generate a sizable rise in credit relative to GDP in nations where it occurred. This therefore points to strong incentives to abuse regulation in favour of a political business cycle, along with the sizable potential losses relative to GDP of such increases.

[7]In the US political context, this point has been made most clearly by Senator Ted Kaufman. He argues that when regulators have failed, as with the US financial sector, it is not a good idea to just renew or expand their mandate. Legislators should instead write simpler, tougher rules that are easier to enforce, such as a size cap on the largest banks.

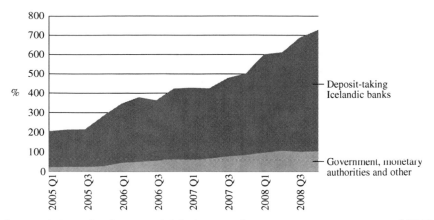

Figure 10.4. Iceland: external debt by main borrowers (as a percentage of GDP).
Source: Statistics Iceland.

US. Ultimately, they took advantage of the European Economic Area rules that allowed them 'passports' into the UK, the Netherlands and parts of Scandinavia.

Figure 10.4 shows the huge increase in external debt since 2005— mostly the result of borrowing by private banks. Total bank assets (and liabilities) peaked at between eleven and thirteen times GDP (while as shown in figure 10.4 external debt of banks reached over six times GDP) right before the crisis of September 2008. How did Icelandic banks manage to raise such large funds? The answer lies in the structure of financial sector moral hazard in wealthy Europe and in the US, along with our collective lax regulatory requirements for foreign bank branches under international treaty.

Icelandic banks first raised their finance by accessing European bond markets. Once it became difficult to raise funds there, banks turned to US markets. This came just as collateralized debt obligations came to the fore in the US. These securitized obligations packaged together bonds from many nations. Icelandic banks were fortunate enough to be rated highly by rating agencies due to the implicit backing of its highly prudent sovereign, but they still carried high yields due to market concerns for their large debt (see the executive summary and chapter 21 of Hreinsson *et al.* (2010)).[8]

---

[8]For example, in May 2007 Kaupthing Bank issued three-year bonds in euros paying 7.7% and rated A− by Fitch at issuance, with a similar rating by Moody's. At the time, European A/A− rate financial institution bonds had average yields of 4.7% on three-year paper. This 300 basis point premium over the sector reflected the bond market's view that rating agencies were too generous.

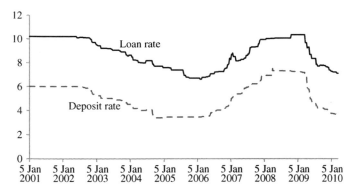

Figure 10.5. Average domestic deposit and loans rates at Icelandic banks.
Source: Central Bank of Iceland.

To further gain funds Icelandic banks then turned to Nordic and UK deposit markets. Under European Free Trade Association rules these banks were permitted to set up branches and internet banking in European deposit markets without being fully regulated by those national supervisory agencies. By offering higher deposit rates, they attracted funds from the local banks.

The three main Icelandic banks used their funds to go on a global buying spree. Their main focus remained speculative real estate, but they also bought high street retailers in the UK, large industrial manufacturers in Europe, and much more. The local regulator turned a blind eye to the risk involved in these transactions, and to the lack of adequate reporting on connected loans which in retrospect dogged all the major banks. For Iceland, these were boom years, and there was a general feeling that nothing could go wrong.

Then credit markets began to dry up. Figure 10.5 shows deposit and loan rates in Iceland. The rising deposit rates in 2008 reflect the growing liquidity problems at Iceland's banks. The banks were gradually being cut from foreign wholesale credit markets, so they increased deposit rates in their foreign branches in the hope of winning funds away from UK and Nordic banks.

The collapse came in 2008. The government and banks were madly searching for alternative funding, including some calls to join the Eurozone so the ECB could be the lender of last resort and thus give greater confidence to credit markets, but none of these actions came soon enough.[9] When creditors finally caught on to this large Ponzi game and

---

[9] As the Icelandic prime minister famously reported, on returning home after a fruitless overseas search for a foreign economic bailout, 'we are all going back to fishing'.

251

stopped providing new funds, the banks collapsed. Senior creditors lost well over 90% of their funds as it became apparent that the bank's assets were worth less than a fifth of their reported value.

Iceland may seem small and rather extraordinary, but its experience contains a much broader cautionary tale that is relevant for the global economy. The easy regulatory policies in Iceland can be interpreted as a form of 'beggar-thy-neighbour' policy. Loose regulation creates a credit boom, but it is often taking funds from other nations and can lead to misallocation of capital. The competition provided by the Icelandic banks may also have weakened regulation elsewhere. With heavy competition coming from lightly regulated Iceland, banks in other nations naturally argue that they too need 'light regulation' in order to survive and compete.

In the end, Iceland also played an important role in sparking the financial panic and contagion that enveloped Europe and the US in autumn 2008 and 2009. If a small little island in the Atlantic Ocean can cause shockwaves through global finance, how could investors be confident that there weren't much larger problems lurking ahead? After Iceland's fall, every creditor of other nations with large deficits and substantial external debt looked for ways to reduce exposure. The obvious risks included much of Eastern Europe, Turkey and parts of Latin America.

Iceland's crisis also made clear that creditors' rights and effective protection remain poorly defined in our integrated financial world. With European governments turning down his appeals for assistance, Iceland's prime minister, Geir Haarde, warned that it was now 'every country for itself'. This smacked of the financial autarchy that characterized defaulters in the financial crisis in Asia in the late 1990s. Similarly, when Argentina defaulted on its debt in 2001–2, politicians there faced enormous pressure to change the rule of law to benefit domestic property holders over foreigners, and they changed the bankruptcy law to give local debtors the upper hand. In Indonesia and Russia after the crises of 1998, local enterprises and banks took the opportunity of the confusion to grab property, then found ways to ensure that courts sided with them.

10.3.2 *Canada*

Defenders of the new banking status quo in the US today—more highly concentrated than before 2008, with six megabanks implicitly deemed 'too big to fail'—often lead with the argument that 'Canada has only five big banks and there was no crisis'. The implication is clear: we should embrace concentrated megabanks and even go further down the route; if the Canadians can do it safely, so can we.

It is true that during 2008 four of Canada's major banks managed to earn a profit, all five were profitable in 2009 and none required an explicit taxpayer bailout. In fact, there were no bank collapses in Canada even during the Great Depression, and in recent years there have only been two small bank failures in the entire country.

Advocates for a Canadian-type banking system argue that this success is the outcome of industry structure and strong regulation. The chief executive officers (CEOs) of Canada's five banks work literally within a few hundred meters of each other in downtown Toronto. This makes it easy to monitor banks. They also have smart-sounding requirements imposed by the government: if you take out a loan over 80% of a home's value, then you must take out mortgage insurance. The banks were required to keep at least 7% Tier 1 capital, and they had a leverage restriction so that total assets relative to equity (and capital) was limited.

But is it really true that such constraints necessarily make banks safer, even in Canada?

Despite supposedly tougher regulation and similar leverage limits on paper, Canadian banks were actually significantly more leveraged—and therefore more risky—than well-run American commercial banks. For example, according to reported balance sheets, J.P. Morgan was thirteen times leveraged at the end of 2008, and Wells Fargo was eleven times leveraged. Canada's five largest banks averaged nineteen times leveraged, with the largest bank, Royal Bank of Canada, being twenty-three times leveraged. It is a similar story for Tier 1 capital (with a higher number being safer): J.P. Morgan had 10.9% at end 2008 while Royal Bank of Canada had just 9%. J.P. Morgan and other US banks also typically had more tangible common equity—another measure of the buffer against losses—than did Canadian banks. There are differences in accounting that matter: for example, different treatment of repo-loans and derivatives make J.P. Morgan look less leveraged than it would be under Canadian accounting rules, but the general picture still remains that Canadian banks are highly leveraged.

If Canadian banks are highly leveraged and less capitalized, did something else make their balance sheets safer? The answer is yes—guarantees provided by the government of Canada. Today over half of Canadian mortgages are effectively guaranteed by the government, with banks paying a low price to insure the mortgages. Virtually all mortgages where the loan-to-value ratio is greater than 80% are guaranteed indirectly or directly by the Canadian Mortgage and Housing Corporation (i.e. the government takes the risk of the riskiest assets). The system works well for banks; they originate mortgages, then pass on the risk to government agencies. However, that does not change the total risk for the nation. Indeed, this only transfers the risk to taxpayers, and makes the role of regulators all the more important to prevent losses. The US, of course, had Fannie Mae and Freddie Mac, but lending standards slipped and those agencies could not resist a plunge into assets more risky than prime mortgages.

The other claimed systemic strength of the Canadian system is camaraderie between the regulators, the Bank of Canada and the individual banks. This oligopoly means banks can make profits in rough times—they can charge higher prices to customers and can raise funds more cheaply. This profit incentive should induce banks to take less risk because their license to generate long-run oligopolistic profits is valuable. However, the concentration can also generate risks for taxpayers as each bank is too big to fail. During the height of the crisis in early 2009, the CEO of Toronto Dominion Bank brazenly pitched investors: 'Maybe not explicitly, but what are the chances that TD Bank is not going to be bailed out if it did something stupid?' In other words, don't bother looking at how dumb or smart we are, the Canadian government is there to make sure creditors never lose a cent. With such ready access to taxpayer bailouts and a stable government that guarantees their riskiest mortgages, Canadian banks need little capital, they naturally make large profit margins, and they can raise money even if they act badly.

Proposing a Canadian-type model to create stability in the US or European banking systems is hardly plausible given these conditions. Icelandic banks managed to blow up without all this direct government support—would the country have been better off if the nation had explicitly backed mortgages too and so recorded even less 'risk' on their bank balance sheets? We doubt it. This would have only made creditors more ready to lend to the banks.

The US would need to merge banks into even fewer banking giants, and then re-inflate Fannie Mae and Freddie Mac to guarantee some of the riskiest parts of the bank's portfolios. Then, with this handful of new 'hyper megabanks', they'd each have to count on their political system to prevent banks from running excessive risk.

Europe already has all the hallmarks of a Canadian system. For example, the British have a handful of large banks that each earn long-run rents which should, theoretically, check their risk-taking. These banks are close to the regulator too. However, to match the Canadian system, the British system would have needed to guarantee virtually all the new

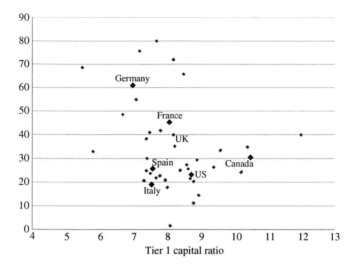

Figure 10.6. Leverage and Tier 1 capital at top five major banks and averages for each nation (end 2006 according to reported balance sheets).

Note: data show levels for the top five banks in each nation. Country data show the weighted average ratios for all five. *Source*: Bloomberg and authors' estimates.

housing mortgages in the last years of the bubble as they soared above 80% loan-to-value ratios. Had Britain done that, we could be sure that the banking system itself would have been safer, but for the nation as a whole the implications are of course much more dire.

The stakes would be even greater with these mega banks. When such large banks collapse they can take down the finances of entire nations. We don't need to look far to see how 'Canadian-type systems' eventually fail. Britain's largest bank, the Royal Bank of Scotland, grew to control assets equal to around 1.7 times British GDP before it spectacularly fell apart and required near-complete nationalization in 2008–9. In Ireland the three largest banks' assets combined reached roughly three times GDP before they collapsed.

So why did Canada not suffer a bank failure during this crisis when so many others did? Canada did provide an enormous liquidity programme to banks as they bought mortgages from them, but they did avoid new capital increases. Figures 10.6 and 10.7 show that Canadian banks were more highly capitalized than other banks ahead of the crisis, but these levels of capital were, in reality, no higher than other entities that subsequently failed (including Lehman Brothers and Washington Mutual).

Figure 10.7 shows why Canada did well. As a natural resource producer, it suffered badly in the 1990s as oil prices troughed in 1998 around $10

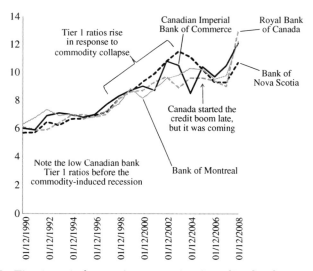

Figure 10.7. Tier 1 capital over time at major Canadian banks.

Note: Toronto Dominion was excluded due to accounting issues in 2003 that make the data incomparable. It generally followed similar trends to the other banks. *Source*: Bloomberg.

per barrel and metals did similarly. In the early 1990s, Canadian banks had little capital, but they suffered when commodity prices fell in the late 1990s and Canada suffered a severe recession. As always, banks raised their capital adequacy during the period while they avoided lending.

Only around 2005, when commodity prices started to take off, did the economy start growing rapidly. Western Canada, where the resources are concentrated, boomed. So did Toronto—the heart of the financial sector. Banks responded similarly: the total loan portfolio of the five major Canadian banks grew by 49% from 2005 to 2008 and their capital adequacy fell. During this period the Canadian Imperial Bank of Commerce entered into the subprime market, buying US mortgages. This probably would have ended in tears, like everywhere else, if it had been permitted to continue. What rescued Canadian banks and taxpayers was not good regulation or a 'safer' system. Indeed, Canada's system is inherently very risky due to its taxpayer-guaranteed mortgages that could finance an enormous housing boom plus their 'too big to fail' banks. Rather, Canada simply got lucky because the commodity boom came so late in the cycle.

Today all the major Canadian banks have ambitious international expansion plans—let's see how long their historically safe system survives the new hubris of its managers. The lesson for policymakers is simple: the Canadian banking system is not the holy grail.

10.3.3 *Ireland*

How did a country once renowned as the 'Celtic Tiger', with one of the most rapid growth trajectories and one of the most prudent governments in Europe, suddenly collapse? Ireland illustrates how all banking systems, regardless of the probity of their sovereigns, are capable of rapidly taking down national economies.

Irish annualized nominal GNP declined by 26% to 2010 Q1 from its peak in 2007. House prices have fallen 50% and continue to fall. The government's official budget deficit in 2009 was 14.3% of GDP, or 17.8% of GNP.[10] While stuck in the Eurozone, Ireland's exchange rate cannot move relative to its major trading partners—it thus cannot improve competitiveness without drastic wage cuts. Ireland serves as a cautionary tale regarding what could go wrong for all of us.

Ireland's difficulties arose because of a massive property boom financed by cheap credit from Irish banks. Ireland's three main banks built up three times the GNP in loans and investments by 2008; these are big banks (relative to the economy) that pushed the frontier in terms of reckless lending. The banks got the upside and then came the global crash in autumn 2008: property prices fell over 50%, construction and development stopped and people started defaulting on loans. Today roughly a third of the loans on the balance sheets of banks are non-performing or 'under surveillance': that's an astonishing 100% of GDP, in terms of potentially bad debts.

The government responded to this with what is now regarded—rather disconcertingly—as 'standard' policies. They guaranteed all the liabilities of banks and then began injecting government funds. The government has also bought the most worthless assets from banks, paying them government bonds in return. Ministers have also promised to recapitalize banks that need more capital. The ultimate result of this exercise is obvious: one way or another, the government will have converted the liabilities of private banks into debts of the sovereign (i.e. Irish taxpayers).

Ireland, until 2009, seemed like a fiscally prudent nation. Successive governments had paid down the national debt to such an extent that total debt to GDP was only 25% at end 2008 (figure 10.8)—among industrialized countries, this was one of the lowest. But the Irish state was also carrying a large off-balance-sheet liability, in the form of three huge banks that

---

[10]Regarding the large gap between GDP and GNP in Ireland, see Boone and Johnson (2010).

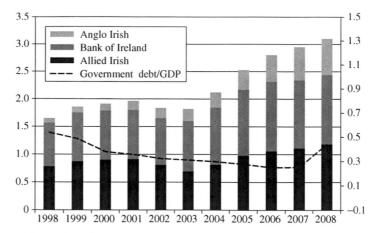

Figure 10.8. Ireland bank assets/GDP by bank (left-hand axis) and government debt/GDP (right-hand axis).

Sources: Central Bank of Ireland; Department of Finance, Ireland; Bloomberg; Ireland Growth and Stability Program; authors' forecasts.

were seriously out of control. When the crash came, the scale and nature of the bank bailouts meant that all this changed. Even with their now famous public wage cuts, the government budget deficit will be an eye-popping 15% of GNP in 2010.

The government is gambling that GNP growth will recover to over 4% per year starting in 2012—and they still plan further modest expenditure-cutting and revenue-increasing measures each year until 2013, in order to bring the deficit back to 3% of GDP by that date. The latest round of bank bailouts (swapping bad debts for government bonds) dramatically exacerbated the fiscal problem. The government will in essence be issuing a third of GDP in government debts for distressed bank assets which may have no intrinsic value. The government debt/GDP ratio of Ireland will be over 100% by the end of 2011 once we include this debt. If we measure their debt against GNP, that number rises to 125%.[11]

---

[11] Ireland has created a corporate tax system which permits companies to reduce their global tax burden by transferring profits through Irish subsidiaries. As a result, GDP includes a large amount of these profit transfers which are not related to local economic activity. These profit transfers contribute little to Irish tax collection since the subsidiaries are usually structured in such a manner that their ultimate location for tax residency is a zero-tax regime, such as Bermuda or the Bahamas. Therefore, the tax base for Ireland is best represented by GNP rather than GDP. Irish GDP is 25% higher than GNP. The standard convention of reporting fiscal deficits and debt as a fraction of GDP, rather than GNP, therefore makes these burdens look less onerous for Ireland than they truly are.

Ireland had more prudent choices. They could have avoided taking on private bank debts by forcing the creditors of these banks to share the burden—and this is now what some sensible voices within the main opposition party have called for. However, a strong lobby of real estate developers, the investors who bought the bank bonds, and politicians with links to the failed developments (and their bankers), have managed to ensure that taxpayers rather than creditors will pay. The government plan is—with good reason—highly unpopular, but the coalition of interests in its favour it strong enough to ensure that it will proceed, at least until it either succeeds and growth recovers, or ends in complete failure with the default of banks or the sovereign.

On its current programme, each Irish family of four will be liable for €200,000 in debt by 2015. There are only 73,000 children born into the country each year. These children will be paying off debts for decades to come—plus, they must accept much greater austerity than has already been implemented. There is no doubt that social welfare systems and health care, plus education spending, will decline sharply. The calamity of the Irish banking system will be felt for decades and paid for by many as-yet-unborn children.

How did Ireland manage to create such a spectacular failure? The answer is simple: when joining the euro, their banks gained access to the 'implicit promises' of the Eurozone system. Under this system, all banks regulated under their national supervisory systems can access lending programmes of the ECB. This gives creditors great confidence that they will never fail: the ECB provides emergency finance, and the ECB naturally does not want to see its member banks, which it may be lending billions to, fail to repay. So the ECB provided the moral hazard backstop that gave Irish banks nearly unlimited access to credit.

With that backing, Irish banks were able to rapidly expand their balance sheets, so, starting around 2002, the great Celtic Tiger turned into a simple, externally financed, real estate bubble. The banks enjoyed the bubble as they made profits, citizens were fooled into thinking their property had really increased greatly in value and they had become wealthy, and the government enjoyed a tax boom driven by a myriad of property-related taxes. When all this stopped, it had become clear that the nation was, collectively, bankrupt.

When Irish-type banks fail, you have a dramatic and unpleasant choice. Either take over the banks' debts, creating a very real burden on taxpayers and ever more drag on growth. Or restructure these debts, forcing creditors to take a hit. The government is attempting, through so-far highly unsuccessful policies, to avoid default by transferring all the liabilities of the banks to future taxpayers.[12]

If the Irish continue with these policies, then in a few years' time the nation will be burdened with levels of debt to income that exceed almost anything ever seen in history for sovereign nations. The problems are strikingly reminiscent of Latin America in the 1980s. Those nations borrowed too heavily in the 1970s (also, by the way, from big international banks) and then—in the face of tougher macroeconomic conditions in the US—lost access to capital markets. For ten years they were stuck with debt overhangs, just like the weak Eurozone countries, which made it virtually impossible to grow. Debt overhangs hurt growth for many reasons: business is nervous that taxes will go up in the near future, the cost of credit is high throughout society, and social turmoil looms because continued fiscal austerity is needed to reduce the debt. In Latin America, some countries lingered in limbo for ten years or more.

The lessons for the world are different: banking systems like those in Ireland or Iceland, which are inherently less risky for taxpayers than systems like Canada's—as those governments did not guarantee national mortgages—will regularly fail. The Eurozone in this case acted as a litmus test: those nations prone to use excessive credit through banks, like Spain and Ireland, embarked on credit booms the moment credit markets were opened with the arrival of the Eurozone. The less profligate nations, such as Germany, did not. The Eurozone has sixteen member nations and is still growing. No wonder many nations want to join this zone: its member banks will get cheap funds and a potential credit boom. It is a system that is doomed to regularly suffer similar failures.

10.4 THE EUROZONE: WILL ITS MORAL HAZARD SINK THE WORLD?

When the Soviet Union collapsed, an elite IMF team rushed to Moscow with a programme to save the ruble zone. Creating money is not easy in a currency zone. The IMF came up with a voluntary solution. In essence, each new nation would have been able to print money as they wished, but with some oversight from other members and the IMF.

The Russians, rightly, rejected this plan. Their point was simple: other nations would abuse this system by printing too much money to finance their spending and credits to banks, and so would destroy the value

---

[12]Honohan (2009), who is now the governor of the Central Bank of Ireland, supports a view that equity holders and subordinated creditors should first take losses before the government.

of the ruble. The Russians wanted complete control, or they would not accept it.[13]

This, in essence, illustrates the key flaw of the Eurozone today. The underlying problem is the rule for creating credit: in the Eurozone, any government can finance itself by issuing bonds directly (or indirectly) to commercial banks, and then having those banks 'repo' them (i.e. borrow using these bonds as collateral) at the ECB in return for fresh euros. The commercial banks make a profit because the ECB charges them very little for those loans, while the governments get the money—and can thus finance larger budget deficits. The problem is that the government and banks eventually have to pay back their debt or, more modestly, at least stabilize public debt levels.

This same structure directly distorts the incentives of commercial banks: they have a backstop at the ECB, which is the 'lender of last resort', and the ECB and the European Union (EU) put a great deal of pressure on each nation to bail out commercial banks in trouble. When a country joins the Eurozone, its banks win access to a large amount of cheap financing, along with the expectation that they will be bailed out when they make mistakes. This, in turn, enables the banks to greatly expand their balance sheets, ploughing into domestic real estate, overseas expansion or anything else they deem appropriate. Given that the Eurozone provides easy access to cheap money, it is no wonder that many more nations want to join. No wonder also that it blew up.[14]

To make this system safe, the Eurozone has a Herculean task. The Eurozone needs to demand that all nations spend 'within their means'. This was the logic behind the growth and stability pact, however the politics of implementing that proved impossible in the Eurozone. This failure to stick to tough standards is directly reflective of the failure to regulate banks well around the world, but they are on a whole different political dimension. It is difficult to stick resolutely to tight regulation, but much

---

[13]See Dabrowski (1995) for a discussion of the contemporaneous debate and the reasons for the downfall of the ruble zone.

[14]As Iceland moved towards its disastrous collapse, Richard Portes in a *Financial Times* editorial in October 2008 argued that one solution for Icelandic banks was for the government to seek membership of the Eurozone so that the banks could gain access to the ECB as a lender of last resort. This recommendation, which in retrospect seems unconscionable, reflects the great difficulty in understanding whether a nation faces a solvency crisis versus a liquidity crisis in the midst of a collapse in credit markets. Such difficulties make it ever more apparent just how hard it will be for the ECB to avoid bailouts and the substantial moral hazard that ensues as member states suffer more crises in the future.

harder to convince voters that you should tighten fiscal spending because politicians in Berlin and Brussels are demanding it.

The Eurozone must also demand that all banks operate safely. For now, that task is largely devolved to the national regulators in each nation. Who can truly monitor each regulator in the sixteen Eurozone nations to make sure each one is not permitting banks to take excessive risk? The answer so far is no one. The regulatory agencies at the Eurozone level are simply too politically weak and confused to be able to maintain tough standards for decades, as is required in the common currency zone. We already know it is difficult to do this at a national level, and we should be sure it will be even more difficult when we add a layer of politics above that. The far more likely scenario is that, in a few years' time, we will start a new race to the bottom as some regulators relax regulations—thereby generating local credit booms—and political expediency then encourages other regulators to start relaxing too.

The problem today is even more severe because even the route out of this short-term fiasco is unclear. The ECB has created several new lending facilities, while keeping its repo window open so as to allow profligate sovereigns to continue refinancing their banks and public debts by building more debts. The governments issue bonds and European commercial banks buy them and then deposit them at the ECB as collateral for freshly printed money. This is the pattern for Ireland, Spain, Greece and Portugal. The ECB has become the silent facilitator of profligate spending in the Eurozone.

The ECB had a chance to dismantle this doom machine when the board of governors announced new rules for determining what debts could be used as collateral at the ECB. Some observers anticipated that the ECB might plan to tighten the rules gradually, thereby sending a message that the institution would refuse to live up to the 'implicit promises' of bailouts which credit markets have been fed on. But the ECB did not do that. In fact, the ECB's board of governors did the opposite: they abolished ratings requirements for Greek debt in order for it to be used as collateral at the ECB, and they announced they would buy the debts of other troubled nations, essentially making it clear that every nation in the Eurozone was backed by the money-printing machine at the ECB.

What is likely to happen next? The Eurozone authorities are hoping that further bailouts, matched by calls for near-term fiscal austerity, will permanently solve the deep flaws in the structure of the Eurozone. This seems highly wishful thinking. We have observed around the world how bank regulation, which is much simpler, is watered down over time as interest groups and governments collude to make changes. Now that the Eurozone has upped the ante by bailing out all creditors, creating ever greater moral hazard, why should anyone believe that they can dramatically raise regulatory standards permanently, as would be needed, to make such a system safe?

There seems to be no logic in the system, but perhaps there is a logical outcome. The EU, with more funding coming from the IMF, is now planning ever larger bailout programmes. With each successive bailout the debts of the indebted nations will grow, while their economies will be held back by their 'debt traps', like the one we observe today in Ireland (and also in Greece). Europe will eventually grow tired of bailing out its weaker countries. The troubles in the periphery will spill over into the core countries from time to time. Italy will one day have trouble rolling over debts, and France could easily lose its 'safe-haven' status in bond markets. The potential bailout or liquidity requirements for these nations are enormous.

The Germans will probably pull that bailout plug first. The longer we wait to see true incentive structures established that convincingly encourage national fiscal probity and safe banking, including through the operations and rules of the ECB and the EU, the more debt will be built up, and the more dangerous the situation will become. When the plug is finally pulled, at least one nation will end up in a painful default; unfortunately, the way we are heading, the problems could be even more widespread.

This matters for the entire world because the Eurozone is a large part of the global economy. Also, as Eurozone banks are likely to exist on a form of life support for the indefinite future, this changes the competitive landscape—all major banks throughout the world will demand similar levels of government support. And the Eurozone remains fragile, thus representing a serious potential cause of future international financial instability.

10.5 WHY THE COMING GLOBAL REGULATORY REFORMS ARE UNLIKELY TO WORK

Based on experience over the past forty years, it is clear that the current global financial system is at greater risk than it ever has been. The moral hazard in the system has undoubtedly risen: our recent bailout of all major financial institutions, the failure of regulatory reform in the US and the operation of the Eurozone system have created levels of moral hazard which have never been seen before. Unless we prove to creditors that these systems do not provide implicit bailouts by letting creditors lose funds when they lend, we need to create a tougher regulatory system than has ever been seen in our history.

This regulatory system cannot afford to break down as it has in the past. That means we need to somehow break the desire or ability of politicians to gradually permit the system be relaxed. They have a natural desire to do this due to the credit boom that comes with relaxation. We also need to make sure that, in our interconnected world, our neighbours do not let their financial systems get out of control. The examples of Ireland and Iceland both show how small nations can, through multiple channels, cause large costs and encourage regulatory relaxation in other nations. Finally, we need to make sure that the financial system itself does not find new ways to circumvent our regulation. This means that constant surveillance is required.

When considering this list, it becomes obvious that current reforms will not work. The present reform programme is based primarily on changes to national regulation. The programme of the G20's Financial Stability Board and the new Basel III plans all introduce tighter regulatory requirements. We are confident that capital requirements at banks are set to be raised, and many of the most egregious errors in bank regulation, such as the treatment of hybrid securities as capital, will be adjusted. There is no doubt that liquidity requirements will be improved too.

However, none of these reforms change the incentive structures in the system. Politicians will still face a desire to relax the system in several years' time in every single nation. Even if all nations agree to adhere to the G20 recommendations, there is no chance that we will be able to enforce these regulations across nations. The troubles in Ireland and Iceland, and at Lehman Brothers, show how difficult it is to know whether these rules are being enforced.[15] So we need to assume that some nations will relax regulations, and we can also assume that that will encourage others to relax.

The political power of the financial sector also remains largely intact. It is still dominated by large banks that are too big to fail. They will be a major source of tax finance, employment and campaign funds in all nations. They are now better able to access funds in credit markets due to their explicit backing from sovereigns. When banks complain that other nations are easing bank regulation and claim that their authorities therefore need to follow, who is going to stand up to this in favour of greater

---

[15] See Haldane (2010) for a regulator's view on the difficulties regulators face.

taxpayer protection? We can be certain that nations which depend on large financial centres, such as the UK and US, will not be able to fight these pressures ad infinitum.

10.5.1   The Failure of Reform in the US

At least in the US, this is about the money at stake.[16] From 1948 until 1979, average compensation in the banking sector was essentially the same as in the private sector overall, then it shot upwards until, in 2007, the average bank employee earned twice as much as the average private-sector worker.[17] Even after taking high levels of education into account, finance still paid more than other professions. Thomas Philippon and Ariell Reshef (2008) analysed financial sector compensation and found that, after correcting for differences in educational level and risk of unemployment, the 'excess relative wage' in finance grew from zero in the early 1980s to over 40% earlier this decade, and that 30–50% of that differential cannot be explained by differences in individual ability. They also found that deregulation was one causal factor behind the recent growth of the excess relative wage.

Between 1978 and 2007, the financial sector grew from 3.5% of the total economy to (measured by contribution to GDP) to 5.9%.[18] Its share of corporate profits climbed even faster. From the 1930s until around 1980, financial sector profits grew at roughly the same rate as profits in the non-financial sector. But from 1980 until 2005, financial sector profits grew by 800%, adjusted for inflation, while non-financial sector profits grew by only 250%. Financial sector profits plummeted during the peak of the financial crisis, but quickly rebounded; by the third quarter of 2009, financial sector profits were over six times 1980s levels, while non-financial sector profits were little more than double 1980s levels.

As of early 2010, there are at least six banks that are too big to fail in the US—Bank of America, Citigroup, Goldman Sachs, JPMorgan Chase,

---

[16]The recent rise of Wall Street's political power is covered in detail by Johnson and Kwak (2010). Ideology was also important—as was the revolving door between Wall Street and Washington—but behind all this lies the vast fortunes that could be made in modern finance.

[17]Data are from Bureau of Economic Analysis's 'National Income and Product Accounts' (tables 1.1.4, 6.3 and 6.5; available at www.bea.gov/national/nipaweb/index.asp). We begin with the finance, insurance and real estate sectors and exclude insurance, real estate and holding companies. Figures are converted to 2008 dollars using the GDP price index.

[18]Data taken from the Bureau of Economic Analysis's 'National Income and Product Accounts (table 1.5.5; available at www.bea.gov/national/nipaweb/index.asp).

Morgan Stanley and Wells Fargo—even leaving aside other institutions such as insurance companies (see figure 10.12). There is nothing in the package of financial reforms—likely to become law in July 2010—that will substantively change this situation. The big banks were able to effectively block or substantially water down attempted reforms at every stage—in large part through their lobbying and through their actual and potential future political contributions. The same forces that pushed successfully for deregulation in the 1980s and 1990s—contributing directly to the development of a much more risky financial system in the US—were able to effectively prevent reregulation.

10.5.2 *In the Absence of Adequate Regulatory Reform*

There is no simple solution to our problems, but we could reduce the potential troubles through reforms. Some combination of the following would undoubtedly make it easier.

1. A treaty for international financial regulation. We should enshrine regulatory powers in an international treaty, similar to the WTO for trade in goods and services, so that all nations are required to follow similar rules. This would make it harder for national legislatures and regulators to relax regulation, and so would reduce the 'beggar-thy-neighbour' costs imposed on others when one nation deregulates. It would also reduce the incentives for a 'race to the bottom' in regulation. The treaty would need to have simple rules, including large capital requirements. It would also need to have a body that monitored implementation, similar to the IMF or BIS today. This body would also need to have clear powers to impose new regulations so that rules can be modified to reflect changes in problems.

2. Macro-prudential supervision needs to be enhanced at the international level. There is no doubt that moral hazard inherent at the national level, or in entities such as the Eurozone, are threatening global stability. Despite this, very little is done at the international level to monitor and pre-empt these potential crises.

A good place to start would be to enhance the IMF's programme of fiscal assessments to include measuring the potential fiscal obligations that arise from both implicit and explicit guarantees from such institutional and regulatory structures.

The overriding principle behind IMF fiscal assessments is the need to capture the true total fiscal costs of existing policies. All subsidies and taxation—including the entire expected and potential costs of supporting the contingent liabilities—should be reflected transparently so policy-makers and taxpayers understand the potential liabilities that they face.

Our current accounting for guarantees and governments' assumption of other contingent liabilities create the impression that government actions to support the broad financial system are costless. Even Ben Bernanke, who surely knows better, recently remarked that 'there will be no more public funds needed to bailout banks'.[19] This is a danger-ous illusion—as seen in the recent increase in government deficits and debts in the most troubled nations. We are all at risk of private debt if we assume that, when crises come, our governments need to bail out this debt.

If we cannot be honest and recognize these costs explicitly, we run the risk of taking on ever more contingent liability. If the financial system reaches the point where its failure cannot be offset by fiscal (and mone-tary) stimulus, then a second Great Depression threatens.

In order to achieve this, an international body, with a strongly inde-pendent manifesto, would need to be charged to monitor and report on these risks. It is not at all clear whether such an institution could trump the politics of denial. For example, while the IMF is the natural institution to conduct such work, it is conflicted by the European/US control of the institution that makes complete and full reporting of problems in those nations unlikely in our current political environment. To make the IMF work better, the process for selecting top management would need to be depoliticized. We do have institutions that function, such as the WTO, so perhaps this could be achieved. However, this specific task would be more controversial and more difficult.

Such an institution would need to be forward looking, and innovative, in a manner that is not common for international organizations. For exam-ple, in their prescient book, aptly entitled *Too Big To Fail*, Stern and Feld-man (2004) mapped out exactly the kinds of problems that US policymak-ers later faced in the autumn of 2008 and early 2009. But their lists of vulnerable financial institutions did not include any of those that just a few years later turned out to be the most prone to failure—Bear Stearns,

---

[19]Speech at the Center for the Study of the Presidency and Congress (8 April 2010). Bernanke is clearly referring to explicit spending lines on the federal budget. However, proper accounting of the public costs of bailouts would need to include the transfers to banks from savers used to recapitalize banks outside the budget, along with the oppor-tunity cost of buying mortgage-backed securities in open market operations. Of course, contingent liabilities which should bear an amortized cost as a result of future bailouts are never recorded in budgets.

Lehman Brothers and AIG are not mentioned at all (although they do accurately foreshadow the issues around Fannie Mae and Freddie Mac).

Stern and Feldman provide compelling analysis with regard to regulated commercial banks, but they missed the interface between more lightly regulated investment banks and commercial banks, and they definitely did not foresee how an insurance company, operating in the derivatives market, could throw the global financial system into disarray.

Discouraging debt. Since our political system finds it difficult to let private creditors default on debt, we should consider ending the myriad of incentives to accumulate debt across the world. The most important change would be to end the deductibility of interest on debt for corporate and personal income tax purposes. This deduction currently encourages corporations and individuals to use debt finance in favour of equity finance. If we end the tax deductibility of interest we would 'level the playing field'. This might discourage debt, and so reduce the growth of implicitly backed private debt. We could also discourage debt contracts in our general financial system by putting large capital requirements on long-term nominal promises. For example, the practice of defined benefit pension schemes needs to be reduced as much as possible, as these encourage large debt backing. To the extent that we discourage debt and encourage equity, the global financial system will become less risky. This should reduce the volatility of equity and make it more of a debt-like instrument. Through these measures we would therefore reduce some of the perceived risks in equity which reflect a historical period of higher leverage.

4. Letting defaults happen. Perhaps the most simple, but most critical, reform is to relax the actual and perceived costs of letting defaults happen. The recent crisis illustrated how difficult it is for politicians not to bail out entities once a crisis starts. In the US, the government could not even take the simple step of making sure equity holders were wiped out when they provided funds to Citigroup and Bear Stearns to keep them afloat. The creditors were fully compensated. The US government argues that lack of a national resolution authority made it difficult to share burdens with creditors, but in reality the more important concern was that causing one entity to fail would lead to contagion in debt markets, thereby causing a large financial crisis. This second concern is not resolved by recent legislation in the US that creates a bank resolution authority, and so creditors are fully aware that the US and European governments will almost surely bail out creditors at financial institutions each time they are in trouble in the future. We see little scope for this to change. The problem of contagion is a serious one and we cannot expect creditors to anticipate that they will face losses when national costs of contagion are high. However, we can reduce the risks of contagion. The most important way of doing this is to raise capital requirements so that the financial system as a whole is safer when single entities have problems. Second, we could, in conjunction with an international treaty, introduce contingent debts which convert to equity when banks need assistance to meet regulatory capital. This would make it clear to those creditors buying contingent instruments that they do bear part of the costs. Such rules would require banks to keep a substantial fraction of risk-weighted capital in such contingent instruments.

5. Depoliticizing finance. One reason for the repeated failures of our regulatory environment is the political strength of our large financial institutions. The close relations between the German chancellor, Angela Merkel, and the CEO of Deutsche Bank, Josef Ackerman, the legacy of Goldman Sachs's relations with the US Treasury and the revolving door from the Treasury to the financial sector and back again each pose threats to sound regulation. We believe many steps need to be taken to reduce these threats. Big banks should be broken up into smaller entities. This will make them less able to lobby individually, and it will make it more apparent to creditors that there is a real risk that the banks may be permitted to default. The usual counterarguments to this policy, e.g. that nations with big corporations need big banks, are surely wrong. Large transactions can always be divided into several parts, or syndicated, meaning corporations may well be better off with competition.

There is little evidence that large banks gain economies of scale beyond a very low size threshold. A review of multiple empirical studies found that economies of scale vanish at some point below $10 billion in assets (see Amel *et al.* 2004; Rhoades 1994; Berger and Humphrey 1994). The 2007 Geneva Report on *International Financial Stability*, coauthored by former Federal Reserve vice chair Roger Ferguson (2007), also found that the unprecedented consolidation in the financial sector over the previous decade had led to no significant efficiency gains, no economies of scale beyond a low threshold, and no evident economies of scope.[20] Finance professor Edward Kane has pointed out that since large banks exhibit constant returns to scale (they are no more or less efficient as they grow

---

[20]There remains an active debate on this topic (see Wheelock and Wilson 2009).

larger), and since we know that large banks enjoy a subsidy due to being too big to fail, 'offsetting diseconomies must exist in the operation of large institutions'—that is, without the too big to fail subsidy, large banks would actually be less efficient than medium-sized banks (Kane 2009). As evidence for economies of scope, Calomiris (2009) cites a paper by Kevin Stiroh (2000) showing that banks' productivity grew faster than the service sector average from 1991 to 1997, 'during the heart of the merger wave'. However, the paper he cites, and other papers by Stiroh (2002), imply or argue that the main reason for increased productivity was improved use of information technology—not increasing size or scope.

A second reform would be to reduce the close relations between regulators and the financial sector. For example, there is a revolving door between the US Treasury and the financial sector. This is even encouraged through tax rules, such as a tax break which permits newly hired public servants to not pay capital gains tax on assets which they sell when they go to work for the Treasury. It should be no surprise that Goldman Sachs partners with large unrealized capital gains are pleased to take a stint at the Treasury!

We believe there should be legal requirements that no public officials involved in regulation, or legislation related to regulation, be permitted to work in industries that they were involved in regulating for extended periods before and after they join public services. This period could be 3–5 years. While such rules would reduce the number of experienced financial experts able to work in regulation, it would promote the cadre of sound regulators that are being built up in our systems.

10.6 Implications for the Global Economy

Of the five points listed above, we would argue that none are currently being implemented. The best we are achieving is to moderately tighten regulation, as we always do, after the fact of a major crisis. We are essentially driving the structural risks of our system underground for a temporary period, with predictable and potentially dangerous consequences for the future when they resurface, as they surely will.

This is the biggest danger: by seeking to decree that 'there shall be no more crises', we will in fact create exactly the conditions for an even more damaging crisis to develop, unseen until it is too late. This is a lesson that many emerging markets learned the hard way in the 1980s and 1990s—for example, with various forms of offshore borrowing in Thailand, Indonesia and Korea—and the good news is that they are being careful to keep financial risks well within the perimeter of the regulated system. But will industrialized countries today be so careful?

10.6.1 *The Coming Boom*

We can already see the outline of the next crisis. The Federal Reserve is, just like in 2002 and 2003, preaching the need for low interest rates in order to recapitalize banks and encourage risk-taking. The deep dangerous flaws in Europe mean the ECB is also going to err on the side of keeping rates low and providing large liquidity. Our financial system, if Europe stabilizes this time and avoids an immediate crisis, will be flush with cash.

Loose credit and money will promote good times and generate growth and more surplus savings in many emerging markets. But rather than intermediating their own savings internally through fragmented financial systems, we'll see a large flow of capital out of those countries, as the state entities and private entrepreneurs making money choose to hold their funds somewhere safe—that is, in major international banks that are implicitly backed by US and European taxpayers.

These banks will in turn facilitate the flow of capital back into emerging markets—because they have the best perceived investment opportunities—as some combination of loans, private equity, financing provided to multinational firms expanding into these markets, and many other portfolio inflows.

So our banking system will soon become a major creditor and debtor to the growing emerging markets. We saw something similar, although on a smaller scale, in the 1970s with the so-called recycling of petrodollars. In that case, it was current-account surpluses from oil exporters that were parked in US and European banks and then lent to Latin America and some Eastern European countries with current-account deficits.

The recycling of savings around the world in the 1970s ended badly, mostly because incautious lending practices and (its usual counterpart) excessive exuberance among borrowers created vulnerability to macroeconomic shocks.

This time around, the flows will be less through current-account global imbalances, partly because few emerging markets want to run deficits. But large current-account imbalances are not required to generate huge capital flows around the world.

This is the scenario that we are now facing. For example, savers in Brazil and Russia will deposit funds in American and European banks, and these will then be lent to borrowers around the world (including in Brazil and Russia).

Of course, if this capital flow is well managed, learning from the lessons of the past thirty years, we have little to fear. But a soft landing seems unlikely because the underlying incentives, for both lenders and borrowers, are structurally flawed.

10.6.2 Misreading the Boom

Our largest financial institutions, in those nations where the sovereign is capable of backing them and is sure to do so, will initially be careful. But as the boom goes on, the competition between them will push towards more risk-taking. Part of the reason for this is that their compensation systems will remain inherently procyclical and, as times get better, they will load up on risk. Equity holders will also demand more risk-taking, since that raises short-term returns on equity.

The leading borrowers in emerging markets will be quasi-sovereigns, either with government ownership or a close crony relationship with the state. When times are good, everyone is happy to believe that these borrowers are effectively backed by a deep-pocketed sovereign, even if the formal connection is pretty loose. Then there are the bad times—think Dubai World today or Russia in 1998.

The boom will be pleasant while it lasts. It might go on for a number of years, in much the same way many people enjoyed the 1920s. But we have failed to heed the warnings made plain by the successive crises of the past thirty years and this failure was made clear during 2009.

The most worrisome part is that we are nearing the end of our fiscal and monetary ability to bail out the system. We are steadily becoming vulnerable to disaster on an epic scale.

REFERENCES

Amel, D., C. Barnes, F. Panetta and C. Salleo. 2004. Consolidation and efficiency in the financial sector: a review of the international evidence. *Journal of Banking and Finance* **28**, 2493–519.

Berger, A. N., and D. B. Humphrey. 1994. Bank scale economies, mergers, concentration, and efficiency: the US experience. Wharton Financial Institutions Center Working Paper 94-24. Available at http://fic.wharton.upenn.edu/fic/papers/94/9425.pdf.

Biais, B., J.-C. Rochet and P. Woolley. 2009. Rents, learning and risk in the financial sector and other innovative industries. Paul Woolley Centre Working Paper 4 (September).

Boone, P., and S. Johnson. 2010. Irish miracle—or mirage. *New York Times* (20 May).

Calomiris, C. W. 2009. In the world of banks, bigger can be better. *Wall Street Journal* (19 October).

Calomiris, C. W., and P. J. Wallison. 2008. Blame Fannie Mae and congress for the credit mess. *Wall Street Journal* (23 September).

Dabrowski, M. 1995. The reasons for the collapse of the ruble zone. Case Research Foundation Working Paper (December).

Ferguson Jr, R. W., P. Hartmann, F. Panetta and R. Portes. 2007. *International Financial Stability*. Geneva Reports on the World Economy, volume 9, pp. 93–94. Geneva/London: CEPR/ICMB.

Goodhart, C. A. E. 2010. Cuckoo for CoCos. London School of Economics mimeo.

Haldane, A. 2010. The $100 billion question. Speech to the Institute of Regulation and Risk, North Asia (IRRNA), Hong Kong (March).

Haldane, A., and P. Alessandri. 2009. Banking on the state. Presentation at the Federal Reserve Bank of Chicago 12th Annual International Banking Conference, The International Financial Crisis: Have the Rules of Finance Changed?, Chicago (25 September).

Honohan, P. 2009. Resolving Ireland's banking crisis. UCD-Dublin Economic Workshop Conference, 'Responding to the Crisis' (January).

Hreinsson, P., T. Gunnarsson and S. Benediktsdóttir. 2010. *Report of the Special Investigation Commission*. Icelandic Parliament. Available at http://sic.althingi.is/.

Johnson, S., and J. Kwak. 2010. *13 Bankers: The Wall Street Takeover and The Next Financial Meltdown*. New York: Pantheon.

Kane, E. J. 2009. Extracting nontransparent safety net subsidies by strategically expanding and contracting a financial institution's accounting balance sheet. *Journal of Financial Services Research* 36, 161–68.

McWilliams, D. 2009. *Follow the Money*. Dublin: Gill & Macmillan.

O'Brien, J. 2007. *Redesigning Financial Regulation: The Politics of Enforcement*. John Wiley & Sons.

Philippon, T., and A. Reshef. 2008. Wages and human capital in the US financial industry: 1909–2006. Working Paper (December). Available at http://pages.stern.nyu.edu/~tphilipp/research.htm.

Rhoades, S. A. 1994. A summary of merger performance studies in banking, 1980–93, and an assessment of the 'operating performance' and 'event study' methodologies. Federal Reserve Board Staff Studies 167 (summarized in *Federal Reserve Bulletin* (July)). Available at www.federalreserve.gov/Pubs/staffstudies/1990-99/ss167.pdf.

Rochet, J.-C. 2008. *Why Are There So Many Banking Crises? The Politics and Policy of Bank Regulation*. Princeton University Press.

Sorkin, A. R. 2009. *Too Big to Fail: Inside the Battle to Save Wall Street*. London: Allen Lane.

Stern, G. H., and R. Feldman. 2004. *Too Big to Fail: The Hazards of Bank Bailouts*. Washington, DC: Brookings Institution.

Stiroh, K. J. 2000. How did bank holding companies prosper in the 1990s? *Journal of Banking and Finance* **24**, 1703–45.

Stiroh, K. J. 2002. Information technology and the US productivity revival: what do the industry data say? *American Economic Review* **92** (2002), 1559–76.

Tett, G. 2009. *Fool's Gold: How Unrestrained Greed Corrupted a Dream, Shattered Global Markets and Unleashed a Catastrophe.* London: Little, Brown.

Wheelock, D. C., and P. W. Wilson. 2009. Are US banks too large? Federal Reserve Bank of St Louis Working Paper 2009-054A (October). Available at http://research.stlouisfed.org/wp/more/2009-054/.

About The Paul Woolley Centre for Capital Market Dysfunctionality

The Paul Woolley Centre for the Study of Capital Market Dysfunctionality was established within the Financial Markets Group at the London School of Economics in September 2007. Its founder is Paul Woolley and its director is Dimitri Vayanos.

Research at the centre aims at understanding the workings of financial markets and the effect of these markets on the broader economy. The research emphasizes the role of financial institutions in influencing market outcomes, and examines whether these institutions serve society at large well.

About The Centre for Economic Performance

The Centre for Economic Performance is an interdisciplinary research centre at the London School of Economics. It was established by the Economic and Social Research Council in 1990 with Richard Layard as its first director, and is one of the leading economic research groups in Europe.

The Centre for Economic Performance studies the determinants of economic performance at the level of the individual, the company, the nation and the global economy. Its work covers labour markets, education, productivity, macroeconomics, international trade and well-being. It has contributed seven present or former members of the Monetary Policy Committee of the Bank of England.

LaVergne, TN USA
09 September 2010
196508LV00002B/17/P

9 780853 284581